SpringerBriefs in Ps

MW01537444

Psychology and Cultural Developmental Science

Series editors

Giuseppina Marsico, DISUFF, University of Salerno; Centre for Cultural Psychology, Aalborg University, Salerno, Salerno, Italy;

Jaan Valsiner, Centre for Cultural Psychology, Aalborg University, Aalborg, Denmark

SpringerBriefs present concise summaries of cutting-edge research and practical applications across a wide spectrum of fields. Featuring compact volumes of 50 to 125 pages, the series covers a range of content from professional to academic. Typical topics might include:

- A timely report of state-of-the-art analytical techniques
- A bridge between new research results as published in journal articles and a contextual literature review
- A snapshot of a hot or emerging topic
- An in-depth case study or clinical example
- A presentation of core concepts that readers must understand to make independent contributions

SpringerBriefs in Psychology showcase emerging theory, empirical research, and practical application in a wide variety of topics in psychology and related fields. Briefs are characterized by fast, global electronic dissemination, standard publishing contracts, standardized manuscript preparation and formatting guidelines, and expedited production schedules.

SpringerBriefs in Psychology and Cultural Developmental Science is an extension and topical completion to*IPBS: Integrative Psychological and Behavioral Science Journal* (Springer, chief editor: Jaan Vasiner) expanding some relevant topics in the form of single (or multiple) authored book. The Series will have a clearly defined international and interdisciplinary focus hosting works on the interconnection between Cultural Psychology and other Developmental Sciences (biology, sociology, anthropology, etc). The Series aims at integrating knowledge from many fields in a synthesis of general science of Cultural Psychology as a new science of the human being.

The Series will include books that offer a perspective on the current state of developmental science, addressing contemporary enactments and reflecting on theoretical and empirical directions and providing, also, constructive insights into future pathways.

Featuring compact volumes of 100 to 115 pages, each Brief in the Series is meant to provide a clear, visible, and multi-sided recognition of the theoretical efforts of scholars around the world.

Both solicited and unsolicited proposals are considered for publication in this series. All proposals will be subject to peer review by external referees.

More information about this series at http://www.springer.com/series/10143

Tania Zittoun

Sociocultural Psychology on the Regional Scale

A Case Study of a Hill

Springer

Tania Zittoun
Institute of Psychology and Education
Faculty of Arts and Humanities
University of Neuchâtel
Neuchâtel, Switzerland

ISSN 2192-8363   ISSN 2192-8371   (electronic)
SpringerBriefs in Psychology
ISSN 2626-6741   ISSN 2626-675X   (electronic)
SpringerBriefs in Psychology and Cultural Developmental Science
ISBN 978-3-030-33065-1   ISBN 978-3-030-33066-8   (eBook)
https://doi.org/10.1007/978-3-030-33066-8

© The Author(s), under exclusive license to Springer Nature Switzerland AG 2019
This work is subject to copyright. All rights are reserved by the Publisher, whether the whole or part of
the material is concerned, specifically the rights of translation, reprinting, reuse of illustrations, recitation,
broadcasting, reproduction on microfilms or in any other physical way, and transmission or information
storage and retrieval, electronic adaptation, computer software, or by similar or dissimilar methodology
now known or hereafter developed.
The use of general descriptive names, registered names, trademarks, service marks, etc. in this publication
does not imply, even in the absence of a specific statement, that such names are exempt from the relevant
protective laws and regulations and therefore free for general use.
The publisher, the authors, and the editors are safe to assume that the advice and information in this book
are believed to be true and accurate at the date of publication. Neither the publisher nor the authors or the
editors give a warranty, express or implied, with respect to the material contained herein or for any errors
or omissions that may have been made. The publisher remains neutral with regard to jurisdictional claims
in published maps and institutional affiliations.

This Springer imprint is published by the registered company Springer Nature Switzerland AG
The registered company address is: Gewerbestrasse 11, 6330 Cham, Switzerland

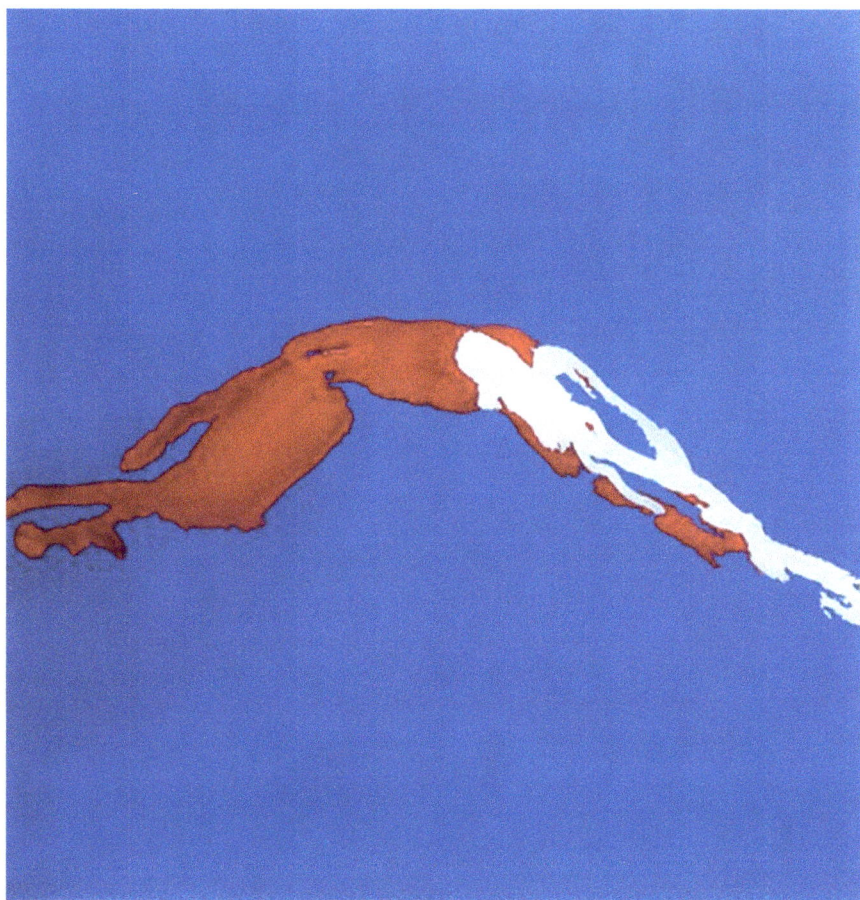

Mariana Alasseur, Říp 2010. (Courtesy of the artist. Source: www.galerieroudnice.cz)

To all my real and imaginary grandmothers:
Rachel, Pia, Savta Sura, Helenka,
and Tonička.

Preface of the Series Editors

Symbolic Places: Cultural Psychology of Human Life Course

This book reveals the intricacies of how human lives are interwoven with symbolic places created out of natural environments. Its author is on the forefront of our contemporary cultural psychologies movement—building new science of specifically *human* psychology ("Yokohama Manifesto"—Valsiner, Marsico, Chaudhary, Sato & Dazzani, 2016). In this new trans-disciplinary work, artificial borders between various sciences—psychology, geography, sociology, anthropology, history, and folklore—vanish. Instead we have an image of a unique texture of human beings living in their self-constructed life-worlds embedded in community, society, and—last but not least—the geological textures of their given natural environments. We—temporary inhabitants of Denmark—have often wondered about "where these nice wide open fields end", desiring to see at least a glimpse of a mountain somewhere on the horizon. There is none—one needs to cross over to Sweden or Norway to feel at home with some granite formations rising up from the sea. In a similar way—our Danish friends visiting Switzerland have reported feeling ill at ease about being surrounded by mountains on all sides. Yet there is no way to escape—the mountains are there, and they stay. The human beings build meanings with the landscapes and seascapes of one's natural habitats.

As Tania Zittoun eloquently demonstrates in this book, Říp is not just a mountain—and even not only a symbolic mountain for the Czech people—but it is also the real meaningful world for persons who live on and around it. It is the silent observer of life dramas brought by societal turmoils of politics during war and peace. Taking a perspective on the whole of human life courses naturally involves the study of life stories of older-age people whose wisdom in coping with all the complexities of the past would otherwise be lost. Most of psychology, driven by the social institutional "prediction and control" imperatives, has attempted to do what fortune tellers have been doing: predicting the future happiness of the now younger generation—*if it does what these institutions require*. This social order for the social sciences has led to the myopic look at the latter part of human life course—where the lived-through experiences of one's life lead to contemplations about what the realities of living are about. Both suffering and happy moments in life are intricately linked by the person himself—and cannot be changed *post factum*. It is the developmental look at the human life course that makes understanding of the wisdom based on experience possible (Zittoun, Valsiner, Vedeler, Salgado, Gonçalves, & Ferring, 2013). There is a lesson for our general scientific look at what we are doing—instead of an "evidence-based" science, we might need an *experience-explicating science*. Or—in other terms—the evidence psychology needs is the documented richness of personal life courses, together with the personal meaning systems built over such life courses. Otherwise it is difficult to see how many real sufferers (of wars) can arrive at personal reconciliation with their lived-through horrors, while their grandchildren would protest publicly against such horrors that are societally repeated some generations later.

Geographical places are made symbolic by people in their cultural lives all over the world—and history. Mountains have been sacred (Reichel-Dolmatoff, 1990), so are forests, or rivers (Eck, 1998), or the areas of the sea. Within such meaningfully organised landscapes, human beings build sacral architecture—temples, mosques, churches, museums, monuments, and seasonal rituals and festivity. Economic and political interests in the same geographical places lead to social conflicts—be it Amerindian demand that their rivers be returned to them, or the public defences of natural park territories against opening those for oil explorations. The most dramatic of such conflicts are the ones of appropriating one's established sacred place for building up a sacral architectural place of an opposing belief system. Culturally *affectivated*—meaningfully constructed and affectively fixated (Cornejo, Marsico, & Valsiner, 2018)—landscapes are not neutral. They are fought for—in riots, wars, and legal disputes—or they are celebrated, and at the time, they become the symbolic "great frontier between the human and the divine, the ordinary and the mythological, the known world and the world to be conquered" (Dazzani & Marsico, 2017, p.220) as in the case of the Yemanjá Festival in Salvador, Bahia. Yemanjá is the "Goddess of the Waters," and the main part of the festival is the "giving of presents" to the divinity which are taken by fishermen out to the open sea. Seascape is here the arena for the collective meaning-making process and the link among past, present, and future. This festival, indeed, is related to the way that the local culture represents the sea—through which thousands of Africans, kidnapped to work as slaves in the New World, arrived in Brazil.

Landscape is the ground for our ornamented lives (Valsiner, 2018). It is the *Umwelt* of our psychological existence. It is the perceivable part of the human environment that we make meaningful as we proceed within it (Lyra & Pinheiro, 2018).

Symbolic geography is accessible everywhere—we carry it in the tacit affective knowledge in our minds. The symbolic role of a mountain or a river can be maintained anywhere in the world—as we carry our own symbolic desires across oceans and continents:

> I leave the computer and open a jug of Ganga water. It pours like ordinary tap water over my fingers and I feel it entering me, origin returning. There is no space but half the world between representation and real. The river writes upon its landscape—geophysical fact both

practical and metaphorical. The flow of water, within and without, is not only life itself but also the expression of that life, effects and their expression inextricably bound one to another. (Prasher, 2005, p. 420)

In a similar vein, the mountain in the middle of the Czech countryside has acquired over centuries the role of the symbolic unifier of the various tumultuous life courses of ordinary human beings over history. Tania Zittoun's masterful weaving of the sacred geography of the mountain together with personal life courses of the people who have lived under its view is a new form of scholarship in cultural psychology that lives up to the original standards of world exploration of Alexander von Humboldt—albeit in twenty-first century new ways of cultural psychology.

Remich, Luxembourg   Giuseppina Marsico
Remich, Luxembourg   Jaan Valsiner
June 2019

References

Cornejo, C., Marsico, G., & Valsiner, J. (Eds.) (2018). *I activate you to affect me*. Vol 2. In Annals of Cultural Psychology series. Charlotte, NC: Information Age Publishing.

Dazzani, M. V., & Marsico, G. (2017). Imagined Sea. In O. Lehmann, N. Chaudhary, A. C. Bastos, & E. Abbey (Eds.), *Poetry and imagined worlds* (pp 209–222). Cham, Switzerland: Palgrave Studies in Creativity and Culture. Palgrave Macmillan. https://doi.org/10.1007/978-3-319-64858-3_12.

Eck, D. (1998). The imagined landscapes: Patterns in the construction of Hindu sacred geography. *Contributions to Indian Sociology, 32*(2), 165–188.

Lyra M., & Pinheiro, M. (Eds.). (2018). *Cultural psychology as basic science: Dialogues with Jaan Valsiner*. New York: Springer.

Prasher, P. P. (2005). The Ganges river: Metaphor and mythopoesis. In S. Akhtar (Ed.), *Freud along the Ganges: Psychoanalytic reflections on the people and culture of India* (pp. 397–423). New York: Other Press.

Reichel-Dolmatoff, R. (1990). *The sacred mountain of Colombia's Kogi Indians*. Leiden, Netherlands: E. Brill.

Valsiner, J. (2018). *Ornamented lives*. Charlotte, NC: Information Age Publishing.

Valsiner, J., Marsico, G., Chaudhary, N., Sato, T., & Dazzani, V. (Eds.) (2016). *Psychology as the science of human being*. Cham, Switzerland: Springer.

Zittoun, T., Valsiner, J., Vedeler, D., Salgado, J., Gonçalves, M., & Ferring, D. (2013). *Human development in the lifecourse. Melodies of living*. Cambridge: Cambridge University Press.

Acknowledgements

The people I would like to thank first are the villagers that I met and gave me time, attention, and warm welcome, satisfied my curiosity, and trusted me enough to share something about their lives to me. This book took a long time to write, and the useful and precious feedbacks I received actually kept me going when I was close to giving up. I am especially thankful to Sophie Zadeh for organising the Cambridge workshop on generalization and Pernille Hviid for proposing a symposium on life courses and history at the 10th Dialogical Self Conference in Braga. Moreover, I would also like to thank my academic and personal friends, Alex Gillespie, Flora Cornish, Ivana Marková, Jaan Valsiner, Janine Dahinden, and Pernille Hviid, for the hours of discussion and critical comments on the topics raised in this book. In particular, Jaan actually believed in this peculiar project from the very beginning, and it actually played an important role in its completion. Special thanks also go to my colleagues at la MAPS and at our CURIOUS centre, both at the University of Neuchâtel, centre for creating spaces for discussion and for their support; rich dialogues are reflected here. I am grateful to Markéta Machková for her patience in editing the English translations of the interviews conducted in Czech and to Mariana Alasseur for her trust and for allowing her powerful paintings to be reproduced here. I am also thankful to Ms Jindřiška Waňková and Ms Jitka Löblová from Langweil project for their kind help and to Pavel Novak for allowing me to use his pictures. Accomplishing this project required me to have time and space. Thus, I would like express my deepest gratitude to my University of Neuchâtel that still guarantees freedom in all sorts of projects one wishes to undertake during a scientific leave. And of course, I would not have dreamed of starting such a case study without Milan Mazourek – my main informant, translator, and guide in the meanders of the Czech village life…

Contents

List of Figures

List of Table

Chapter 1
Introduction: Říp

According to legend the patriarch Czech climbed up the hill protruding from an old bosky crater and told his exhausted tribesmen: "Here is the land rich with milk and honey; here will we stay". But in reality the ancient Czechs colonized a country that was already inhabited.

—(Pospec, 2003, p. 16)

Approaching Prague by plane from the West, the land appears very flat around the capital. Far up north can be seen a small chain of indented hills, but between these and Prague lies a large plain, extensively cultivated. Only one little hill emerges, a little bump – Říp (Fig. 1.1). This almost invisible hill is however far from being insignificant – strangely, as we will see, it has been defined as the umbilicus of the Czech nation: it is its birth mark and grounding place, to which many turn in times of uncertainty.

Contemporary Czech Republic is a land of 78,866 km^2 and 10.5 million inhabitants, located at the centre of Europe mainland. A chain of mountains borders Czech Republic with Germany, Austria, Slovakia and Poland. It is irrigated by three main rivers that connect it to the North, Baltic and Black seas. Prague is located in the western half of the country, Bohemia – the other half being Moravia.

At 30 km north (NNW) from Prague, in the direction of Dresden, stands Říp, 459 m above the sea level in the plains of Bohemia – when the surrounding land is at about 200 m (Fig. 1.2). It is covered by a thick forest and is now a protected natural reservation; it has a very characteristic shape, which makes it easily recognisable from far away and from all directions (Figs. 1.3, 1.4, and 1.5).

On the top of Říp can be found a roman chapel – a rare rotunda – and a small pub, open a few hours a day for hikers and tourists. Right under the forest line, the hill is bordered by fields, and scattered on the plain are a series of villages, proudly named "villages of under-Říp" – the Podřispsko region. Located at 30 minutes from Prague, these villages are inhabited by a mixture of local families working in agriculture or factories, and commuters. Located at a distance of 7 km north is the town of Roudnice nad Labem. The whole region developed around the eleventh century; Roudnice is a mid-size town of 12,000 inhabitants and the villages range between 300 and 600 inhabitants (Table 1.1).

© The Author(s), under exclusive license to Springer Nature Switzerland AG 2019
T. Zittoun, *Sociocultural Psychology on the Regional Scale*, SpringerBriefs in Psychology, https://doi.org/10.1007/978-3-030-33066-8_1

Fig. 1.1 Říp from the
plane, copyright author,
2016

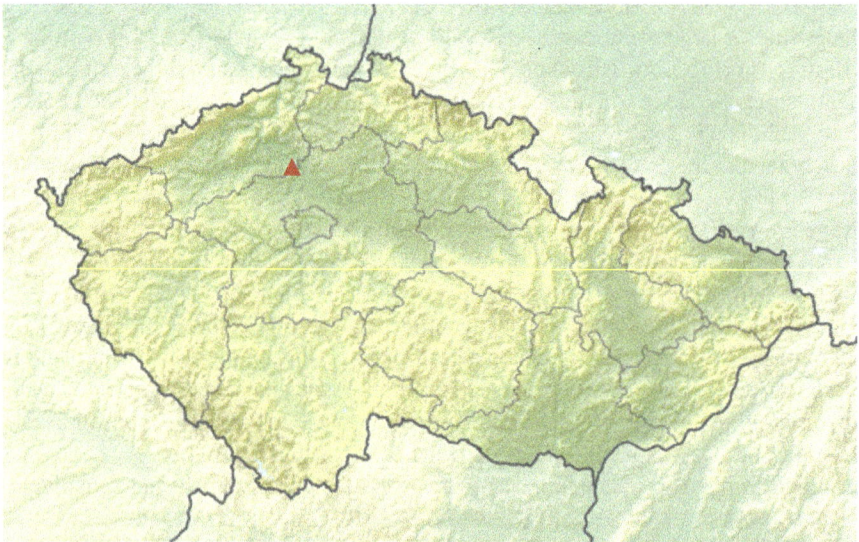

Fig. 1.2 Czech Republic and location of Říp, relief map of Czech Republic, Wikipedia, under
creative commons

Each village has usually a small shop, a pub and a church; children from two
villages are often grouped for one school.

People circulate from village to village: they have relatives in one or the other,
bring children, visit friends, attend an event or go to the pub; they also cross villages
by foot, bike or car, and drive or take the bus or train go to Prague or Roudnice

Fig. 1.3 Říp from south-east, copyright author, 2016

Fig. 1.4 Říp from south, copyright author, 2016

Fig. 1.5 Říp from west, copyright author, 2016

Table 1.1 Podřípsko localities

Village	Year of foundation	Number of inhabitants
Ctiněves	1318	328
Černouček	1100	287
Straškov-Vodochody	990	1100
Vražkov	1100	429
Mnetěš	1226	579
Roudnice nad Labem	1167	12,000

Information from Wikipedia (2016)

(Fig. 1.6). Under the hill, before the villages, the fields are bordered by country roads, which connect the villages by shorter distances than the roads. On these country roads, local families walk their children, their dogs or their horses. Bikers and hikers also use them, as well as people collecting berries or fruits growing along these roads or the occasional driver who wants to avoid the other roads after drinking alcohol.

At mid-way up on the slope of Říp has been created a circular pathway, which joins by a few vertical paths the lower field ways; the circular pathway is about 3 km long (see Fig. 1.7), and allows to connect the villages, see a few viewpoints, and have a nice stroll in the woods (Fig. 1.8). This circular pathway is used by locals, daily joggers and mothers walking their prams; only on weekends and holidays, it is crowded by people from towns going for an excursion in the green. Finally there

Fig. 1.6 Aerial view of Říp and Podřípsko region, © Seznam.cz, a.s mapy.cz, 2016

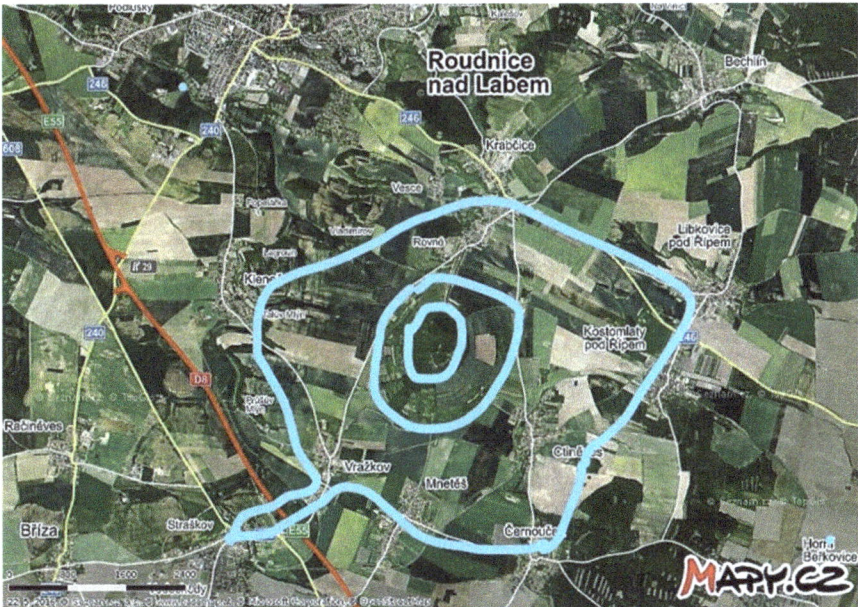

Fig. 1.7 Podřípsko region, with main circulation added: across villages, fields under Říp, "circular" pathway mid-hill, © Seznam.cz, a.s mapy.cz, 2016

Fig. 1.8 Circular pathway around Říp, mid-hill, copyright author, 2018

are two accesses from the villages to the top of Říp (Fig. 1.9), one covered with cement going from a parking in a quasi-straight line to the top – the "highway" taken by tourists and weekenders, starting with a beautiful and historical linden alley (Fig. 1.10) – and another one, a steep and muddy pathway zigzaging between trees, their roots offered as natural steps.

Why should anyone be interested in this region? Because, I believe, it is a small region, self-bounded, which may teach us a lot about sociocultural dynamics and human lives, like any other region. However, there are a few specificities to it. First, as we will see, it is heavily thematised in social discourses, national representations of the past and various mythical sayings, as well as in people's everyday activities and life choices. In that sense, it is a good case study to explore phenomena which are omnipresent – the mutual shaping of social and historical movements and of everyday lives. But this is not enough; second, to justify a study such as the one I undertook, and now propose to the reader, there needed to be a surprise: bewilderment is, I believe, the main and most powerful trigger for any scientific enquiry (Zittoun, 2017). Let me explain my surprise.

The Podřipsko villages are all located at about 30 km – that is, 30 min by a direct highway – from Prague. Prague is an international, vibrant, quickly developing, highly touristic European city and a centre of education, politics, arts and finance. The region is located on major circulation axes, the Dresden-Prague road and train line. It is also about 40 km from the region once annexed by the Germans and commonly named "the Sudetenland" from 1938 to 1945; it was on the axis of the

Fig. 1.9 Aerial view from Říp with walking pathways to the top, © Seznam.cz, a.s mapy.cz, 2019

Fig. 1.10 Linden Allee, main access to Říp from Krabčice, copyright author, 2018

intervention of the Union of Soviet Socialist Republics (USSR) armed forces in 1968. In other terms, the region is located at the border of the epicentre of major events of modern and contemporary history. However, life in the villages and around Říp does not reflect this historicity and modernity at first glance. Indeed, a large part of the population cultivates fields, as main or free-time activity; each village has its ponds, with jumping carps and lazy ducks; women make jams and men are part of their village's hunting society; villagers gather at the pub, where they drink large jugs of beer; they grill pigs for birthdays, work as firemen during their free time and organise dance balls on the football pitch or in the old dance hall. In other words, life seems very similar to that described beautifully by film director Miloš Forman in his comedy "Fireman's ball" (1967) (*Hoří, má panenko*).

So my initial surprise came from the contrast between what seems to be a fluid, moving, evolving, historical environment, and the apparent calm and undisturbed traditional quality of a standard village life – as if it was, at first glance, relatively protected from the acceleration of time and social history. Of course, inhabitants have Internet at home, new playgrounds are built and, also, a few people move away from the region to live in the city or abroad; some shops are held by second-generation Vietnamese migrants, people come to retire in the region, and the hill is visited by hordes of tourists in the summer; hence, the villages are not out of time. Yet, the impression of a strong contrast remains – and this, the slowing down of time or the possible layering of temporalities, is what motivates this enquiry. Furthermore, the very shape of the hill and the region, the fact that it affords circular movements, that it seems to attract people from close and from far, that it retains many people in its close proximity and that it once in a while lets go an inhabitant is also intriguing and suggests a form of circular, orbital movement. This double impression, the first of the layering of temporalities, the second of circularities, might actually be combined in a first intuition: that Říp is the axis around which centripetal and centrifugal forces are at work. How much can this intuition be further developed then becomes a theoretical question: is it a useful guiding metaphor, does it allow to see and understand things? And if so, what are these forces made of, what animates them and what are their consequences? And if this is a wrong metaphor, what alternatives can we propose? This will be the guiding threads of this enquiry.

This small book is an attempt to theorise a regional case study in sociocultural psychology. It pursues an interest in the intermeshed history and life stories (Zittoun & Gillespie, 2015); yet rather than observing people moving through time and space, the limits of the present analysis are given by a geographical space. It is also an attempt to expand the reflection on case study construction through abductive reasoning – the effort to identify, based on astonishment, configurations or patterns in the infinity diversity of elements we are confronted with when we observe the world (Zittoun, 2017). Chap. 2 sets the theoretical frame for this enquiry; it defends the scale of the analysis, fixes three sets of concepts and justifies the search for patterns that diffuse across sociogenetic, ontogenetic and microgenetic dynamics. In Chap. 3, I present my posture as a researcher and the methodology of the present exploratory case study. The next three chapters present the case itself: in Chap. 4, I propose an analysis of sociogenetic dynamics, that is, historical events, as these affected the life around the hill, as well as the history of the uses of the hill on a more symbolic level. Chapter 5 presents the parallel analysis of the courses of life of two women in their 90s, whose trajectories have been marked by the historical events described in Chap. 4, and who, however, have each developed unique melodies of living. In Chap. 6, I adopt a microgenetic perspective and try to understand daily lives of people around Říp; how people circulate, how time is marked and eventually, how various persons organise their lives. This brings me to identify two core patterns whereby people organise their daily lives: one is stable and the other is unstable. Stability is, I propose, dependent on each person's configuration of proximal and distal spheres of experience, which may be more or less adjusted to the demands of life around the hill; eventually, the hill may act as a centripetal or centrifugal force. In Chap. 7, I articulate these chapters together and try to unpack the semiotic logics at work. Eventually, I suggest, the scale of a hill or a region allows to show how redundant semiotic patterns diffuse through all layers of change – socio, onto and microgenetic – and how these can be more or less internalised and thus participate in people's courses of lives.

References

Forman, M. (1967). *Hoří, má panenko* [Comedy, Drama]. Retrieved from http://www.imdb.com/title/tt0061781/

Pospec, M. (2003). *Verifik 1*. Kostelec, Czech Republic: Verifik.

Zittoun, T. (2017). Modalities of generalization through single case studies. *Integrative Psychological and Behavioral Science, 51*(2), 171–194. https://doi.org/10.1007/s12124-016-9367-1

Zittoun, T., & Gillespie, A. (2015). Integrating experiences: Body and mind moving between contexts. In B. Wagoner, N. Chaudhary, & P. Hviid (Eds.), *Integrating experiences: Body and mind moving between contexts* (pp. 3–49). Charlotte, NC: Information Age Publishing.

Chapter 2
Building a Theoretical Frame: Towards Patterns

> *...if, for instance, one is confronted by a single hill, which is set into the plain as a "spatial form" with its base below the surface, one can also imagine that it is merely a curvature in the plain, a bump in the ground; one can also see the hill as a "planar form." Or if the pedestrian sees the fields and meadows before him as nature in the aesthetic sense, he can also well imagine the quite different landscape that the farmer would encounter here...*
>
> —(Lewin, 1917/2009, p. 201)

This is a book about a hill, Říp. As I approach it as a sociocultural psychologist, it is a book about the lives of people and a community on and around a hill, in changing times. Approaching this hill with certain theoretical assumptions, my slow acquaintance of the hill and the cultivation of my theoretical intuitions brought me to identify some forms of configuration in the richness and chaos of life. In this chapter, I build the sociocultural psychological approach that allows me to construct a hill and its region as object of study. After defining an epistemological stance that combines four perspectives on dynamic processes (Sect. 2.1), I explain why I believe that a hill gives us a good entrance in sociocultural dynamics: it gives a unity of place to observe the intermeshed dynamics occurring at sociogenetic, microgenetic and ontogenetic scale (Sect. 2.2). I then propose a few more analytical distinctions and define three sets of notions to account for each of these dynamics (Sect. 2.3). Using these, I finally briefly sketch the typical developmental dynamics of a person in a given region (Sect. 2.4). The question is, do we learn something specific about development, when we study it in a specific region, and approach it a three levels of analysis? Does such anchoring of lives allow seeing things we would not have seen otherwise? I believe so, and in the last section (Sect. 2.5), I present the idea that will run through the book: studying lives under a hill, some specific patterns of living emerge.

© The Author(s), under exclusive license to Springer Nature Switzerland AG 2019
T. Zittoun, *Sociocultural Psychology on the Regional Scale*, SpringerBriefs in Psychology, https://doi.org/10.1007/978-3-030-33066-8_2

2.1 Defining A Sociocultural Psychological Epistemology

Sociocultural psychology – with it, cultural-historical psychology and cultural psychology – has, as overall project, to understand the mutual making of societies and subjectivity or the evolution of cultural, social and historical worlds and the life of persons (Cole, 1996; Rosa & Valsiner, 2018; Valsiner, 2019; Valsiner & Rosa, 2007). Such project has also been shared by many close disciplines – such as social anthropology or cultural geography – and sub-disciplines, especially critical psychology (Teo, 2015) or psychosocial approaches (Stenner & Brown, 2009). These sub-disciplines share many assumptions, such as the interactive or dialogical nature of human and social life, a processual or historical or genetic approach to human experience and societies, and a critical stance upon theorisation and in psychology. However, these psychological approaches also tend to draw on different ancestors and traditions and to choose different entry points in their analysis of the meeting of the cultural and the subjective. Over time and trends, the focus has been put on activities, practices, discourses, narratives, interactions or institutions, to cite only a few. Some of these concepts allow to foreground the *psychological* counterpart of culture, while others emphasise the *social* component of human action, with the risk of eliminating subjectivity – a long-standing debate in cultural psychological approaches, with deep philosophical roots. Currently, human experience comes to the fore again, either through the rehabilitation of Vygotsky's notion of *Perezhivanie* (Blunden, 2016; Salmi & Kumpulainen, 2017; Zavereshneva & van der Veer, 2018), through a rediscovery of existential philosophy (Hviid, 2012, 2015), as a reaction to the previous focus on discourse (Stenner, 2017), or as part of a long-standing interest for semiotic processes (Salvatore, 2016; Valsiner, 2007b, 2014, 2019). But how to consider, at the same time as human experience, the social at work, cultural tensions, as well as historical dynamics in which the person is embedded, and which create the very conditions of people's living, the semiotic streams in which they have to learn to swim, the matter in which they will grow and that, in turn, they will use and shape?

As a sociocultural psychologist, I believe that it is fundamental, in any analysis of human experience, to combine a description and analysis of the social and cultural, as it participates in the making of the life environment of the person or the people we study, together with a description and analysis of the psychological aspects of that life (Benson, 2001). To do that, I propose, following others, to combine four perspectives, or aspects of the studied phenomena. The first one implies a description of elements that, from an analytical point of view, constitute people's environment – understood in the systemic sense of what is relevant for a specific phenomenon (Van Geert, 2003) – and may become relevant for people, even if they do not mention or consider them – a description from a "third person perspective". Note here that this point is controversial in psychology: Lewin (2000) and others after him suggest that as psychologists we should only account for the world as it is given to the person, or the context as the person is apprehending it (Grossen, 2001; Marková, 2015). My stance here is that, although only the part of the world that directly impinges upon the person is part of their psychological world, it is still necessary to describe society and culture in wider terms: for there are forces, representations and material arrangements that define and participate in the making of the person, far beyond the immediately visible or consciously identifiable. People resist, ploy and define their spaces of freedom within these complex constraints and contradictory streams (Ratner, 2012; Zittoun & Gillespie, 2015a). The second aspect aims at accounting for the person's perspective – a "first-person perspective", although this is never fully reachable: this is about giving room to the person's experience, ways of externalising about events and life, emotional reactions, thoughts and activities – how the world resonates in him or her, how the person turns it into something unique and how, from this very unique experience of the world, she or he acts, creates or simply imagines (Hviid, 2012; Zavereshneva & van der Veer, 2018; Zittoun, 2007). This is why both depend on a third entrance, an "n-person perspective": that of the distancing power provided by theory (Gillespie & Zittoun, 2015; Zittoun, 2016c). Concepts, models or theories are indeed distancing and elaborating mediators that allow to bind and articulate the two other perspectives, make hypothesis about the relations between the world given to people and what they make out of it (Zittoun & Gillespie, 2015a; Zittoun et al., 2013). A fourth viewpoint is necessary for dialogical and ethical reason, the one accounting for the researcher's position and perspective upon the phenomena at hand, and especially, his or her relation to the persons and the field. Such "second-person perspective" thus designates reflections on the intersubjective or dialogical nature of any research endeavour (Grossen, 2010; Marková, 2016), which meets up with the current discussion on researchers' reflexivity (Brinkmann, 2013; de Saint-Laurent & Glaveanu, 2016; Denzin, 2001). Thus, these four perspectives are triangulated not to verify against each other, but to build a complex case, with depth and breadth, through their combination (Flick, 1992). Only with such epistemological stance can we understand, analytically and in the light of theory, how the sociocultural worlds creates conditions for living, but also, how people navigate in these – ignoring some aspects, being shaped against their will, or on the contrary, how they actively use, oppose or create – and how these dynamics appear to the researcher.

2.2   The Region as a Sociocultural Unit

Beyond such epistemological position, whose methodological implications I will examine later (chap. 3), what analytical tools do we dispose of to identify "the social" or "the cultural" in such a way, that we can then link them to the analysis of individual lives?

Many comparable efforts have been done in social and cultural psychologies. Recent attempts have been made to reintroduce societal dynamics, or macro-cultural forces on a larger scale in cultural psychology (Ratner, 2012, 2014), interestingly connecting them to intergroup dynamics (Moghaddam, 2018), but with the difficulty of connecting these forces to the persons' lives. Some authors have articulated at least theoretically traditions and specific contexts of activity guiding people's actions (especially children's motives) but gave little consideration for the creative role of the person (Hedegaard, 2012; Hedegaard & Chaiklin, 2005). Other authors have rather proposed to focus on specific contexts or frames of activities (Perret-Clermont, 2015), with less attention to larger sociohistorical dynamics, while some have focused on the specific local communities or institutions (Clot, 2002; Engeström, 2011; Gillespie, Cornish, Aveling, & Zittoun, 2008). Combining an analysis of historico-cultural dynamics with that of individual lives has also been recently undertaken (Zittoun, 2017; Zittoun & Gillespie, 2015a) but with less attention to local communities and interactions.

Although these approaches cannot usually hold "everything" – the social in all its ramifications and the person – the typical foregrounds of these studies suggest that the sociocultural as relevant for psychology implies dynamics and processes that can be analytically distinguished as part of three main streams (Duveen & Lloyd, 1990; Gillespie & Cornish, 2010). The first stream includes the making of the social and cultural world, from the more diffuse social representations and ideologies to specific nation-states, institutional, groups or intergroup dynamics: these dynamics participate to what can be called sociogenesis. The second stream examines more specific interactions and dynamics: that of actual encounters, activities and negotiations between people, or between people and the material world; this is the microgenesis of the social world and of people. It is actually through microgenesis that sociogenesis is generated and also that it participates in the transformation of people (Gillespie & Cornish, 2010). Indeed, the third stream of movements examines the processes and dynamics by which people themselves make sense, act, feel and through it, keep becoming – changing, learning or developing: this is an ontogenetic dynamic. There are alternative propositions to define layers of analysis, such as the one made by Wilhelm Doise to distinguish four levels of analysis – the intrapsychological, the interpersonal, the groupal or positional and the ideological (Doise, 1980; Doise & Mapstone, 1986; Perret-Clermont, 2004); the idea was then to combine at least two levels to be able to account for psychosocial dynamics. My reason to opt for the three-part division is the actual emphasis on processes and also for operationalisation purposes. I leave out here analytical frames which are more static, such as the largely used one proposed by Urie Bronfenbrenner (Bronfenbrenner, 1979).

This division is a matter of entry point. Let us consider these three streams from a fundamental dynamic perspective, assuming that things out there and within us are in constant motion and made out of flows of elementary stuff – atoms, signs or other – in a constant process of composition and stabilisation into configurations or patterns, themselves evolving, transforming and decomposing (Bergson, 1938; James, 2007; Spinoza, 1677; for a recent account, see Stenner, 2017). From such stance, these three levels or streams observe different points of friction or different types of evolution. Thus sociogenesis is about the making and unmaking of ideas and values, as these are diffused in a wide diversity of material and immaterial means and crystallised in others, as well as about the evolution of these more or less solid, more or less stable configurations – castles, flags and anthems. Microgenesis operates at the border or the boundary of specific human beings and their immediate world, which appear to them in material or symbolic forms (Valsiner, 2019). Ontogenesis is about the transformation of the person herself/himself, body and mind, material and symbolic, but so to say from within, from what makes the unicity of the person – what holds him/her together as such – within him/her specific location in semiotic and material streams (Cole, 2016; Martin & Gillespie, 2010; Zittoun et al., 2013). Another way to articulate these three streams is to say that their flow usually operates on different physical timescales: sociogenesis often operates at speeds not perceivable in a lifetime, like the erosion of a touristic site, or slowly enough to confer to the world as offered to humans some form of stability – as for instance the slow evolution of the Swiss government. Of course, there are always breaches in this slow time – the fire of a monument, a major terrorist attack – which suddenly can accelerate sociogenesis and have repercussions at all other levels (see for instance Wagoner, Moghaddam, & Valsiner, 2018). Sociogenesis is bounded by the history of humankind, and as such, only one section at a time can be considered by a researcher. Microgenesis is conceived in such way, that dynamics are observable in the "real-time" of research, in the unfolding of a dialogue, a football match or a seasonal ritual. Microgenesis is constant, yet specific units start, unfold and end – of course in what terms, is specific to each possible type of activity or conduct. Because of their infinity, a researcher usually studies one or a few of them. Ontogenesis is always about a specific person; its speed can be variable along the way. Some periods may imply very rapid developments, such as during the first years of life, or any later period of transition, while others seem to unfold relatively slowly at human scale – such as when we see an old friend after 10 years and they appear to have not changed at all. The course of human life is what bounds ontogenesis, and a researcher rarely has access to the whole of a lifecourse.

For theoretical, empirical and analytical reasons, it is difficult to give sociogenesis, ontogenesis and microgenesis an equal status in a research project, so as to examine how they co-define, shape and transform each other. One of the reasons of that difficulty is that it is often difficult to "hold" enough the phenomena at hand to look at it from all three perspectives at once. Hence, if one does a very careful analysis of the sociogenesis of a social representation, it is clear that such dynamic semiotic-enacted configuration is, like a cloud, moving across places or people and groups (Moscovici, 2008); alternatively, it can be examined at a microgenetic scale, yet losing sight of people's development (Psaltis, 2012). When carefully examining the evolving lifecourse of a person during a long, documented historical period, it becomes impossible to account for all the interactive and group dynamics he/she traverses (Zittoun & Gillespie, 2015a). Another possible explanation for that difficulty may be that, because of their focus on changing psychosocial realities, these studies usually do not give much consideration to the geographical places and the material reality where these take place. It is as if time and space were treated as fluid entities – people appear as moving and evolving through an undefined time-space, or through spaces and places along time. So what about changing the entry point, and instead, starting by anchoring our analysis in the more stable material reality of a place, in order to make time visible?

My proposition here is thus to circumvent the difficulties of combining three layers of change by stabilising one aspect – the sociomaterial space – through which time may run; a place large enough to see all these three dynamics operate, and participate to each other. Some studies have stabilised places by studying a village (Jodelet, 1989); the proposition here is to examine a region.

Regions can be small localities, villages, microregions and town areas – heteromorphic portions of the geographical-material reality that have some unity at a social or symbolic level, that people consider as relevant (Baidal, 2016; Clough, 2008). There is a wide discussion in social and political sciences on the definition of regions; here I will focus on what some call a "vernacular region":

> Regions are artificial constructs that geographers use to divide the world into sections which can then be compared with other units or studied in more detail on their own. Their defining feature is that the phenomena being studied exists in greater concentration within the boundaries than it or they do outside of it. (…) Rather than size, it is the criteria chosen that establishes the boundaries. There are several different kinds of regions. (…) Vernacular regions are constructed by peoples' perception and therefore vary in extent from person to person. They exist because people refer to them as if they are real. (Clough, 2008, para. 3)

Strangely, regions have been very little addressed in psychology; they are treated as geographical, political (Mandal, 2016) or possibly cultural and cross-national entities, but in no way is the concept of region itself addressed (Obschonka et al., 2015). Regions have thus not been addressed as part of what makes a subjectively relevant environment and therefore may be worth analysing from a sociocultural perspective. This is what I propose here; I will examine a vernacular region, resulting from a mixture of self-definition by inhabitants and communities, as well as a geographical-historical reality, whereby that portion seemed to have evolved in a more or less organic way.

Hence, a vernacular region can be considered as an open system; it is a relatively stable condensation of the social and cultural world, where local group dynamics, daily interactions – public and private – and individual trajectories take place; within, local social representations and a sense of community develop. It is also held by social dynamics, relating it to the wider environment, such as institutions defined at the level of the state, and it is anchored in a geographical and material space. Finally, a region, as sociomaterial reality, is not immutable: but the speed at which it usually changes is slower than, say, children, and it reflects historical transformations, while appearing as relatively stable from the perspective of people.

2.3 What Is a Region Made of?

Assuming that a region can be defined and that it offers a manageable scale to observe, describe and analyse sociogenetic, ontogenetic and microgenetic dynamics, then what is it made of? At a descriptive level, as we will see, it is made of a geographical space, with its specific geological, ecological and urbanistic arrangements: stones, trees, villages and roads. It is then made of people, living, acting, moving in that space but also, dreaming, voting, cultivating their fields and raising children. Finally, it is about stories, values, institutions and identities. How to organise all these elements and avoid building lists à la Prévert (1946)? Admitting that theories give us the categories and concepts to reveal, describe, deconstruct and reconstruct the world in certain ways, a theoretical entrance needs to be defined. It is clear that a biologist could offer a detailed classification of the flora of a hill, and a geologist could describe the properties of its floor. Similarly, anthropologists, sociologists or economists would address a region with their own vocabulary, and theoretical or empirical goals. What, then, is the theoretical entrance of a sociocultural psychologist on a hill? My aim is to address the mutual making of lifecourses and the evolution of a hill; I thus propose an order which will make visible socio-, micro- and ontogenetic dynamics. I will thus theoretically organise that field, so that I can then use smaller scale, mid-range concepts to make psycho-sociocultural processes visible.

In order to define a range of actionable notions and concepts, I operate three analytical distinctions. The first one is the more substantial: I propose to distinguish, analytically, notions and concepts primarily intended to describe the material and geographical reality, from those primarily used to describe semiotic or semantic realities. Differently said, there are concepts and notions needed to account, from an observer's perspective, in a given sociocultural and material reality, for places, houses, stones, as well as notions to account for things such as social representations or values. It is important to note that this proposition is not based on the claim of an ontological division between matter and meaning; on the contrary, I consider them as constituting a continuum – both in accordance with dynamic approaches and non-dualistic ontologies and with the evidence that for humans, one cannot be perceived or conceived without the other. However, the distinction is useful here, first because it draws on different disciplinary traditions – some being more inclined to describe material aspects, other, semiotic ones – and second, because when talking about a region, there is a wide range of phenomena which demands very specific combinations of these two aspects. To take an example which will be of importance in these pages, the notion of landscape is typically one that is meant to designate a portion of the geographical and material world, but it is also always and already semiotically constituted by whoever uses the term, or defines, designates, depicts evaluates or preserves a specific "landscape" (Ingold, 2012; Lewin, 2009; Simmel, 2007). I will thus propose a conceptual space, assuming there can be a gradation from notion primarily useful to describe "stuff" out there and others primarily describing "meaning" – and a full zone of overlap (Fig. 2.1).

A second distinction, introduced above, still needs to be maintained, that between concepts and notions that enable to account for the sociomaterial reality from a third-person perspective, from those to account for specific persons', or first-person perspective. Hence, if a community agrees to find highly significant the landscape constituted by the profile of a hill, each person may have his or her relation to that hill and give a personal sense to the otherwise consensually shared meanings. The implication of this is that a first-person perspective on ontogenetic movement needs a specific vocabulary to be accounted for.

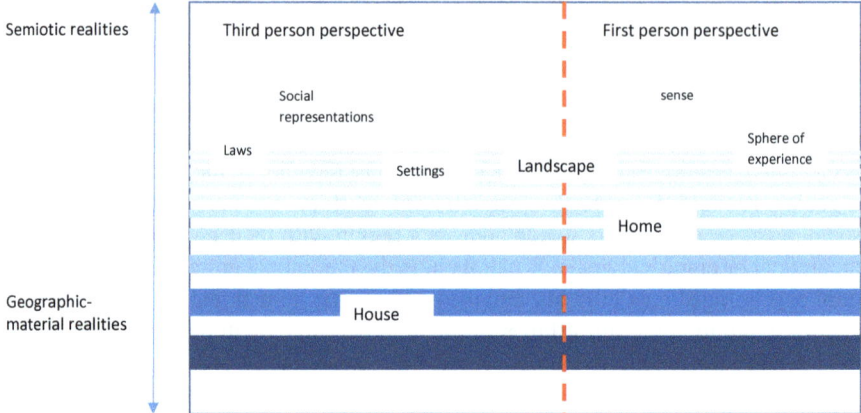

Fig. 2.1 Conceptual space, with a few examples

A third distinction is at the border of redundancy but needs to be signalled: that between notions and concepts that describe stable entities, and those that describe dynamic ones. Again, this is not an ontological statement: I assume here that all is always in becoming and processual, and ideally, even epistemologically, one should accordingly only use processual concepts. However, from the perspective of the observer, and also, from that of observed people, some entities are in principle stable: a hill, a house (or at least their stability is taken for granted, with the exception of state of war and natural disaster). Of course, these could be described as temporary assemblage of matter, energy and meaning, but this would make the writing cumbersome. It may thus be more relevant to use the common-sense notion of a house to account for a stable material reality and to analytically distinguish from the related more theoretical notion of "home", which can be conceived of as accounting for a first-person experience, at the junction of the symbolic and the material, allowing to observe homemaking as a process (Genini, 2016).

These three distinctions being made, I now start to deploy three sets of notions and concepts allowing to account for socio, onto and microgenetic dynamics. I do it quite straightforwardly, only taking the space to defend or present in more nuanced way concepts necessary to account for psychological dynamics and that will ground the further development of this work.

2.3.1 Sociogenesis: Places, Events and Mobilities

On an abstract level, the concept of environment (rather than "context", to avoid the issue mentioned above), in the sense of the environment of a given system (Van Geert, 2003), allows to designate that portion of social and material world that is relevant to account for the lives of people. Sociogenetic dynamics are usually described by historians and sociologists or even social psychologists.

To describe the material-geographical reality from a third-person perspective, I will need to speak about very common-sense stable entities: villages, roads, a hill made of certain geological properties, etc. However, the semantic level is always at the crest of the material entities: fields correspond to cadastres, some houses are churches and thus reflect complex cultural subsystems (see below). Other third-person-perspective entities are mainly symbolic or semantic, such a laws, or political decisions structuring the life of a region. However, these are soon to be materialised in written texts, oral orders and possibly, physical activities or even violence.

To account for the same geographical and semantic realities from a more dynamic perspective, I will use the notions of circulation and mobility (Urry, 2007). These two notions designate both material and semantic dynamics, as it is possible to talk of circulation of ideas (in the semantic field) as well as of persons (in the geographical space) (Zittoun, 2009b), or of actual physical mobilities, as well as imaginary ones (Appadurai, 1996; Salazar, 2011; Zittoun, In press). Interestingly, the distinction allows here to show points of tensions, where for instance a person's geographical mobility is not symbolically acknowledged, as for instance in the case of undocumented or socially excluded migrants (Ellis & Stam, 2017; Gillespie, Kadianaki, & O'Sullivan-Lago, 2012).

At that level, to speak about the more semantic counterpart of what constitutes a region, then one can use notions such as social representations (Moscovici, 2008; Valsiner, 2003), values or socially shared meanings (Zavereshneva & van der Veer, 2018).

Finally, a notion to account for perturbations of sociogenetic moments is needed. In dynamic system theory, this would be designated by the notion of "catastrophe" – that what disturbs a state of equilibrium – but it is too generic to be used at this level. As we have reserved the more empirical notion of rupture for a first-person perspective, I will avoid using it for major sociocultural discontinuities (Zittoun et al., 2013). I thus propose to use here the notion of an "historical event" to account for a catastrophe from a third-person perspective. A historical event designate the disturbance of the order of things, in such way that it is thematised socially and, politically. Finally it has consequences for people (it leaves traces, Capdevila, 2016), which are also addressed retrospectively, historically. A historical event is likely to be experienced as rupture by many, but does not have to be so by everybody.

2.3.2   Microgenesis: Cultural Sub-systems, Frames of Activity, Networks, Boundaries

When we adopt a microgenetic perspective, the social and material environment appears to people in specific encounters, taking place in material and social settings (Gillespie, In preparation). In more dynamic terms, a setting engages people in various social frames – as frames result in and are negotiated by on-going activities and interactions (Goffman, 1974; Perret-Clermont, 2015; Zittoun & Perret-Clermont, 2009; Zittoun et al., 2013).

Very often, these settings can also be characterised by the specific sets of semiotic networks or rules that constitute them, which can be called cultural subsystems. Referring to Geertz's notion of cultural system (Geertz, 1972), I here designate a specific socially shared group of activities and practices, regulated by their rules, with certain values, attributing roles to certain individuals and including some cultural elements. I would not call them cultural systems to avoid, at the level of a region, to turn this into a "regional culture" with the risk of essentialising the notion. The notion of sub-system will thus be useful to designate the informal cultural arrangements around a local pub or the more formalised practices of a hunter association.

The notion of social network designates the complex arrangement of interpersonal relations that can be deployed around people, through time and space – I will use here in a non-technical way (otherwise see Scott & Stokman, 2015).

When, at a microgenetic level, the main dynamic at stance is not the interaction between two persons or the activity of a person with matter, it may also be an intergroup one (Tajfel, 1981). Social anthropologists use the notion of "boundary work" (Dahinden, 2013) to show the processes by which people create or transform symbolic boundaries, understood as distinctions "that can be expressed through normative interdictions (taboos), cultural attitudes and practices, and patterns of likes and dislikes" (Lamont, Pendergrass, & Pachucki, 2015, p. 850).

At this level, catastrophes or disruption of the order of things can happen, as in conflicts, or incidents. I did not witness any directly, and had access only to them through first-person account, so I will treat them as ruptures.

2.3.3   Ontogenesis: Proximal and Distal Spheres of Experience, Imagination and Ruptures

Ontogenetic dynamics can be described from a third-person perspective, statically, in terms of status or positions, and dynamically, in terms of developmental trajectories. However, to enter more in detail on the first-person perspective, one needs a different set of notions.

To describe the first-person perspective at any moment or place – when a person is engaged in any type of activities, in material, social or purely symbolic interactions – we proposed the notion of sphere of experience (Zittoun, 2012; Zittoun & Gillespie, 2015a). As I have here the space, I will retrace how we came to propose that notion, in dialogue with a group of researchers writing almost a century ago.

Let us first recall Kurt Lewin's early work: as a young soldier, he tried to account for the phenomenological experience of the changing landscape as he was moving towards the front. His 1917 paper opens with a distinction between the actual geographical and physical field, and the psychological field – that of the experienced counterpart of the former. The psychological field is the one transformed by action, movement, imagination and emotional experience (Lewin, 1917/2009). In his later work, Lewin foregrounded the psychological field, showing the constant evolution of the life-space of the person, as function of the relation of the person's experience to the environment. The person can explore new regions of the life-space or expand it, through geographical or social movements, and or even imaginary ones, through time (Lewin, 1939, p. 878). Hence, in such descriptions, the actuality of the social and material field is backgrounded. As the anchor points in the person's phenomenological experience, life-space is one, and it continuously morphs into new shapes.

However, knower of early Lewin (in text and in person), Lev Vygotsky tried, towards the end of his life in 1934 (Zavereshneva & van der Veer, 2018, pp. 483–501), to further reflect these initial distinctions. He distinguished two interdependent fields of experience, the field or level of meaning-making, and the field of activity and conduct, taking place in the material and cultural world. He thus reflected on cases of people with disabilities engaging either into meaningless and repetitive activities in the "real field" (Zavereshneva & van der Veer, 2018, p. 497), or in endless meaning and imagination, unbounded to activity. In contrast, proposes Vygotsky, the solution to human conduct would be in the free binding and articulation between these two planes. However, these intuitions were not developed further.

Alfred Schuetz pursued a comparable attempt to describe the person's experienced world and to distinguish it from the social world seen by others (Schuetz, 1944, 1945a, 1945b, 1951). This is what led him to describe the multiple worlds in which the person may be finding herself and which he called provinces of meaning. A person alternates his or her provinces of meaning, which are different while watching a film, daydreaming or walking in the street or working; some are overt, visible to others, and others are covert, as in daydreaming. These can be distinguished from what is external to the person and shared within the social environment surrounding the person; he calls these the cultural patterns of group life (for discussions of Schuetz's work see Stenner, 2017, pp. 151–173; Zittoun & Gillespie, 2015c). Hence, Schuetz seems to have lost the geographical and material counterparts of these cultural patterns of meaning.

What these approaches have in common is a nondualist apprehension of the person in the world: the division is not between person and world, body and mind or affective versus cognitive life. On the contrary, they all follow an idea of on-going experience in flow, and consider experiencing as being more or less engaging in activities with matters and tools, or in interpreting the world. They then, with more or less precision, tried to differentiate this experiencing person from the actual cultural-material world that creates the conditions for these experiences. It is to continue such efforts in theorisation that I have, together with Alex Gillespie, tried to develop a vocabulary that enables to catch these different planes of experience and reality (Gillespie & Zittoun, 2015; Zittoun & Gillespie, 2015a). As shown above, we first propose to adopt a third-person perspective to describe and account for the world as it can be apprehended from a usually socially shared perspective, in terms of environment, settings, places and houses.

To approach the first-person perspective, we have then proposed to call "sphere of experience" a specific configuration of activity, sense, feeling, aspects of self (or dialogical positions, Hermans, 2011) and conducts, which is recurrent enough, for a given person, to be identified as "the same" and as "taken for granted". The notion thus resembles that of a province of meaning by Schuetz, but it adds to it its material, embodied and social grounding. In effect, we consider it partly shaped, but not strictly, by material conditions. Hence, a "family dinner" for a given person may need the presence of an n-number of family members and food, but may not be bound by a place – it can take place in the living room, in the garden or at the restaurant. If x persons are missing or if the food is too informal, the experience of eating may simply not be a "family dinner" configuration for that person. In the same garden, the person may be engaged in another sphere of experience, "reading", which may encompass the same spot under the tree than a dinner, but this time a book of fiction and a different range of affects, activities and engagements. Hence, as in Lewin, we admit that the person's living experience is partly shaped by the environment, but consider that the person is not having *one* life-space endlessly transforming; we consider it useful to distinguish different spheres of experience. Finally, and to account both for the fact that these can be expanded in imagination, to keep the Schutzien's intuition of overt and covert provinces of meaning, and also to account for the fact that these can be more or less anchored in actual activities, as proposed by Vygotsky, we proposed to distinguish proximal from distal spheres of experience.

A "proximal" sphere of experience takes place in a specific place and social activity, during a microgenetic moment or duration, and it is this social and material actuality that is relevant for the person, in consciousness. "Distal" experiences are characterised by the fact that the person's attention or intention is engaged in a foremost symbolic space, which can be ignoring, overwriting, expanding or bracketing (Bogdan, 2013) the actual social and geographical nature of the physical and relational situation. Distal experiences can be experienced bodily as well, but they are in any case achieved by imagination. Imagination is itself defined as the dynamic process of looping out of the here-and-now, of temporarily decoupling the flow of consciousness from the proximal nature of experience (Zittoun & Gillespie, 2016).

The notion of rupture is here designating a person's sense of disruption of spheres of experience. It is more than the "mild shock" identified by Schutz when moving from one sphere of experience to the other, as in transitive transitions; it rather happens when a situation or event makes irruption in an otherwise taken-for-granted experience. Ruptures, which can be caused by external events or incidents or by inner changes or realisations, then call for further changes. They thus are usually followed by transitions, the processes of exploring new ways of handling a situation, defining oneself or making sense of the situation, in such ways that the person may develop a new sphere of experience (Zittoun, 2006, 2009a). Learning and development are quite likely to occur during such transitions (Hedegaard & Edwards, 2014; Märtsin, Chang, & Obst, 2016; Zittoun, 2006, 2014), which have thus a certain liminal quality (Stenner, 2017).

2.4 Human Development in a Region

Human development during the lifecourse can be understood as on-going process of change, from conception to death. Of course it depends on the biological maturation of the organism and its continuous transformations, but as now commonly admitted, this is deeply and intrinsically shaped by socio-relational, cultural and semiotic dynamics (Baltes, Lindenberger, & Staudinger, 2006; Cole, 2007; Zittoun et al., 2013).

2.4.1 Development as Transactions

In the vocabulary defined above, development can be considered as the on-going transactions between the person and his/her environment, translated in the establishment, coordination, transformation and disappearance of spheres of experience; it is thus about the constant evolution of the configuration of a person's proximal and distal spheres of experience. As is well known, psychological development is foremost dependent on interactions and social relationships, as these are always already culturally shaped and take place in specific social, material and cultural environments. With time, as the child moves out of his/her initial close relational circle, he or she explores more and more cultural settings, engages in a diversity of social frames, with demand the learning of new semiotic systems and cultural subsystems, and which, in turn, transform his/her modes of thinking, perceiving, feeling and more generally, modes of conduct. In each of these, he/she is likely to develop one or more spheres of experience. Research has largely shown how modalities of the human relations and interactions, mediated by cultural objects and semiotic systems, are key in the development of the person (Mäkitalo, Linell, & Säljö, 2017; Nelson, 2007; Rogoff, 2003). Of course, with time, the others with which one interacts vary, and can become more general or distant (Gillespie, 2006; Zittoun, 2010); also, progressively, human interactions may become secondary to person-cultural object interactions: from their childhood onwards, people interact with toys, trees, laptops, books and TV programmes, and through all of these, people develop and learn more or less actively (Singer & Singer, 1992, 2005).

2.4.2 Internalisation: How Cultural Meanings Become Psychological

Through these interactions, key processes have been named differently, but I will use here the concepts of internalisation to designate the process by which the cultural becomes recreated from within, or is "ingrown" in the person (Arievitch & van der Veer, 1995; Lawrence & Valsiner, 1993; Valsiner, 1997, 2014; Vygotsky,

1929, 1975; Zavereshneva & van der Veer, 2018), and of externalisation, to designate the process by which the person acts out new cultural forms, through any semiotic and embodied activity.

Internalisation can be further analysed. Valsiner (1997, 2019) proposed a three-layer model of internalisation, suggesting that signs and meanings could be, first, absorbed superficially and then forgotten, second, internalised just enough to be repeatable as they were – that is, ventriloquised (Gillespie, 2005) – or, third, actively synthesised and recreated from within. In addition, and following here Vygotsky's attempt to pinpoint "higher-level" mediation and development, Valsiner shows how signs can generate signs that mediate other signs, or new semiotic creations which create new possible future mediations (Valsiner, 2001, 2007a).

We also tried to account for internalisation of complex social and cultural guidance, as in position exchange (when interactions invite to take the position of the other on oneself (Gillespie & Martin, 2014; Martin & Gillespie, 2010)), and in cultural experiences guided by music, reading or films (Vygotsky, 1971; Zittoun, 2013, 2016d; Zittoun & Gillespie, 2014). In both cases, socially shared semiotic configurations guide and shape the person's flow of experience in certain ways and, so to say, bend it so as to privilege certain feelings, perspectives and new semiotic elaborations. We thus proposed that the two sociocultural patterns, those of position exchange and cultural experiences, do guide a certain movement of the semiotic flow of consciousness, and that it is this movement, rather than the actual interaction or the cultural element, which is then internalised, that is, recreated from within (Zittoun & Gillespie, 2015b).

In addition, people are not only exposed to others and to objects, they are also exposed to settings organised into institutions, and to the environment in the broader sense of geographical and material places and spaces. I will leave here institutions, as they usually appear to people through arrangements of settings, interactions, norms etc.; although promoting certain forms of internalisation, these are less relevant for this study (but see Gillespie & Zittoun, 2013; Marková, 2018; Zittoun, 2016a).

Regarding people's relation to their broader environment, Jaan Valsiner recently highlighted the fact that cultural worlds expose people to redundant motives or ornaments, which may play an invisible yet substantial role in human development. Ornaments are for instance the geometrical patterns on classical temples and buildings, the framing of paintings, or the shapes of hairdos and tattoos. Valsiner identifies four characteristics or ornaments:

> (1) In ornaments, there is high redundancy – *repetition of the form*, either precisely or approximately. (…); (2) Ornaments *involve direction of suggested movement*. It can be horizontal (right or left) or vertical (upwards<>downwards), often both. Furthermore— ornaments can center symmetrically, or guide the experiencing person towards one or another (left or right) direction. (…); (3) Ornaments are *perceptually peripheral but semantically central*. Their redundancy makes it ever-influential and unavoidable. (Valsiner, 2019b, pp. 3–4, emphasis original)

To which he also adds a fourth point:

> The important characteristic of ornaments is their trans-materiality—a similar pattern can be found on the body, on clothing surrounding the body, on the walls of the building where the body lives or works, on the architectural construction that the person experiences in the

public space (Contadini, 2016). Similar patterns can occur in different media-on skin, on textiles, on walls, on paper or wood. This makes it possible for the whole field of the person to be saturated by a particular form—such as a spiral, or a lotus flower. (Valsiner, 2019, p. 236)

Based on this multi-modal semiotic redundancy, Valsiner proposes the following developmental thesis:

My main claim (…) is that external (visual and other—musical, olfactory, etc.) ornaments relate to our deeply subjective worlds that are set up in similar ways— with a focus on the relations of the total field being differentiated by specific actions through the use of signs. (Valsiner, 2019, p. 237)

Hence, ornaments guide another type of experience, and although not internalised per se, the movement they initiate in the organisation of a person's perception may operate from within, creating certain expectations and forms of future orientation. This interesting idea, developed through everyday observations, careful historical and iconographical analysis, Valsiner has not yet fully empirically demonstrated. It is however worth mentioning here for two reasons at least. First, Valsiner proposes here the first systematic account of how the environment[1] may, in a more diffuse way, also participate in the specific developmental trajectory of a person. Hence, one may, for instance, raise the following hypothetic question: assuming that two persons had exactly the same life trajectory – same family, same social networks, same learning and professional choice – with the only difference that one person lives a life surrounded by forests, while the other lives surrounded by the towers of a town, would their experiences be the same? The answer appears obvious, but why and how? Valsiner's idea of redundant ornaments in specific experiential landscapes – shapes, colours, sounds, smells – suggests that the periphery of the experience of these persons has been constantly shaped in very different manner. And perhaps internalising years of changing colours of tree leafs and birdsongs creates a different organisation of mind than years of square blocks and windows and humming of claxons and radios.

The second reason to mention this here is that the analysis of ornamentation as semiotic guidance goes in the same direction than the one we made about complex cultural or interactive guidance: these guide, from without, a specific movement of part of the flow of consciousness, and thus may lead the person to be able to reproduce that same patterned movement from within. Both intuitions will be of importance to study development in the hill region.

2.4.3 Developing in a Region

To sum up, development in the life of people living in a given region is likely to occur in four key points. First, learning in diverse social frames, the person develops – there can be development in each sphere of experience, but there might

---

[1] For Jaan Valsiner, the study of ornaments is a mean to access to our relationship to panorama (personal communication).

also be routines and habits, which are not developmental per se once installed. Second, development is likely to take place as the person moves from one sphere of experience to the next. This is especially the case when the disappearance of a sphere is provoked by a rupture – an event that the person experiences as disruption of one or many spheres of experience, and that demands to engage in the creation of new ones, which eventually occurs through processes of transition. For such new creations, the person never starts from the scratch but draws on existing knowledge, skills or symbolic resources from other spheres of experiences, or provided by the social and cultural environment; the person integrates material into new modes of acting, thinking or presenting herself – we called it horizontal integration. Third, with time, people are also likely to learn from learning, or to learn from lived experience (within, across spheres of experience); these meta-learning can be conceived of as attempts to integrate experience more vertically and these are always semiotic creative synthesis, which may use semiotic forms available in the social and cultural environment. We have thus suggested that people may develop as "personal life philosophies", a term proposed by Vygotsky and then developed by Jaan Valsiner: these may express, for an older person, in one formula, the synthesis of a life time of experience, often through the use of common-sense expressions and proverbs (Zittoun, 2012; Zittoun & Gillespie, 2015a; Zittoun et al., 2013). And fourth, development may also be shaped by the more discrete, but constant, exposure to one's living environment, conceived as semiosphere exposing to redundant shapes, sounds and forms and guiding and organising one's experience according to some patterned movements. What do I mean by that?

2.5   A Theoretical Proposition: Patterned Experiences

The theoretical proposition I am making here is that development in a region renders visible the dynamic patterned nature of human experience. By *dynamic pattern*, I mean a movement that follows a specific configuration of dynamically coordinated elements and that has certain stability. Hence, drawing a circle with one's finger in the air is such a dynamic pattern: it is a movement following invisible points, yet which has a configuration stable enough to be perceived as a circle by an observer (however approximate that circle may be). The proposition is that, similarly, living in a given environment also generates dynamic patterns of feeling, perception, thinking or acting and thus engages experience.

2.5.1   Patterns in Development

The search for patterns in human conduct is by no means new in psychology. It can be considered at two levels. At a metatheroetical level, the very attempt to identify order in the infinite diversity of experience through model building, or generalisation, can be seen as the search for configurations or patterns (Zittoun, 2016b). At a second level, many theories in psychology actually look for patterns in conduct or modalities of interactions. To take two well-known examples, the study of early interactions has thus highlighted the rhythmic and patterned nature of harmonious infant-adult interactions, through careful microgenetic analysis and with the help of dynamic system approaches. Drawing on Daniel Stern's work, Español thus recalls that early infant-parent interactions depend on a mutual, dialogical affective engagement, defined by the circulation of affective experiences' patterns between protagonists:

> *Attunement* (…) is a type of imitation of some chosen features, while others are disregarded. It is not about a faithful translation of the open conduct, but rather of a type of matching, frequently cross-modal, of intensity, temporal or spatial patterns of some conduct. In this manner, there are at least six types of matches: (1) absolute intensity: the level of intensity of conduct A is equal to the level of intensity of conduct B, whatever its modality, (2) profile of intensity: the object to be matched is the changes of intensity in time (for example, acceleration-de-acceleration), (3) pulsation: a regular pulsation is matched in time, (4) rhythm: a pattern of pulsations of unequal emphasis are matched, (5) duration: the lapse of the conduct is matched, (6) spatial pattern: some spatial features of the conducts, susceptible of being abstracted and transformed into different acts, are matched. As opposed to imitation, which keeps attention focused on the external shape of behaviour, attunement brings out that which underlies behaviour, the "character of the shared feeling", to the focus of attention. That is why attunement is the predominant mode of sharing internal states or showing that they are being shared. The matched external conducts may differ in shape and mode but they are interchangeable as manifestations of a recognizable internal state. (Español, 2007, p. 243)

Later with development, these patterns, which are flexible and multimodal, continue to evolve and to be transformed into patterns of conduct, which are culturally mediated and thus form the basis of symbolic externalisations. Comparably, attachment styles have also, to some part, been conceived as preferential relational patterns (Ainsworth, Blehar, Waters, & Wall, 2015). The theory of attachment indeed proposes that some modalities of engaging with others, acting, feeling and trusting, develop through early relationships and constitute then first patterns of feeling, acting and trusting other persons and situations. These theories say something about very early, non-conscious modes of patterning experience, engaging in a quasi-automatic way one's feeling-in and acting-in the world. Yet these patterns are flexible enough to be revised and transformed in future interactions.

What these studies have in common is the idea that a pattern is a certain type of movement, eventually psychologically experienced, which organises a mode of feeling, being, acting, thinking and meaning, and that is, for a large part, built through interactions with the environment – first with the carers (as affectively significant others), then with others and objects. Patterns are multimodal, transformative, and can become more and more semiotically elaborated and complex.

If we now link these observations to the ones made before, regarding cultural guidance, ornaments and internalisation, then we can see very comparable phenomena. Cultural elements, such as song or novels, become internalised symbolic resources as forms of semiotically enabled, patterned movements of experiencing; ornaments are patterns that guide, from without, inner experience. Where I am heading to, here, is that there is some very fundamental developmental process, whereby the world, as it is given to the person, provides guidance of certain patterns of feeling-acting-thinking, that is, experiencing. These patterns are mostly fluid, evolving and can become complex, abstract, differentiated and generalised – as we know about any form of semiotic mediation (Valsiner, 2014).

The notion of pattern will therefore allow me to bind sociogenetic, microgenetic and ontogenetic movements when studying a region. In effect, if human experience can be guided by any aspect of the relational, material and geographical space, we need a notion that may capture "things" that may circulate from what is observable in the world, to what people say or do. The notion of pattern, as guided dynamic movement, may offer us such an analyser. It can enable us to identify forms, shapes, expressions or modes of actions that circulate in and around people within a region and that are made visible by an analysis at three levels of change.

2.5.2 Looking for Patterns

So let us open up a series of questions related to development at three levels in a specific region. First, how is the history of a region organised and when and how is it used symbolically? Are they some dominant features, can we identify patterns here?

Second, at the level of people's lifecourses, if people develop through and from experiences, and if most of these experiences take place in a region, which is itself marked by a series of significant historical events, then how is a person's lifecourse shaped by that history? In what respect is a changing sociocultural environment defining a course of life and its uniqueness, how and in what respect can a person still develop as unique person, with his/her unique life experience – does one develop specific patterns of sense making?

Third, at the level of microgenetic movements, what if a majority of a person's interactions and activities, or proximal spheres of experience, are taking place in a specific, relatively bounded region? The question becomes especially relevant if we consider the embodied, geographically grounded activities in which people engage in that region: people moving between two settings within the region (walking, biking and driving), people participating in the transformation of its materiality (cultivating fields, planting trees, and attending wild animals) or people cultivating the semiotic aspects of the region (maintaining rites or myths, or simply contemplating or representing the landscape). What do people experience, and in what sense can it be said that people's experiences within their geographical and symbolic, specifically delimited region, participate in their development? Is there something specific that comes from that consistency, which is more than the sum and the integration of spheres of experience? And what about people's distal spheres of experience, do they follow proximal ones? Can we see patterns in the organisation of one's lives?

Finally, if put together, sociogenesis, ontogenesis and microgenesis and their mutual determination, what do we see? This is what we will examine in turn.

References

Ainsworth, M. D. S., Blehar, M. C., Waters, E., & Wall, S. N. (2015). *Patterns of attachment: A psychological study of the strange situation* (1st ed.). New York, NY: Psychology Press.

Appadurai, A. (1996). *Modernity at large: Cultural dimensions of globalization*. Minneapolis: University of Minnesota press.

Arievitch, I., & van der Veer, R. (1995). Furthering the internalization debate: Gal'perin's contribution. *Human Development, 38*(2), 113–126. https://doi.org/10.1159/000278304

Baidal, J. A. I. (2016). Region. In J. Jafari & H. Xiao (Eds.), *Encyclopedia of tourism* (pp. 782–783). Cham (Switzerland): Springer. https://doi.org/10.1007/978-3-319-01384-8_486

Baltes, P. B., Lindenberger, U., & Staudinger, U. M. (2006). Life span theory in developmental psychology. In W. Damon & R. M. Lerner (Eds.), *Handbook of child psychology: Vol. 1. Theoretical models of human development* (6th ed., pp. 569–664). New York: Wiley.

Benson, C. (2001). *The cultural psychology of self: Place, morality and art in human worlds*. London: Routledge.

Bergson, H. (1938). *La pensée et le mouvant*. Paris: Presses Universitaires de France.

Blunden, A. (2016). Translating Perezhivanie into English. *Mind, Culture, and Activity, 23*(4), 274–283. https://doi.org/10.1080/10749039.2016.1186193

Bogdan, R. J. (2013). *Mindvaults: Sociocultural grounds for pretending and imagining*. Cambridge, MA: MIT Press.

Brinkmann, S. (2013). Practice of self-observation in the phenomenological traditions. In J. W. Clegg (Ed.), *Self-observation in the social sciences* (pp. 195–222). New Brunswick, NJ/London, UK: Transaction Publishers.

Bronfenbrenner, U. (1979). *The ecology of human development: Experiments by nature and design*. Cambridge, MA: Harvard University Press.

Capdevila, L. (2016). Les temporalités de l'événement en histoire. In D. Alexandre, M. Frédéric, S. Parent, & M. Touret (Eds.), *Que se passe-t-il?: Évènements, sciences humaines et littérature* (pp. 80–89). Rennes: Presses universitaires de Rennes. Retrieved from http://books.openedition.org/pur/35841

Clot, Y. (2002). *La fonction psychologique du travail* (3rd ed.). Paris: Presses universitaires de France.

Clough, L. D. (2008). Region. In *The Encyclopedia of Earth*. Retrieved from https://editors.eol.org/eoearth/wiki/Region

Cole, M. (1996). *Cultural psychology. A once and future discipline*. Cambridge, MA/London: The Belknap Press of Harvard University Press.

Cole, M. (2007). Phylogeny and cultural history in ontogeny. *Journal of Physiology-Paris, 101*(4–6), 236–246. https://doi.org/10.1016/j.jphysparis.2007.11.007

Cole, M. (2016). Designing for development: Across the scales of time. *Developmental Psychology, 52*(11), 1679–1689. https://doi.org/10.1037/dev0000156

Contadini, A. (2016). Threads of ornament in the style world of the fifteenth and sixteenth centuries. In G. Necipoğlu & A. Payne (Eds.), *Histories of ornament: From global to local* (pp. 290–308). Retrieved from https://eprints.soas.ac.uk/19894/

Dahinden, J. (2013). Cities, migrant incorporation, and ethnicity: A network perspective on boundary work. *Journal of International Migration and Integration, 14*(1), 39–60. https://doi.org/10.1007/s12134-011-0224-2

de Saint-Laurent, C., & Glăveanu, V. P. (2016). Reflexivity. In V. P. Glăveanu, L. Tanggaard, & C. Wegener (Eds.), *Creativity: A New Vocabulary* (pp. 121–126). London: Palgrave Macmillan.

Denzin, N. K. (2001). The reflexive interview and a performative social science. *Qualitative Research, 1*(1), 23–46. https://doi.org/10.1177/146879410100100102

Doise, W. (1980). Levels of explanation in the European journal of social psychology. *European Journal of Social Psychology, 10*(3), 213–231. https://doi.org/10.1002/ejsp.2420100302

Doise, W., & Mapstone, E. (1986). *Levels of explanation in social psychology*. New York, NY: Cambridge University Press.

Duveen, G., & Lloyd, B. (Eds.). (1990). *Social representations and the development of knowledge.* Cambridge, UK: Cambridge University Press.

Ellis, B. D., & Stam, H. J. (2017). Cycles of deportability: Threats, fears, and the agency of 'irregular' migrants in Canada. *Migration Studies, 6,* 1–24. https://doi.org/10.1093/migration/mnx049

Engeström, Y. (2011). From design experiments to formative interventions. *Theory & Psychology, 21*(5), 598–628. https://doi.org/10.1177/0959354311419252

Español, S. (2007). Time and movement in symbol formation. In J. Valsiner & A. Rosa (Eds.), *Cambridge handbook of sociocultural psychology* (pp. 238–256). Cambridge: Cambridge University Press.

Flick, U. (1992). Triangulation revisited: Strategy of validation or alternative? *Journal for the Theory of Social Behaviour, 22*(2), 175–197.

Geertz, C. (1972). La religion comme système culturel. In R. E. Bradbury, C. Geertz, M. E. Spiro, V. W. Turner, & E. H. Winter (Eds.), *Essais d'anthropologie religieuse* (pp. 19–66). Paris: Gallimard.

Genini, L. (2016). Home sweet home? *Dossiers de psychologie et éducation, 74.* Retrieved from http://doc.rero.ch/record/258556

Gillespie, A. (2005). Malcolm X and his autobiography: Identity development and self-narration. *Culture & Psychology, 11*(1), 77–88.

Gillespie, A. (2006). *Becoming other: From social interaction to self-reflection.* Greenwich, CT: Information Age Publishing.

Gillespie, A. (In preparation). *Disruption, Self-Presentation and Defensive Tactics at the Threshold of Learning.*

Gillespie, A., & Cornish, F. (2010). What can be said? Identity as a constraint on knowledge production. *Papers on Social Representations, 19,* 5.1–5.13.

Gillespie, A., Cornish, F., Aveling, E.-L., & Zittoun, T. (2008). Living with war: Community resources, self-dialogues and psychological adaptation to World War II. *Journal of Community Psychology, 36*(1), 35–52.

Gillespie, A., Kadianaki, I., & O'Sullivan-Lago, R. (2012). Encountering alterity: Geographic and semantic movements. In J. Valsiner (Ed.), *The Oxford handbook of culture and psychology* (pp. 695–709). Oxford, UK: Oxford University Press.

Gillespie, A., & Martin, J. (2014). Position exchange theory: A socio-material basis for discursive and psychological positioning. *New Ideas in Psychology, 32,* 73–79. https://doi.org/10.1016/j.newideapsych.2013.05.001

Gillespie, A., & Zittoun, T. (2013). Meaning making in motion: Bodies and minds moving through institutional and semiotic structures. *Culture & Psychology, 19*(4), 518–532. https://doi.org/10.1177/1354067X13500325

Gillespie, A., & Zittoun, T. (2015). Social and psychological movement: Weaving individual experience into society. In B. Wagoner, N. Chaudhary, & P. Hviid (Eds.), *Integrating experiences: Body and mind moving between contexts* (pp. 279–294). Charlotte, NC: Information Age Publishing.

Goffman, E. (1974). *Frame analysis: An essay on the organization of experience* (New edition). New York, NY: Harper & Row.

Grossen, M. (2001). La notion de contexte: Quelle définition pour quelle psychologie? Un essai de mise au point. In J.-P. Bernié (Ed.), *Apprentissage, développement et significations* (pp. 59–76). Bordeaux: Presses Universitaires de Bordeaux.

Grossen, M. (2010). Interaction analysis and psychology: A dialogical perspective. *Integrative Psychological and Behavioral Science, 44*(1), 1–22. https://doi.org/10.1007/s12124-009-9108-9

Hedegaard, M. (2012). Analyzing children's learning and development in everyday settings from a cultural-historical wholeness approach. *Mind, Culture, and Activity, 19*(2), 127–138. https://doi.org/10.1080/10749039.2012.665560

Hedegaard, M., & Chaiklin, S. (2005). *Radical-local teaching and learning.* Aarhus: Aarhus University press.

Hedegaard, M., & Edwards, A. (2014). Transitions and children's learning. *Learning, Culture and Social Interaction, 3*(3), 185–187. https://doi.org/10.1016/j.lcsi.2014.02.007

Hermans, H. J. M. (2011). The dialogical self. In S. Gallagher (Ed.), *The Oxford handbook of the self*. Oxford: Oxford University Press. Retrieved from http://www.oxfordhandbooks.com/view/10.1093/oxfordhb/9780199548019.001.0001/oxfordhb-9780199548019-e-29

Hviid, P. (2012). 'Remaining the same' and children's experience of development. In M. Hedegaard, K. Aronsson, C. Hojholt, & O. Ulvik (Eds.), *Children, childhood, and everyday life: Children's perspectives* (pp. 37–52). Charlotte, NC: Information Age Publishing, Inc.

Hviid, P. (2015). Borders in education and living–A case of trench warfare. *Integrative Psychological and Behavioral Science, 50*(1), 44–61. https://doi.org/10.1007/s12124-015-9319-1

Ingold, T. (2012). Introduction. In M. Janowski & T. Ingold (Eds.), *Imagining landscapes: Past, present and future* (1st ed., pp. 1–18). Farnham, Surrey, England/Burlington, VT: Routledge.

James, W. (2007). *The principles of psychology*. New York, NY: Cosimo Classic.

Jodelet, D. (1989). *Folies et représentations sociales*. Paris: Presses universitaires de France.

Lamont, M., Pendergrass, S., & Pachucki, M. (2015). Symbolic boundaries. In J. D. Wright (Ed.), *International encyclopedia of the social & behavioral sciences* (2nd ed., pp. 850–855). https://doi.org/10.1016/B978-0-08-097086-8.10416-7

Lawrence, J. A., & Valsiner, J. (1993). Conceptual roots of internalization: From transmission to transformation. *Human Development, 36*(3), 150–167. https://doi.org/10.1159/000277333

Lewin, K. (1939). Field theory and experiment in social psychology: Concepts and methods. *American Journal of Sociology, 44*(6), 868–896. https://doi.org/10.1086/218177

Lewin, K. (2000). Field theory and learning. In *Resolving social conflicts & Field theory in social science* (Original publication 1942, pp. 212–229). Washington, D.C.: American Psychological Association (APA).

Lewin, K. (1917/2009). The landscape of war. *Art in Translation, 1*(2), 199–209.

Mäkitalo, Å., Linell, P., & Säljö, R. (Eds.). (2017). *Memory practices and learning: Interactional, institutional, and sociocultural perspectives*. Charlotte, NC: Information Age Publishing.

Mandal, A. (2016). Size and type of places, geographical region, satisfaction with life, age, sex and place attachment. *Polish Psychological Bulletin, 47*(1), 159–169. https://doi.org/10.1515/ppb-2016-0018

Marková, I. (2015). On context. In B. Wagoner, N. Chaudhary, & P. Hviid (Eds.), *Integrating experiences: Body and mind moving between contexts* (pp. 53–62). Charlotte, NC: Information Age Publishing.

Marková, I. (2016). *The dialogical mind: Common sense and ethics*. Cambridge, UK: Cambridge University Press.

Marková, I. (2018). From imagination to well-controlled images: Challenge for the dialogical mind. In T. Zittoun & V. P. Glăveanu (Eds.), *Oxford handbook of culture and imagination* (pp. 319–344). Oxford: Oxford University Press.

Martin, J., & Gillespie, A. (2010). A neo-meadian approach to human agency: Relating the social and the psychological in the ontogenesis of perspective-coordinating persons. *Integrative Psychological and Behavioral Science, 44*(3), 252–272. https://doi.org/10.1007/s12124-010-9126-7

Märtsin, M., Chang, I., & Obst, P. (2016). Using culture to manage the transition into university: Conceptualising the dynamics of withdrawal and engagement. *Culture & Psychology, 22*(2), 276–295. https://doi.org/10.1177/1354067X15621476

Moghaddam, F. M. (2018). *Mutual radicalization: How groups and nations drive each other to extremes* (1st ed.). Washington, D.C.: American Psychological Association.

Moscovici, S. (2008). *Psychoanalysis. Its image and its public* (G. Duveen, Ed.; D. Macey, Trans.). Cambridge: Polity Press.

Nelson, K. (2007). *Young minds in social worlds. Experience, meaning, and memory*. Cambridge, MA/London: Harvard University Press.

Obschonka, M., Stuetzer, M., Gosling, S. D., Rentfrow, P. J., Lamb, M. E., Potter, J., et al. (2015). Entrepreneurial regions: Do macro-psychological cultural characteristics of regions help solve the "knowledge paradox" of economics? *PLoS One, 10*(6), e0129332. https://doi.org/10.1371/journal.pone.0129332

Perret-Clermont, A.-N. (2004). Articuler l'individuel et le collectif. *Nouvelle Revue de Psychologie Sociale, 3*, 94–102.

Perret-Clermont, A.-N. (2015). The architecture of social relationships and thinking spaces for growth. In C. Psaltis, A. Gillespie, & A.-N. Perret-Clermont (Eds.), *Social Relations in Human and Societal Development* (pp. 51–70). New York: Palgrave Macmillan.

Prévert, J. (1946). Inventaire. In *Paroles*. Paris: Gallimard.

Psaltis, C. (2012). Social representations of gender in peer interaction and cognitive development. *Social and Personality Psychology Compass, 6*(11), 840–851. https://doi.org/10.1111/j.1751-9004.2012.00466.x

Ratner, C. (2012). *Macro cultural psychology. A political philosophy of mind*. New York, NY: Oxford University Press.

Ratner, C. (2014). Macro cultural psychology. In T. Teo (Ed.), *Encyclopedia of critical psychology* (pp. 1095–1111). https://doi.org/10.1007/978-1-4614-5583-7_413

Rogoff, B. (2003). *The cultural nature of human development*. New York, NY: Oxford University Press.

Rosa, A., & Valsiner, J. (Eds.). (2018). *The Cambridge handbook of sociocultural psychology* (2nd ed.). Cambridge: Cambridge University Press. Retrieved from https://doi.org/10.1017/9781316662229

Salazar, N. B. (2011). The power of imagination in transnational mobilities. *Identities, 18*(6), 576–598. https://doi.org/10.1080/1070289X.2011.672859

Salmi, S., & Kumpulainen, K. (2017). Children's experiencing of their transition from preschool to first grade: A visual narrative study. *Learning, Culture and Social Interaction., 20*, 58. https://doi.org/10.1016/j.lcsi.2017.10.007

Salvatore, S. (2016). *Psychology in black and white. The project of a theory driven science*. Charlotte, NC: Information Age Publishing.

Schuetz, A. (1944). The stranger: An essay in social psychology. *American Journal of Sociology, 49*(6), 499–507. https://doi.org/10.2307/2771547

Schuetz, A. (1945a). On multiple realities. *Philosophy and Phenomenological Research, 5*(4), 533–576. https://doi.org/10.2307/2102818

Schuetz, A. (1945b). The homecomer. *American Journal of Sociology, 50*(5), 369–376. https://doi.org/10.2307/2771190

Schuetz, A. (1951). Choosing among projects of action. *Philosophy and Phenomenological Research, 12*(2), 161–184. https://doi.org/10.2307/2103478

Scott, J., & Stokman, F. N. (2015). Social networks. In J. D. Wright (Ed.), *International encyclopedia of the social & behavioral sciences* (2nd ed., pp. 473–477). https://doi.org/10.1016/B978-0-08-097086-8.32101-8

Simmel, G. (2007). The philosophy of landscape. *Theory, Culture & Society, 24*(7–8), 20–29.

Singer, D. G., & Singer, J. L. (1992). *The house of make-believe: Children's play and the developing imagination (reprint)*. Cambridge, MA: Harvard University Press.

Singer, D. G., & Singer, J. L. (2005). *Imagination and play in the electronic age*. Cambridge, MA/London: Harvard University Press.

Spinoza, B. d. (1677). *L'éthique*. Paris: Gallimard.

Stenner, P. (2017). *Liminality and experience. A transdisciplinary approach to the psychosocial*. London: Palgrave Macmillan.

Stenner, P., & Brown, S. D. (2009). *Psychology without foundations: History, philosophy and psychosocial theory*. London: Sage. Retrieved from http://knowledge.sagepub.com/view/psychology-without-foundations/SAGE.xml

Tajfel, H. (1981). Social categorization, social identity and social comparison. In *Humans groups and social categories* (pp. 254–287). Cambridge: Cambridge University Press.

Teo, T. (2015). Critical psychology: A geography of intellectual engagement and resistance. *American Psychologist, 70*(3), 243–254. https://doi.org/10.1037/a0038727

Urry, J. (2007). *Mobilities*. Cambridge: Polity Press.

Valsiner, J. (1997). *Culture and the development of children's action* (2nd ed.). New York, NY: John Wiley and Sons.

Valsiner, J. (2001). Process structure of semiotic mediation in human development. *Human Development, 44*, 84–97.

Valsiner, J. (2003). Beyond social representations: A theory of enablement. *Papers on Social Representations, 12*, 7.1–7.16.

Valsiner, J. (2007a). Constructing the internal infinity: Dialogic structure of the internalization/ externalization process – A commentary on Susswein, Bibok, and Carpendale's "reconceptualizing internalization". *International Journal for Dialogical Science, 2*(1), 207–221.

Valsiner, J. (2007b). *Culture in minds and societies: Foundations of cultural psychology.* New Delhi: Sage.

Valsiner, J. (2014). *An invitation to cultural psychology.* London: Sage.

Valsiner, J. (2019). *Ornamented lives.* Charlotte, NC: Information Age Publishing.

Valsiner, J., & Rosa, A. (Eds.). (2007). *The Cambridge handbook of sociocultural psychology.* Cambridge: Cambridge University Press.

Van Geert, P. (2003). Dynamic systems approaches of modeling of developmental processes. In J. Valsiner & K. J. Conolly (Eds.), *Handbook of developmental psychology* (pp. 640–672). London: Sage.

Vygotsky, L. S. (1929). The problem of the cultural development of the child. *Journal of Genetic Psychology, 36*, 415–432.

Vygotsky, L. S. (1971). *The psychology of art.* Cambridge, MA/London: MIT press.

Vygotsky, L. S. (1975). Internalization of higher psychological functions. In M. Cole (Ed.), *Mind in society* (pp. 52–57). Cambridge, MA: Harvard University Press.

Wagoner, B., Moghaddam, F. M., & Valsiner, J. (2018). *The psychology of radical social change: From rage to revolution.* Cambridge: Cambridge University Press.

Zavereshneva, E., & van der Veer, R. (2018). *Vygotsky's notebooks. A selection.* Singapore: Springer.

Zittoun, T. (2006). *Transitions. Development through symbolic resources.* Greenwich, CT: Information Age Publishing.

Zittoun, T. (2007). Dynamics of interiority. Ruptures and transitions in the self development. In L. M. Simão & J. Valsiner (Eds.), *Otherness in question: Development of the self* (pp. 187–214). Greenwich, CT: Information Age Publishing.

Zittoun, T. (2009a). Dynamics of life-course transitions – A methodological reflection. In J. Valsiner, P. C. M. Molenaar, M. C. D. P. Lyra, & N. Chaudhary (Eds.), *Dynamic process methodology in the social and developmental sciences* (pp. 405–430). New York, NY: Springer.

Zittoun, T. (2009b). La circulation des connaissances: Un regard socioculturel. *Revue Économique et Sociale, 67*(2), 129–138.

Zittoun, T. (2010). How does an object become symbolic? Rooting semiotic artefacts in dynamic shared experiences. In B. Wagoner (Ed.), *Symbolic transformations. The mind in movement through culture and society* (pp. 173–192). London: Routledge.

Zittoun, T. (2012). Lifecourse. In J. Valsiner (Ed.), *Handbook of culture and psychology* (pp. 513–535). Oxford: Oxford University Press.

Zittoun, T. (2013). On the use of a film: Cultural experiences as symbolic resources. In A. Kuhn (Ed.), *Little Madnesses: Winnicott, transitional phenomena and cultural experience* (pp. 135–147). London: Tauris.

Zittoun, T. (2014). Transitions as dynamic processes — A commentary. *Learning, Culture and Social Interaction, 3*(3), 232–236. https://doi.org/10.1016/j.lcsi.2014.02.010

Zittoun, T. (2016a). Living creatively, in and through institutions. *Europe's Journal of Psychology, 12*(1), 1–11. https://doi.org/10.5964/ejop.v12i1.1133

Zittoun, T. (2016b). Modalities of generalization through single case studies. *Integrative Psychological and Behavioral Science, 51*, 1–24. https://doi.org/10.1007/s12124-016-9367-1

Zittoun, T. (2016c). Studying "higher mental functions": The example of imagination. In J. Valsiner, G. Marsico, N. Chaudhary, T. Sato, & Dazzani (Eds.), *Psychology as a science of human being: The Yokohama Manifesto* (pp. 129–147). Dodrecht: Springer.

Zittoun, T. (2016d). The sound of music. In S. H. Klempe (Ed.), *Cultural psychology of musical experience* (pp. 21–39). Charlotte, NC: Information Age Pub.

Zittoun, T. (2017). Imagining self in a changing world – An exploration of 'studies of marriage'. In M. Han & C. Cunha (Eds.), *The subjectified and subjectifying mind* (pp. 85–116). Charlotte, NC: Information Age Publishing, Inc.

Zittoun, T. (In press). Imagination in people and societies on the move: A sociocultural psychology perspective. *Culture & Psychology*.

Zittoun, T., & Gillespie, A. (2014). Sculpture and art installations: Towards a cultural psychological analysis. In B. Wagoner, N. Chaudhary, & P. Hviid (Eds.), *Cultural psychology and its future: Complementarity in a new key* (pp. 167–177). Charlotte, NC: Information Age Publishing.

Zittoun, T., & Gillespie, A. (2015a). Integrating experiences: Body and mind moving between contexts. In B. Wagoner, N. Chaudhary, & P. Hviid (Eds.), *Integrating experiences: Body and mind moving between contexts* (pp. 3–49). Charlotte, NC: Information Age Publishing.

Zittoun, T., & Gillespie, A. (2015b). Internalization: How culture becomes mind. *Culture & Psychology, 21*(4), 477–491. https://doi.org/10.1177/1354067X15615809

Zittoun, T., & Gillespie, A. (2015c). Transitions in the lifecourse: Learning from Alfred Schütz. In A. C. Joerchel & G. Benetka (Eds.), *Biographical ruptures and their repairs: Cultural transitions in development* (pp. 147–157). Charlotte, NC: Information Age Publisher.

Zittoun, T., & Gillespie, A. (2016). *Imagination in human and cultural development*. London: Routledge.

Zittoun, T., & Perret-Clermont, A.-N. (2009). Four social psychological lenses for developmental psychology. *European Journal for Psychology of Education, 24*(2), 387–403.

Zittoun, T., Valsiner, J., Vedeler, D., Salgado, J., Gonçalves, M., & Ferring, D. (2013). *Human development in the lifecourse. Melodies of living*. Cambridge: Cambridge University Press.

Chapter 3
Methodology

> *The behavioral scientist must learn to admit that he never observes the behavior "that would have taken" place in his absence, nor hears an account identical with what which the same narrator would give to another person. Fortunately, the so-called disturbances created by the observers' existence and activities when properly exploited, are the cornerstone of a scientific behavioral science, and not – as is currently believed – deplorable contretemps, best disposed of by hurriedly sweeping them under the rug.*
> —(Devereux, 1967, pp. 6–7)

This project was built over the years, from my first disquieting experiences in end-of-communist Czechoslovakia in 1989, then in the mid-1990s just after the Revolution and the birth of Czech Republic and during my progressive inside discovery of life in rural Czech life from about 2002. At that time, in effect, I started to regularly visit the country with my husband, himself born in the Říp region. Even with biannual trips to my new extended family and language courses, years were necessary to gain familiarity with the ways of life around Říp, so close and so different. During these past 15 years, I read about the history of the country, heard life stories, saw exhibitions, enjoyed novels and an innumerable amount of Czech films from the past 80 years. Thanks to my husband's deep knowledge of the Czech Republic, I visited the country by foot, bus, car and boat, from picturesque baroque Southern-bohemian villages and post-soviet god-forsaken towns, to romantic Moravian hills and endless castles, as well as painful traces of destructions of villages, landscapes and lives all around the country. Like locals would do, I went down rivers, up hills, shared family dinners and celebrations, grilled pigs, went to village fairs and music open air festivals and ate home-made dumpling and cakes, cheap pub food and posh restaurants meals – and tried many beers.

This book, however, reflects a more specific period of systematic data gathering in spring and summer 2016, during a scientific leave offered by my University. It was the last moment, I felt, to draw on my surprises, bewilderment and irritations in the Říp region I describe here – sooner or later I would become an insider. The decision was thus made to build a regional case-study. In this chapter, I expose some of

© The Author(s), under exclusive license to Springer Nature Switzerland AG 2019
T. Zittoun, *Sociocultural Psychology on the Regional Scale*, SpringerBriefs in Psychology, https://doi.org/10.1007/978-3-030-33066-8_3

the rationale for building a case study (Sect. 3.1), and I then expose the data collected (Sect. 3.2), the analysis made, my positions within and the possible generalisation that can be done on the basis of such work (Sect. 3.3).

3.1   Case Studies in the Social and Psychological Sciences

Sociocultural psychology has a complex relationship with issues of methodology. On the one hand, it claims holding a specific object of research, which demands both a consideration of the cultural and the psychological, and that therefore implies devising smart methodologies allowing to capture dynamics and changes. On the other hand, it does spend a lot of energy to criticise the inertia and limitation of "mainstream" psychology, which imposes techniques and standards of data collection and proof-making, which often destroy the very phenomena at hand (Toomela & Valsiner, 2010). However, sociocultural psychology could also remember that it is anchored not only in the sciences of the psyche but also in the studies of the social (from the *Völkerpsychologie* proposed by Wundt or developed by Lazarus and Steinthal [Diriwächter, 2004; Kalmar, 1987], up to current social sciences). It could also realise that, as such, there is much more methodological freedom and reflection to draw on that in the tight closet of academic psychology. Such movement is reflected both in epistemological terms, for instance, in Jaan Valsiner's inspiring methodological cycle, that shows the constant possibility to rethink methodologies and data in the light of intuitions and theories, themselves nourished by the empirical field (Valsiner, 2017a), and in more methodological terms.

3.1.1   The Reflexive Turn in Methodology

During the 1960s and 1970s, a large diversification of research practices took place, where sociologists and social psychologists threw themselves in their fields (from "breaching experiments" à la Garfinkel to full-time immersion à la Goffman); during the early second millennium, in contrast, social scientists became more reflexive on their practices – from the anthropologists questioning their implication in the fields, now that these were much closer than before, to researchers inspired by psychoanalysis or feminism, or any theory inviting to question the false evidence on which our reading of the world is based (Alvesson & Sköldberg, 2009; Anderson, 2006; Bourdieu, 2004; Denzin, 2001; Ghasarian, 2002; Glowacki-Dudka, Treff, & Usman, 2005). In parallel, researchers who felt free to use anything that goes to document the social fields they wanted to investigate – from pictures to movies, from films to sound-recording, from map to sketch made by interviewees – were progressively followed by researchers engaging in justification and theorisation of these techniques (Bauer & Gaskell, 2000; Reavey, 2011). It has also more concretely been explored by authors opening research to everyday life (Brinkmann, 2009, 2012, 2014, 2016) and accounting for the subjective experience of the researcher.

3.1.2 On What Makes a Case Study and Other Preliminary Questions

Among the intense reflection and justification of practices, case studies have also been debated: if, in front of the dominant need for quantity and repeatability as guarantee of "good science", these may seem amateurish and relatively modest, there is, however, an increased awareness of the strength and power of good case studies – which demand not less serious work than any other techniques, and this, in all domains and especially social sciences (Eisenhardt, 1989; Flyvbjerg, 2011; George & Bennett, 2005; Gomm, Hammersley, & Foster, 2000; Yin, 2009). Case studies or, more specifically, regional case studies, have been built in many disciplines of the social sciences: anthropology that classically studied the organisation of social and symbolic life in specific geographic places; sociology, interested in social transformations at the scale of a village or region (Morin, 1967); geography and local development, interested in space and flows of goods and people in them; and, more recently, economics and tourism studies, which are more interested in the circulations of goods and people, and their economic and cultural consequences.

The methodology and epistemology of case studies is now largely discussed; these have been grounded philosophically, defended, proven to be powerful and, therefore, established as such. However, what defines and constitutes a good case study is still being actively discussed. Questions raised include: the epistemological nature of the case study and its link to the ontological status of the object of study; the question of how, empirically or theoretically, to define a case study (Ragin, 1992, p. 9); whether the limits of a case have to be clearly defined, or not (Yin, 2009); what are the criteria of quality of a case study; and a set of three riddles: "What is it a case of?", "What is the stuff that my case is made of?" and "what does my case do?" (Dumez, 2013, p. 16). Finally, other questions follow, such as: what can we learn from a case study? And, more specifically, how and what can be generalised from a case study?

These questions, I have tried to address in Chap. 2. In guise of summary, let us recall that I work with an ontology that admits process and a continuum of matter and semiotic stuff. Epistemologically, I attempted to identify notions and concepts which allow capturing the processual nature of phenomena, at various points of such continuum. I also assumed that it was necessary to distinguish sociogenetic, ontogenetic and microgenetic dynamics, with the presupposition that they all co-determine each other and play a core role in people's courses of life. The case I build is thus understood as an open system (Valsiner, 2019), within its wider socio-cultural and historical environment; that case is made of the things I choose to analyse at each level. Here, the limits of the case are defined by the "region" as perceived by locals and that corresponds to administrative divisions. The case itself is an extreme case of people living their lives in a region; in effect, because Říp and its region are so clearly thematised in history, mythology, social representations, daily practices and discourses, the role and place of its material-symbolic reality in people's lives become particularly salient, and it facilitates the identification of internalisation and externalisation dynamics. Consequently, what the case "does" is, hopefully, to bring to the fore psycho-sociocultural dynamics otherwise hard to identify – dynamics I have so far designated under the generic notion of "patterns" (see Chap. 2).

3.1.3   On the Quality of a Case Study

In what regards the quality of a case study, the criteria proposed are the same than for any other methodology; only the ways in which these are accomplished vary. Hence, Yin (2009, pp. 40–45) states that case studies need to establish validity, both internal and external, as well as reliability. Overall validity is achieved first at the level of data collection, in terms of building the case on the basis of existing theories and checking the operationalisation on the background of other studies. Tactics to increase validity include multiple sources of evidence and checking it with insiders (Yin, 2009, p. 42). Second, internal validity is about grounding inferences as relations; tactics to address these are "pattern matching", building explanations, addressing rival explanations and using logical models while analysing the data (Yin, 2009, p. 43). External validity is achieved on the basis of analytical generalisation, where "the investigator is striving to generalize a particular set of results to some broader theory" (Yin, 2009, p. 43). Finally, reliability is related to replicability – that does not imply recreating the same case, but providing the information for another researcher to be able to do the same analysis on the basis of the same case – "a good guideline for doing case studies is therefore to conduct the research so that an auditor could *in principle* repeat the procedures and arrive at the same result" (Yin, 2009, p. 45, my emphasis).

The two next sections attempt to make transparent the processes leading to the construction of the present case study and analysis, both in terms of the step taken and, also, of my own implication in the field.

3.2   Studying a Region: Fieldwork

Data were collected during years and, more specifically, during an intensive 7-month-long, quasi-ethnographic fieldwork in the Říp region. It is quasi-ethnographic in the sense that I was living in the region, experiencing it, meeting people, using services, shopping, attending events, etc. When I decided to engage in more formal interviews, I was already known to people. This I need to rapidly specify.

3.2.1 Positionality

Entering in a field and, especially, in a relatively isolated village life, challenges every newcomer, and this has been largely discussed and reflected upon by anthropologists. My entry in the Říp region was greatly facilitated by also what caused my interest for the region. As mentioned, my husband is from one of the Říp villages; although he left the region for over 15 years, he kept regular contacts with people – an extended family network and also a more loosely built network of acquaintances of his generation through the villages. During my stays in the region, we were either living in one of the villages under Říp or staying in a garden actually located on one of the sides of a hill. Thanks to this, when we met people in pubs or informal meetings, I was introduced, and immediately acknowledged, as "the wife of". Not talking Czech fluently, I was, however soon accepted, albeit as vaguely strange (for my language, my habits and my profession), but with benevolence – a benevolence manifested in people's generous gifts of fresh vegetables or pickled food or informal invitations. People who accepted to be later interviewed by me therefore knew me through family connections or from the pubs, and they trusted me enough to be ready to be part of the research leading to a book "about life around Říp", even though they would not be able to read it. Part of my plans is therefore to prepare a shorter, less theoretical version of the present case study, in Czech, for the participants.

3.2.2 Data Collection

As part of this fieldwork, I collected a large amount of material, some I use and some not. As mentioned, I read a great amount of books that could help me to get acquainted with life in Czechoslovakia and the Czech Republic, during and after the war, during the communist years, as well as more recent academic writings, autobiographical accounts, novels, magazines, etc. I attended museum exhibitions about the region, the hill, or art exhibition of the region. I also used online material to document the current lives of the villages and other punctual information. During my intensive stay, I kept a research diary, used both for my observations and for informal meetings, and for more reflexive and auto-ethnographic observations. I also made a lot of pictures of places and aspects of the village life which, with time, appeared interesting and relevant. Finally, I made a series of semi-structured interviews, including two repeated biographical interviews with women in their 90s, and a small number of more specific interviews, combining problem-based questions and biographical aspects, with a group of active adults. These interviews were audio-recorded and transcribed by me; more information about these can be found in Chaps. 5 and 6.

3.2.3   Saturation?

For this fieldwork, I conducted a very limited number of interviews, and in no way, I attained the so-called saturation mostly expected in qualitative research (Schreier, 2018). What does that imply?

First, the quality of the present case study is not attained through exhaustivity: I do not want to cover all forms of life around the hill or give a full picture of everything going on. Rather, here, the accuracy of the more sketchy form of my account of life on the hill is done through the multiplication of perspectives, as visible in the type of data collected and elaborated. Second, my primary goal is not to give a full and exhaustive account of the hill: this is not a historical writing or a full ethnography. My primary goal is epistemological and theoretical: it is an exploration of the interest to work with a region as a unit of analysis, so as to observe the interplay of sociogenetic, ontogenetic and microgenetic dynamics, and to reflect on the theoretical implications of such analysis. Double checking of the data and my analysis with people knowing the region guarantees the consistency and internal validity of the facts; my duty is to make the analysis and the theoretical elaboration sound enough, and it is through theoretical work that I wish to attain external validity.

Finally, the notion of saturation has recently raised some epistemological criticism (e.g. Saunders et al., 2018); it also raises an ethical conundrum, as recently pointed out by Sophie Zadeh (Zadeh, 2018). Looking for "saturation" (whether data based, thematic or theoretical) when conducting an interview, the researcher actually waits to feel "saturated", that is, for the moment where he or she starts to consider what the research participant he or she is having a conversation with says as mere variation or repetition of what was heard so far. How then still to consider and respect the uniqueness of the other, and maintain a genuine dialogical interest? Hence, if one wants to maintain a full engagement in an interview, one should precisely avoid saturation, or stop just before – so as to keep engagement and full acknowledgement of the other (Abbey & Zittoun, 2010; Marková, 2016). Here, I believe, the partiality of the data collected preserves the dialogical relations of the person I interviewed – people whom I still meet occasionally and who share with me the new adventures of their lives – conversations in which I still participate with the same genuine interest.

3.3   Building a Theoretical, Exploratory Case Study

Of course, data collection is not all, and the creation of a case study is for a large part made through the process of transforming it into a written text, which itself relies on analysing data, that is, entering in an endless dialogue with what was observed, experienced, noted down (or not) or remembered as relevant as time goes, as well as with theoretical ideas and intuitions. Here, I distinguish two moments – the actual process of analysis, and the dynamic of generalisation.

3.3.1 Analysing Data

Analysis goes on during the whole process of research – before, with initial intuitions; during data collection, in an actual analytical phase; as well as during the process of writing. Intuitions, here, were linked to my feeling of strangeness and also, and mainly, with my various surprises, related to the fact that life so close from Prague could be so different (see Chaps. 1 and 6). Then, as this fieldwork extended over the years, I had time to come back to my "normal" life, reflect upon what I had seen, read more about both the region and theory, present some aspects of the work to various audiences, work on other projects, which, per indirect echo, changed my understanding of what I was doing. The analytical process, here, is thus for a good part a long process of decantation, maturation of intuitions, and progressive elaboration of impressions and experiences.

In what regards the interviews themselves, they were analysed more systematically with the help of atlas.ti to identify the chronology of events and to capture emerging themes, and then, by working from emerging theoretical intuitions back to the data (see Chaps. 5 and 6). Finally, and this became more clear in the process of writing up the cases, the life-course interviews were analysed so as to follow the main structure of historical events depicted in the sociogenetic account in Chap. 4, but the events selected in Chap. 4 were also developed so as to give the background of these life stories. The microgenetic account (Chap. 6) was then analysed in dialogue with the development of the sociogenetic part (Chap. 4) and the elaboration of the theoretical chapter (Chap. 2). Hence, the overall endeavour was simply abductive – with a constant care for internal consistency, keeping the methodological cycle going; writing these pages, I ended far from where I started.

3.3.2 Towards Generalisation

Currently, a discussion on the importance of case studies in sociocultural and dialogical psychology is taking place; it also raises the issue, of generalising from single cases (Demuth, 2018; Flyvbjerg, 2006, 2011; Marková, Zadeh, & Zittoun, 2019; Valsiner, 2017b). Single cases, when understood as open systems, that is, when built so as to capture dynamics both within the case and at the boundary of the system and its environment, are likely to reveal processes that then can be reflected upon (Valsiner, 2019). Based on the readings of Baldwin and Peirce, the process of generalisation itself has been described in various ways, and it is mostly related to the process of abduction (Marková, 2017; Valsiner, 2017b, 2019; Zittoun, 2017). It demands to see and identify patterns, on the ground of something known, and using surprise as a leverage (Zittoun, 2017). Patterns can be progressively generalised, thinking through metaphors or across cases; such generalisation, thus, demands focusing on some aspects of what has been observed, and deliberately leave out, or ignore others (Valsiner, 2019).

What sorts of generalisation do I expect from a regional case study? I identify three lines of generalisable findings. The first one concerns the very study of small regions as a relevant unit of analysis for a sociocultural psychology, where I hope that the three levels of analysis applied here may reveal itself to be a relevant entry to highlight dynamics of co-emergence of the social and the psychological. Second, I hope to contribute, through such analysis, to our understanding of lifecourses, and thus, I pursue an effort of theorisation undertaken in previous work, with a focus here on what people do learn as their lives unfold along history. Third, I hope to identify something more undefined, which I so far have called "patterns" (Chap. 2), which designate semiotic configurations that circulate from sociogenesis to people via microgenetic dynamics and back, and that, I believe, could only be identified through such case constructions. Hence, the generalisation here concerns both methodology – how to study sociocultural dynamics – and theory – how is mind shaped by, and shaping the sociocultural world. Whether such ambitions are achieved or not will be made clear to the reader in the next chapters. Before this, I need to share a last reflection on such methodological chapter.

3.4   Coda: But Why So Much Effort?

Making one's methodological choices as explicit as possible, and retracing one's steps and decisions, are a necessity when working qualitatively (Flick, 2008). However, there is one step from transparency to justification. Writing these pages, I felt compelled to justify my choices more than usually, which leads me to the following reflection (the reader not interested in issues of production of science can skip this section).

It seems to me that, the more time passes, the more one has to justify his or her methodological choices if these are non-"mainstream" – mainstream being often a synonym of large-scale, quantitative research (Toomela & Valsiner, 2010). There might be two reasons to that. The first reason is institutional and connected to the whole machinery of publications, quotation, hiring business, money allocation to Universities, etc. In that system, "value" comes with numbers and visibility, and because of the social preponderance of certain domains based on numbers and quantitative results, these come with "large numbers". Others have largely denounced this industry standardising research and its negative consequences (for instance, Stengers, 2013), and some Universities and research agencies try to resist to these forces.

There is, however, a second reason, which, I daresay, is more psychological. Engaging in well-grounded, theoretically based research, or research bringing to theory, whatever the methodology is – quantitative or qualitative – requires both a leap of faith and the hard work of thinking. Theoretical work requires going beyond what is known, let oneself be surprised, at times disturbed, and wait until one starts seeing patterns – even where nobody else sees them or even when others doubt about the relevance of the enquiry itself. This in itself is a source of anxiety – the uncertainty of fieldwork, of not knowing where it goes, the self-doubt and feeling of erring – which adds to the usual "anxiety of the behavioural sciences" (Devereux, 1967). It then needs the painstaking work of translating the intuition in a language that reflects these experiences and observations, that can be understood, thus producing a discourse that perhaps has its own voice or "ethos" (Pildal Hansen, 2016). Readers or audiences who do not see or understand these two aspects, the leap and the theoretical work, either because they are not familiar to the domain, the topic or the mode of thinking, or because they think that there is nothing to see if there is just a bit of qualitative facts, tend not to see anything. In contrast, there always seems to be "something" if there are large numbers – at least there are quantities. Imagine the following analogy: a reader not familiar with poetry, both as a specific way to observe reality and as an attempt to communicate it playing with common linguistic rules, may think that a poem is actually a badly written prose with no respect for grammar. Similarly, a reader not familiar with a qualitative research – both as questioning stance and a style of presenting evidence – may think that such study is simply bad science.

Of course, the two aspects are related: the vast diffusion of one specific modality of science induces the widely shared belief that this is the *only* right way of doing science; the fact that many ways coexist tends to be occulted. In addition, this long-term shadowing of qualitative approaches and especially case studies – for about hundred years – has also slowed down the theorisation of methods and ways of presenting research. Quantitative approaches have had time to develop a high level of technique and standards of exposition; however, over the past 50 years, qualitative methods have themselves developed standards, sometimes aligned on the former – that is, as a set of standardised techniques – sometimes accompanied by an intense epistemological reflection, bringing to weaken the division and accompanied by an "intellectualisation of method" (Alvesson & Sköldberg, 2009, pp. 1–14).

Nowadays, this tension between two main streams of work – a dominant stream of quantitative approaches, mostly grounded in a naïve empirical epistemology, questioned by a stream of more qualitatively oriented approaches, usually grounded in alternative epistemologies (constructionist, pragmatist etc.) – has been largely commented upon and discussed. This discussion still goes on, and it produces a lot of discourses and not enough integrative studies. Here, although I am not blind to these debates, I simply focus on epistemological and methodological issues related to the case at hand; if I try be reflexive on my practice as researcher, I also chose to, rather to pose myself contra other approaches, concentrate on building what I need to develop mine. In that sense, I will engage in R-reflexivity (aimed at proposing new ways of seeing the world), rather than D-reflexivity (aimed a deconstructing) (Alvesson & Sköldberg, 2009, pp. 312–314). This is why I will not defend more the position taken, and I invite the reader to see in the next chapters whether it functions at all.

References

Abbey, E., & Zittoun, T. (2010). The social dynamics of social science research: Between poetry and the conveyer belt. *Qualitative Studies, 1*(1), 2–17.

Alvesson, M., & Sköldberg, K. (2009). *Reflexive methodology: New vistas for qualitative research* (2nd ed.). London: SAGE.

Anderson, L. (2006). Analytic autoethnography. *Journal of Contemporary Ethnography, 35*(4), 373–395. https://doi.org/10.1177/0891241605280449

Bauer, P. M. W., & Gaskell, G. (2000). *Qualitative researching with text, image and sound.* London, etc.: Sage.

Bourdieu, P. (2004). *Esquisse pour une auto-analyse.* Paris: Raisons d'agir.

Brinkmann, S. (2009). Literature as qualitative inquiry: The novelist as researcher. *Qualitative Inquiry, 15,* 1376. https://doi.org/10.1177/1077800409332030

Brinkmann, S. (2012). *Qualitative inquiry in everyday life: Working with everyday life materials.* London: Sage.

Brinkmann, S. (2014). Doing without data. *Qualitative Inquiry, 20*(6), 720–725.

Brinkmann, S. (2016). Methodological breaching experiments: Steps toward theorizing the qualitative interview. *Culture & Psychology, 22*(4), 520–533. https://doi.org/10.1177/13540 67X16650816

Demuth, C. (2018). Generalization from single cases and the concept of double dialogicality. *Integrative Psychological and Behavioral Science, 52*(1), 77–93. https://doi.org/10.1007/s12124-017-9399-1

Denzin, N. K. (2001). The reflexive interview and a performative social science. *Qualitative Research, 1*(1), 23–46. https://doi.org/10.1177/146879410100100102

Devereux, G. (1967). *From anxiety to method in the behavioral sciences.* The Hague/Paris: Mouton & Company.

Diriwächter, R. (2004). Völkerpsychologie: The synthesis that never was. *Culture & Psychology, 10*(1), 85–109. https://doi.org/10.1177/1354067X04040930

Dumez, H. (2013). Qu'est-ce qu'un cas, et que peut-on attendre d'une étude de cas? *Le Libellio d' AEGIS, 9*(2), 13–26.

Eisenhardt, K. M. (1989). Building theories from case study research. *Academy of Management Review, 14*(4), 532–550. https://doi.org/10.5465/AMR.1989.4308385

Flick, U. (2008). *Managing quality in qualitative research.* London/Thousand Oaks, CA: Sage.

Flyvbjerg, B. (2006). Five misunderstanding about case-study research. *Qualitative Inquiry, 12*(2), 219–245.

Flyvbjerg, B. (2011). Case study. In N. K. Denzin & Y. S. Lincoln (Eds.), *The Sage handbook of qualitative research* (4th ed., pp. 301–316). Thousand Oaks, CA: Sage.

George, A. L., & Bennett, A. (2005). *Case studies and theory development in the social sciences.* Cambridge, MA/London: MIT Press.

Ghasarian, C. (2002). *De l'ethnographie à l'anthropologie réflexive: Nouveaux terrains, nouvelles pratiques, nouveaux enjeux.* Paris: Armand Colin.

Glowacki-Dudka, M., Treff, M., & Usman, I. (2005). Research for social change: Using auto-ethnography to foster transformative learning. *Adult Learning, 16*(3–4), 30–31. https://doi.org/10.1177/104515950501600308

Gomm, R., Hammersley, M., & Foster, P. (2000). *Case study method: Key issues, key texts.* London: SAGE.

Kalmar, I. (1987). The Völkerpsychologie of Lazarus and Steinthal and the modern concept of culture. *Journal of the History of Ideas, 48*(4), 671–690. https://doi.org/10.2307/2709693

Marková, I. (2016). *The dialogical mind: Common sense and ethics.* Cambridge, UK: Cambridge University Press.

Marková, I. (2017). Case studies and dialogicality. *Journal of Deafblind Studies on Communication, 3*(1). Retrieved from http://jdbsc.rug.nl/article/view/29193

Marková, I., Zadeh, S., & Zittoun, T. (2019). Introduction to the special issue on generalisation from dialogical single case studies. *Culture & Psychology*, 1354067X19888193. https://doi.org/10.1177/1354067X19888193

Morin, E. (1967). *La métamorphose de Plozevet, commune en France*. Paris: Fayard.

Pildal Hansen, S. (2016). Commonplace and character. In J. Bruun & J. Lieberkind (Eds.), *Challenges of citizenship education – A Danish case study* (pp. 93–113). Copenhagen: U Press.

Ragin, C. C. (1992). Introduction: Cases of 'what is a case?'. In C. C. Ragin & H. S. Becker (Eds.), *What is a case? Exploring the foundations of social inquiry* (11th ed., pp. 1–17). Cambridge, UK/New York, NY: Cambridge University Press.

Reavey, P. (2011). *Visual methods in psychology: Using and interpreting images in qualitative research*. London: Routledge.

Saunders, B., Sim, J., Kingstone, T., Baker, S., Waterfield, J., Bartlam, B., et al. (2018). Saturation in qualitative research: Exploring its conceptualization and operationalization. *Quality & Quantity, 52*(4), 1893–1907. https://doi.org/10.1007/s11135-017-0574-8

Schreier, M. (2018). Sampling and generalisation. In U. Flick (Ed.), *The SAGE handbook of qualitative data collection* (pp. 86–98). London: Sage.

Stengers, I. (2013). *Une autre science est possible!* Paris: La Découverte.

Toomela, A., & Valsiner, J. (Eds.). (2010). *Methodological thinking in psychology: 60 years gone astray?* Greenwich, CT: Information Age Publishing.

Valsiner, J. (2017a). Methodology in the new key: The methodology cycle. *From Methodology to Methods in Human Psychology* (pp. 21–30). Cham (Switzerland): Springer.

Valsiner, J. (2017b). Generalization from single instances. In *From Methodology to Methods in Human Psychology* (pp. 81–85). Cham (Switzerland): Springer.

Valsiner, J. (2019). Generalization in science: Abstracting from unique events. In C. Højholt & E. Schraube (Eds.), *Subjectivity and knowledge: Generalization in the psychological study of everyday life*. New York: Springer.

Yin, R. K. (2009). *Case study research: Design and methods* (4th ed.). Los Angeles, etc.: Sage.

Zadeh, S. (2018, April). *Towards a dialogical approach to social research*. Invited lecture presented at the Studio, Institute of psychology and education, University of Neuchâtel, Neuchâtel, Switzerland.

Zittoun, T. (2017). Modalities of generalization through single case studies. *Integrative Psychological and Behavioral Science, 51*(2), 171–194. https://doi.org/10.1007/s12124-016-9367-1

Chapter 4
Sociogenesis: The Making of a Land and a Symbolic Space

> *The notion of an entity moving through time gives rise to the notion of history as always history of something, this something being in particular case the Czech nation (…). When the object of history is the nation, it is its imagined existence over time which makes it possible the construction of the enduring "we" who imagine "our history" and unproblematically utter, as Czechs do, the phrase "We have suffered for three hundred years".*
>
> —(Holý, 1996, pp. 116–117)

In this chapter, I propose a sociogenetic view of Říp. I do this in three steps. First, I sketch a short history of the region. Rather than retracing simply the history of the Czech Republic, I will try to do so with "Řipocentrism" – that is, trying to highlight the history as it affected Říp and its region and, conversely, the role it played in Czech history (Sect. 4.1). Second, I show how, across this history, Říp has been used symbolically, both intentionally by political powers and also more incidentally in shared representations and discourses (Sect. 4.2). Third, I propose a first analytical interpretation of these two movements – the historical time and the symbolic streams accompanying them (Sect. 4.3).

4.1 A Short History of the Czech Lands from the Perspective of Říp and Its Region

In this first section, I try to give a factual account of the evolution of the Říp region, within the general history of the Czech Republic. I privilege here historical sources, academic and grey,[1] yet my attention goes to facts that have specific relevance to the lives of people around Říp, as will appear in the next chapters. Here, I try to remain

---

[1] My limited access to the Czech language brings me to rely on English translations or secondary literature; the fact that I do not recourse to archival sources will be excused, I hope, by the fact that I have no intention to replace the work of historians.

© The Author(s), under exclusive license to Springer Nature Switzerland AG 2019
T. Zittoun, *Sociocultural Psychology on the Regional Scale*, SpringerBriefs in Psychology, https://doi.org/10.1007/978-3-030-33066-8_4

at the level of the "objective" facts, that is, at the level of events and configurations of elements that have been considered as historical events and, thus, treated as history, - they are socially acknowledged as such, or have durable consequences for the country, the region, and people's conditions of living.

4.1.1   Origins and Early History

Říp is the remnant of an old volcano, composite of various stones, including magnetite,[2] that cause magnetic perturbations on the hill (compasses do not point correctly to the north). Erosion explains the round shape of the hill. Being 459 m high, it must have always been visible far from the plain land, which is about 250 m lower, even though it was probably covered only by grass for most of its history. The name Říp itself is "of pre-Slavic origin and probably comes from the Germanic stem *rīp- which means 'an elevation, a hill'".[3]

Indications of inhabitants go back far in time. There are traces of settlements from the late Stone Age and the early Bronze Age around Říp – houses and burial sites – and bones and objects from these old inhabitants can be found in the local museum in Roudnice nad Labem, the immediate main town at 5 km, or in Litoměřice, the subregion capital that is 20 km north-west. "The Romans called the Celtic tribes in the Czech lands *Boii*" (Bažant, Bažantova, & Starn, 2010, p. 7) from which are derived the names Bohemia in Czech and *Böhmen* in German. It is generally admitted that Celts and Germans left the region around 530 CE, and the inhabitants becoming the ancestors of Czechs and Moravians arrived in Eastern Europe soon after. The name "Czechy" is said to have been attributed at that time, in the honour of the leader of the settlers.

The pagan tribes were progressively Christianised. The next three or four centuries are agitated by numerous clans and dynastic wars in the Czech lands, poorly documented and too complicated to be retraced. The region was a buffer zone between Western and Eastern Europe (Bažant et al., 2010, p. 7), and the Church progressively became increasingly powerful between the eighth and ninth centuries. The heart of the Czech land moved to Prague in the tenth century, from when there are enough sources to retrace the history of the country (Bažant et al., 2010, pp. 8–9).

With Prague being the capital centre, the region and the country quickly developed. Kings built a network of castles in Bohemia, and the regions must have been flourishing. Roudnice nad Labem, the closest town to Říp, was created in the twelfth century, and so were most of the villages around the hill. It is at that time as well that Cosmos of Prague, Dean of the Church of Prague (1024–1125), wrote the "*Chronicles on the Nation*" with the aim to ground the sovereignty of the Bohemians

[2] https://www.dub.cz/en/rip-mountain; https://www.geocaching.com/geocache/GC1XE14_geologie-ripu-geology-of-mountain-rip and also on geological anomalies (Ulrych et al., 1998).
[3] Profous, Antonín (1951). Místní jména v Čechách: Jejich vznik, původní význam a změny, díl 3. M-Ř. Prague, Czechoslovakia: Czechoslovak Academy of Sciences as quoted in https://en.wikipedia.org/wiki/%C5%98%C3%ADp_Mountain.

in the Czech land, attributing the birth of the nation in the region close to Prague. Besides his reattribution of the power to a local dynasty, he also wrote what was to become the founding myth of the nation on Říp:

> When man entered this wilderness, and it is not known just who and how many, in search of a suitable place for human habitations, he surveyed the valleys, plains, and slopes, and he built the first settlements, I assume, around the mountain Říp, between two rivers, the Ohře and the Vltava. There he joyously placed on earth the godlings that he had carried there on his shoulders. At that moment the chief, who others accompanied as their master, said to his retinue, among other things, this: "Friends, who many times endured with me the troubles of journeys through impassable forests, let you make a stop and sacrifice a pleasant offering to your godlings, with the miraculous help of whom you finally came to this homeland, which was foreordained to you by fate. This is it, this is the land that I have, as I remember, often promised you, a land subjected to no one, land filled with game and birds, wet with sweet milk and honey, and as you can see, its climate is pleasant to live in. Water is abundant everywhere here and it is uncommonly rich in fish. You will be lacking nothing here because no one will do you wrong. And when such a fine and great land is in your hands, think what would be a suitable name for this county". Then immediately, as if from divine inspiration, they all shouted out: "Because your name, father, is Čech, [Latin *Boemus*], where do we find better and more fitting name but to call this country Čechy [Latin Boemia]"? (Cosmos of Prague, 2010, pp. 20–21)

This founding myth, based on the figure of "Praotec Čech", "forefather Czech", would be later reactivated every time the power in place needed to refresh the myth of the nation (in the sixteenth and eighteenth centuries),[4] as we will see (Sect. 4.2). Note here the biblical connotation: the "land of milk and honey" is a clear reference to Exodus 3:2, when God promises Moses a land where milk and honey would flow. Cosmos of Prague could not ignore this; immediately, this "Christianises" the Pagan ancestors of the nation, and also, confers a divine predestination to the country.

It is probably also at the same period that a Romanic church was built at the top of Říp, first dedicated to Saint Vojtěch, and later to Saint-Georges, Rotunda svatého Jiří (Fig. 4.1), which is held to be one of the oldest stone buildings in the country – although its construction date is unknown, its renovation is mentioned in texts at the beginning of the twelfth century.[5] Also, during the twelfth century, a castle was built in Roudnice nad Labem by the nephew of the king at the time – probably on the remnants of an older, tenth-century castle – to protect the commercial route linking Prague to the North via the Elbe, or "Lužice route".[6] In Roudnice, a stone bridge was built over the Elbe in the fourteenth century (it was the third one in the country).

After a period of various kingdoms came the Hussite Wars in the fifteenth century, which opposed the protestant Czechs around Jan Hus to Catholic Germany.[7] Interestingly, it is said that Jan Hus was ordained priest in the castle of Roudnice, at

---

[4] There are thus traces of Říp in other chronicles. See the only book fully written on Říp (Jilík, 2008).

[5] https://en.wikipedia.org/wiki/%C5%98%C3%ADp_Mountain; it was "renewed in 1126 by Czech Prince Soběslav I at the occasion of his victory over the German King Lothar III in the famous battle of Chlumec" http://www.roudnicenl.cz/mesto/sights.

[6] https://www.roudnicenl.cz/mesto/sights

[7] The history of the Czech Republic has a few significant periods and turns, which I can only allude to here; for more details, see the structure of the excellent "*The Czech Reader*" (Bažant et al., 2010).

Fig. 4.1 Rotunda Saint-Georges, copyright author, 2018

the time a residency of the bishops (much later a Jan Hus statue was erected on the "Jan Hus" square in Roudnice); the castle itself was attacked during the wars.[8] The Hussite revolution proposed a type of state close to democracy, unlike anything existing around at that time, but was broken down by Rome. "After the Hussite wars, the city was sold several times, before becoming the property of Zdeněk Václav Popel of Lobkowicz in 1603",[9] an aristocratic family who fully renovated the castle and started to collect art and precious objects, and participated in the development of the town (see Fig. 4.2). The Lobkowiczs also then became the owners of Říp. The town was, however, attacked and destroyed a few times during the Thirty Years' War in the first half of the seventeenth century.

4.1.2   Flourishing to Become a First Republic

During the rule of the Austrian Empire, from the sixteenth to the seventeenth century, Rudolph II moved his capital from Vienna to Prague in 1580, and the country underwent impressive development, benefitting from the Italian and French

---

[8] https://www.roudnicenl.cz/mesto/sights;

[9] https://www.triposo.com/loc/Roudnice_nad_Labem/history/background

Fig. 4.2 Lobkowicz castle in Roudnice nad Labem, copyright author, 2018

Renaissance and the support of Rudolph to scientists and artists. This period was flourishing for the arts, culture and education, interrupted by the Thirty Years' War (1618–1648). Roudnice and the Říp region widely benefitted from the architectural, technological and economic developments of the subsequent period, and the town became a vibrant industrial centre. In 1879, Mořic Lobkowitz had trees planted on Říp, thus transforming its appearance of a hill covered with grass (Fig. 4.3) into the one we are now familiar with (see Chap. 1).

From the eighteenth century onwards, the local economy developed and flourished again, and with it, industry and the arts, until the collapse of the empire during World War I. At its end, with the dismantlement of the Austro-Hungarian Empire, the independence of Czechoslovakia was obtained, thanks to the careful diplomatic work of an intellectual and university professor, Tomáš Garrigue Masaryk. Philosopher and pedagogue, he then became the president of the First Czechoslovak Republic (1918–1938) (for a biographical account see Soubigou, 2002), a country grouping the major industrial capacity of the former Empire. This short period was another time of economic growth as well as cultural and intellectual freedom, during which the country continued its development.

Fig. 4.3 Říp, undated historical postcard (detail), Roudnice nad Labem museum, copyright author, 2019

Roudnice nad Labem became an important industrial centre, located at the beginning of the newly created Prague-Dresden railway. The government of Masaryk pursued the development of compulsory primary schooling and the transport network. Hence, most villages around Říp have their own school buildings (one of the most remarkable ones is named after the president-pedagogue, Fig. 4.4). Most villages are also connected by a small train line around Říp, going to Roudnice. This allowed villagers of the region to commute by train and work in the factories developed in town, and older children to attend the secondary schools there as well. Finally, during that time, a land reform resulted in the nationalisation of parts of Říp, and some fields were offered as family gardens to local inhabitants.

4.1.3   From Munich to the End of World War II

At the end of September 1938, at the outbreak of the war, the Munich agreement between the European powers, led by UK prime minister Chamberlain, had two dramatic consequences for the country and the region we are interested in. First, all

Fig. 4.4 Masaryk School, Krabčice, copyright author, 2019

the border regions of the Czechoslovak countries were taken by Germany, who leveraged the fact that these were inhabited by a large percentage of people of German origin (and also propaganda from inlands through the pro-Nazi Henlein party, see [Luža, 1964]), regions that were known under the term "The Sudetenland" (Fig. 4.5). As a consequence, very soon, the Czech families living in these regions had to leave their houses and goods to be resettled inland. Families of mixed German and Czechs origins, as were many after centuries of cohabitation between Czech and Germans, had to decide: the German partners could leave their Czech partners, or move with them inland.[10] This had direct consequences for the Říp region: Roudnice is located just between Prague and Ústí nad Labem (Aussig), a major industrial town on the Prague-Dresden route, which was considered part of the Sudetenland. Consequently, among the many families who fled from Ústí, some resettled as close as possible to their town, which was right in the Říp region; some other families came also to settle from the annexed region in Southern Bohemia – the choice of destination often depending on family ties.[11]

---

[10] There were some political discussions on who (German, Czechs) had to move or could choose to stay in the territories or resettle (Smetana, 2008, p. 59), but the application of these rules seems to have been varied (see Chap. 5).

[11] Hence, it seems that some Czech families in Ústí/Aussig who were living there for many generations and had cut their ties with possible relatives inland actually remained there during the war; see testimony of Bedřich Brabec (Matějka 2010, p. 149).

Fig. 4.5 Map of Czechoslovakia under the German occupation; the zones in grey are the "Sudetenlands" conceded in 1938 (http://www.schloss-hartheim.at/projekt-sudetenland-protektorat/img/rgs-karte.gif)

The second dramatic consequence of the Munich agreement is that Czechoslovakia, led by President Edvard Beneš,[12] had to accept to totally surrender, and the country was completely occupied by Hitler's army without resistance – it became a German protectorate in March 1939. For the international community, this was expected to be a gesture of appeasement to Hitler, meant to prevent a war – of course, in vain; Hitler needed the industrial strength of the country and its location as basis for his expansion towards the East. For the Czech people, this episode was seen as treason from the allied countries. Also, the path of no resistance chosen by the government has been abundantly questioned and discussed: on the one hand, it preserved the country from combat and destruction – Czechoslovakia is one of the rare Central European nations not to have been bombed during the war – and saved innumerable lives; however, on the other hand, did it not affect the people's morale

---

[12] Beneš apparently felt that he took the only reasonable solution, given the lack of support of his allies. He thus writes in his memoirs: "We were informed [by France and Great Britain] that if we did not accept the plan for the cession of the so-called Sudeten regions, they would leave us to our fate, which, they said, we had brought upon ourselves. They explained that *they* certainly would not go to war with Germany just to '*keep the Sudeten Germans in Czechoslovakia*'". (Beneš, 1954, p. 43, emphasis original). According to Luža, however, "the decision to capitulate haunted him for the rest of his life" (Luža & Vella, 2002, p. 22). See also (Smetana, 2008) for a close analysis of the process leading to the Munich agreement and its consequences.

Fig. 4.6 Butonia Factory, Roudnice nad Labem. (Reproduced with authorisation of Státní oblastní archiv (SOA) Litoměřice. The state district archives Most, workplace Velebudice, archive fund Tovarna na knofliky Butonia, Langweil brothers and Robert Eisler, Roudnice nad Labem, NAD 997, carton no 2, inventory no 44)

and turn them into passivity?[13] Anyway, this marked the end of the First Republic, and was soon followed by the independence from Slovakia.

During World War II, the German protectorate ruled like everywhere, using the country's factories, its mines and its means of production, rationalising the food and ruling according to the racial laws. In Roudnice nad Labem, where an important Jewish community lived, the Nurnberg Laws were applied. Factories owned by Jewish families were handed over to Germans, and soon, Jewish people who did not escape were deported. For instance, the Butonia factory (see Fig. 4.6), a button factory that employed workers from all around the region, was owned by the Jewish family Langweil. They had moved their factory in 1927 to Roudnice, and were running it successfully. When the rise of Hitler was starting to become a threat to Jewish citizens, the Langweil family refused to sell their factory to an American buyer, wanting to protect their nation. However, the factory was "Aryanised" before 1941,[14] and the family was sent to the nearby camp of Terezín (Theresienstadt), then to Auschwitz and other camps, where they all died. One of the owners, Jindřich Langweil, followed the advice of his lawyer and divorced his non-Jewish wife,

---

[13] This question – whether Czechoslovakia, with its small yet strong army, should have fought or not - was discussed in public debate, during the war and after, in historiography and literature (Heimann, 2009, pp. 82–86; Luža & Vella, 2002, pp. 20–24; Mastny, 1971, pp. 17–20). Mamatey reports that after the announcement of the surrender, "a million people milled through the streets of the capital, frenziedly crying: 'We want to fight!'" (Mamatey, 1973, p. 164). See also the accounts of resistance generals (Luža & Vella, 2002; Moravec, 1975), bitter and clairvoyant about the political underpinnings of the situation, and in contrast the novels by Josef Skvorecky that describe the carelessness of some part of the youth under occupation (Skvorecky, 2010).

[14] As shown by a series of letters between the Böhmische Escompte and the Dresder Bank, documents which were made available for the Nürnberg trials https://wiener.soutron.net/Portal/Default/en-GB/Results/SimpleSearchResults.

which saved her life and that of their children.[15] During the protectorate, the country was more generally in a state of occupation. There were collaborators to the regime, and local Gestapo agents, including in the villages of the Říp region. There were also movements of resistance, in contact with the government in exile in the UK; the resistance was met with intimidation and strong repression by the power in place. This was especially strong after the assassination of Reinhard Heydrich, the Reichsprotektor, by three parachutists in Prague in 1942 (Operation Anthropoid).[16] One of the most violent acts of retaliation was the destruction of the village of Lidice, 40 km north of the Říp region – execution of all men, deportation of women and children and village burnt to the root. There were also multiple executions and persecutions that included the students in Roudnice (Podřipske muzeum, 2007).

After the war, in 1945, the country was "officially" liberated by the Soviet army. Technically, the USSR army – the first Ukrainian Front under Marshall Konev – entered only from the north and east of the country, while the American Third Army entered from the south-west, through Pilsen, under the leadership of General Patton. Nevertheless, it did not take long for the local communist party to take the power, and as part of the post-war settlements, Czechoslovakia fell in the zone under Soviet influence following the Yalta agreement in February 1945, and thus behind the Iron Curtain (e.g., Cornej & Pokorny, 2004). The mistrust of the Czech population towards the allies after their "betrayal" in 1938 partly explains why the country relatively easily accepted the dominance of the Soviet Union. The government was, however, soon to be replaced by a clearly USSR-controlled communist regime in 1948, which thus led the country to another type of occupation.

Before we follow these events, it has to be noted that, at the end of the war, the regions called "Sudetenland" came back to Czechoslovakia. This had as massive consequence that the now overall German population was violently, yet legally (McDermott, 2015, p. 46), expelled by the Czech local population, first spontaneously and then in an organised way by the militia, often letting free their anger and thirst for revenge even against civilians after 6 years of German occupation. In a very short lapse of time, people and families had to gather a few goods, leave their houses and properties, and cross the border to Germany or Austria. All the left behind property was soon taken over by the nearby population; also, because so many houses were left empty, people from other places moved in. Hence, some people moved at that time from the Říp region to these former Sudetenland villages. Among them, some had former connections to these places but not all who initially came from these places moved back. Many houses, however, remained empty and entire villages were to disappear in the years to come. Also, in the Czech towns and villages in the Říp region, like elsewhere, many exactions were committed against the last retreating Wehrmarcht soldiers, or anyone suspected to have collaborated with the occupants – if not, in some cases, anyone having German relatives.

---

[15] As retraced on a website devoted to the Langweil family. The story has also been reported by one interviewee. http://zmizelilangweilovi.zstrmice.cz/pages_en/info/daniel-eduard-langweil.php.

[16] An event that inspired literature and cinema (for instance, Binet, 2010; Linskey, 2017; MacDonald, 2011)

4.1.4   Communism

The communism installed in Czechoslovakia lived through a series of waves. The first period, from 1945 to 1948, was still quasi-democratic. However, the currency was changed at the end of the war, and went back to the Czechoslovak krone after having been turned into Reichsmark under the German occupation. Consequently, people who had savings lost most of them[17]; also, the economy being impoverished, food continued to be rationed. In 1948, the communists formally took over, and in the 1950s, a harsh period followed, Stalinist style, with the confiscation and nationalisation of people's property, arrests, deportations, forced "re-education", labour camps, mock trial (doubled with antisemitism[18]), etc. (McDermott, 2015). In 1953, the government imposed another currency reform, "which effectively wiped out people's savings and resulted in heavy price rises" and was considered as a "state theft", or in the collective memory, as the "robbery of the century" (McDermott, 2015, p. 86). However, rationing was officially terminated in 1953 (Krejčí, 1972, p. 18). By that time, communism had radically transformed the society, and also, the life in the villages and small towns around Říp. All the big farmers had to give up their lands and their animals, and their properties were united in extensive exploitations; many of them were arrested. Small-time craftspeople had to destroy their private means of production, that is, butchers or bakers had to give up and destroy their tools, and work now for the collective factories; families were hit by the currency reform. The factories in Roudnice were nationalised (among which was Butonia, which then changed its name[19]). With it, life became organised around factories, which were sending their employees on organised tours and their children to holiday camps.

Also, like in all communist countries, the educational system was revised and politically regulated. It was orienting students to the vocational training needed by the economy. In addition, in what was meant to be an equalisation of access to education, it was promoting access to higher education for young people from modest background families, and forbidding children from "bourgeois" background to receive higher education. This strong policy has the paradoxical effect, on the one hand, of guaranteeing a low unemployment rate, but on the other hand, of training a few generations of young people in professions that did not interest them, or that were far from satisfying their own need to know and to develop (Zittoun, 2017).

---

[17] The money was exchanged to the ration of 1 Reichsmark to 1 Czech krona (CZK); in addition, people could only exchange 500 CZKs; "amounts exceeding CZK 500 were forcibly deposited on bonded deposits. These deposits remained blocked until 1953 (…), when they were canceled without further compensation in the next monetary reform". (https://cs.wikipedia.org/wiki/%C4%8Ce skoslovensk%C3%A1_m%C4%9Bnov%C3%A1_reforma_(1945)).

[18] As in the Slánský trials, which were mock trials that led to the execution of a member of the communist party and 10 other members of his group, himself and a majority of his colleagues being Jewish (McDermott, 2015, pp. 69–73).

[19] Apparently, one of the sons of the owners of Butonia came after the war to try to recover the factory. As it was already nationalised, he decided to work as an employee of the former family factory.

Finally, during this period, people had very little contact with the West, having no media access and no possibility to travel.

After 1956, Stalinism lost its grip and the society slowly relaxed; people recovered some freedom, were able to travel and restore contact with families abroad or in Western Europe. In the large towns, the progressive liberalisation brought to the Prague spring, with its explosion of creativity in culture and the arts in the 1960s. This, however, was considered as too much for the authorities in Moscow, and in 1968, the armies of the "Warsaw Pact" entered the country with tanks and marching troops. Because of its location on the Dresden-Prague line, some people in the villages around Říp remember being woken up by the trembling road under the column of tanks passing by. This violent intervention has also given rise to impressive photographic work, such as the one by Josef Koudelka (Koudelka, 2008) which, via the photographic agency Magnum, shocked the international opinion.

This sudden intervention was a trigger for many Czechs to emigrate to the West. It was also followed by what has been called a period of "normalisation", that is, of bringing back the country to its "normal socialist road". During this period, the regime controlled people less by violence and deportation, a than by psychological and economical pressure, and the times were gloomy (McDermott, 2015, pp. 152–181). People, however, developed various hobbies and activities to compensate the dullness of their work, where they were often well paid not to do much. They developed what was coined as "a quiet life" (Bren, 2010, pp. 87–88), investing family life, weekend houses (*chatá*) or gardens. It is also in the 1970s that women were encouraged to go back to work and that guest workers from allied countries, mainly from Vietnam, came to support the feeble economy (Bren, 2010, p. 163).

4.1.5   The Velvet Revolution and Thereafter

In the 1980s, the countries of the Eastern Bloc entered into a slow process of distancing from the communist regime, and in Czechoslovakia, the "Velvet revolution" took place in 1989, resulting from a combination of political changes, economic opportunities and popular movements (Zittoun, 2018). It led to the reestablishment of a democratic state with Václav Havel, theatre author and philosopher, formerly dissident, elected as president. In the years that followed, there was a vast enterprise of restitution of the goods confiscated by the communist regime, and also, of reprivatisation of state companies (Mlčoch, 2000). This was partly made through the distribution of bonds to all the citizens, who could then organise themselves to redistribute them. With little surprise, many of the bonds were quickly grouped in the hands of former oligarch who understood much more than others what was at stake, and thus some of the former collective services fell into powerful private hands – the result of some "predatory" economic conduct (Sojka, 2000). Then, in 1991, the Slovak Republic obtained its independence after common agreement, and the Czech Republic joined the North Atlantic Treaty Organization (NATO) in 1999 and the European Union (EU) in 2004.

The Czech Republic has a rapidly expanding liberal economy that has benefitted from the help of the EU and also massive investments from the West. However, the liberalisation is unevenly spread, and there are also increasing inequalities within the population (Birčiaková, Stávková, & Antošová, 2014; Kahanec et al., 2012). Hence, in Roudnice nad Labem, many of the factories have been bought and are run by international companies from the West, delocalising their productions in zones in which the work was cheaper and taxes lower, so as to maximise their benefits. These factories also offer employment to unqualified or little qualified workers from the surrounding villages, thus becoming one of the first sources of local incomes. Soon, the wide brands of international supermarkets were developed in the town, and then its outskirts, forcing many shops in the city centre to close. In each of the villages in the Říp region, one local shop usually survives, but it is not uncommon to see the local Vietnamese shop managers fill their stock in the next hypermarket. Hence, the liberal opening of the country has affected, as many others, the life in the Říp region as it can be observed at present (see Chap. 6). However, the overall health of the country is good, and although nationalism and ultra-right movements as well as a nostalgia for communism rise in the country[20], democracy is functioning (Kopeček, 2017); the unemployment rate was, in 2018, the lowest in Europe (2,4% in June 2018)[21].

4.2   The Uses of Říp, in Past and Present Times

The founding history of Říp is frequently drawn upon to recall the foundation of the country or to reinforce its cohesion. The myth of the foundation of the country was thus retold and rewritten in the sixteenth century and in the nineteenth century (Bažant et al., 2010). In simplified versions, it is still narrated, presented by tourist guides and told to children, and it goes more or less as this: as the hordes of Slavs coming from the north arrived at the foot of the hill and then climbed it, their leader, forefather Czech, looked at the plain, rich lands rolling peacefully up to the horizon bordered by the Silver mountain, planted his stick and declared: "This is the Land where flow milk and honey, and this is where we will establish our land". And so they did[22] (see also 4.1.1). The biblical connotation of the sentence is highlighted by the widely diffused painting, where forefather Czech appears very Moses-like with his white beard (Fig. 4.7). This founding myth is also extensively present in painting and iconography. The Chapel of Saint-Georges was also renovated in times of nation building.

---

[20] Since December 2017, I have been surprised by the increase of the Czech flags everywhere in the country, from billboards next to the highways, to pots of yoghourt.

[21] https://countryeconomy.com/unemployment/czech-republic

[22] Oral version as told to me as I started to discover the country. Similar versions can be found in secondary literature ('Czech Republic', 2016; Pospec, 2003).

Fig. 4.7 Josef Mathauser (1846–1917) – Praotec Čech na hoře Říp – public domain (wiki)

4.2.1   Mythical Uses: Říp as Cradle of the Nation

It is especially at the end of the Austro-Hungarian Empire, at the end of the nineteenth century, that the myth accompanying Říp was strongly activated (or at least, many traces of it can be found). In the period during which Europe became a large field of nation bursting, Czechoslovakia was also building its own identity. Říp was thus a frequent theme of stories, paintings and stamps. At that time, as a strong unifying gesture, the National Theatre was built in Prague; one of its foundation stones came from Říp (others from other comparably quasi-sacred mountains in the country). In a spectacular founding act, the stone was laid down on 10 May 1868. It "was laid jointly by historian František Palacký and the composer Bedřich Smetana. On the stone were words that would be repeated again and again: 'in music is the life of Czechs' " (Bažant et al., 2010, p. 154). During the same period, a group of "patriots" created the Czech Tourist Club (KČT) in 1888,[23] and started marking hiking routes in 1889 all around the country. Říp itself became a hiking attraction, and it is crossed by three of these itineraries (Fig. 4.8).

On the top of Říp, a touristic restaurant was built in 1907 by the Sokols (the "falcons", a sportive and nationalist association created in 1862), and it became property of the Czech touristic association in 1910[24] (the Sokol sign remained on the

---

[23] http://www.kct.cz/cms/czech-tourist-klub-kct

[24] This was led by the chairman of the association, at that time Václav Bouma; apparently the cottage is also named "the Bouma hut". https://cs.wikipedia.org/wiki/Boumova_chata.

Fig. 4.8 Touristic
pathways around Říp,
circular pathway, copyright
author, 2018

Fig. 4.9 Řípska, 1954 – original postcard. The "S" over the door stands for "Sokol"

Fig. 4.10 Inscription on the restaurant on Říp, close up, copyright author, 2018

Fig. 4.11 Restaurant on Říp, with its front inscription, copyright author 2018

house for years, see Fig. 4.9). The house was renovated in 1966 and then in 1974 (Tlustá, Pařez, & Michovská, 2006, p. 45). During these years – probably during a gathering that took place there in 1968 – this remarkable sentence was written on the house: "Co Mohamedu Mekka, to Čechu Říp", meaning "what the Mecca is for the Muslims, is Říp for the Czechs"[25] (Figs. 4.10 and 4.11). The hill was thus installed as the origin of the country, and at the same time clearly – even if ironically as it is playing with various religious connotations – installing Říp as a place for pilgrimage. The sign was renovated together with the house and became part of the common legend of the hill itself.[26] The restaurant was returned to its original owner, the family Lobkowicz, in 1990, and it is now exploited by the owner of one of the local restaurants (in 2019 a new renovation took place).

---

[25] Apparently there is no clear attribution of the origin of that inscription http://www.cestomila.cz/clanek/1384-rip-nevypadala-by-posvatna-hora-ceskeho-naroda-lepe-odlesnena, but a picture of 1954 (Fig. 4.9) shows clearly that it was not there yet.

[26] Apparently with the disapproval of the National Heritage Institute (Nejedlý, 2015).

Fig. 4.12 Říp budoucnosti, pohlednice s fotografickou koláží, vydavatel Rudolf Kaška z Roudnice, 1904

4.2.2   Political Uses: *Říp Used as Unifying Resource in Times of Collective Crises*

During periods of intense industrialisation and expansion, Říp, now mythical, was also at the heart of all the fantasies of innovation and technologies (see Fig. 4.12).

The motive of Říp was used at every instance of rupture in the history of the state: it can, for instance, be found on a memorial plaquette at the end of World War I or on ex libris at the beginning of World War II, etc. After the wars, in 1959, Říp was declared a nature reserve and in 1962, a national cultural monument.[27]

4.2.3   Redundant Uses: *Říp as Ornament*

This symbolic nature of the hill is largely used by the region, which is proud of living *podřipem*, "under Říp". The motif of the hill is present in many of the public buildings in the villages around the hill. Hence, the pub in Ctiněves is called Hostinec U praotce Čecha (the pub "at the forefather Czech"); it has reproductions of the classic painting of the forefather within. An old dancehall attached to it, which was and is still used for weddings, village balls and other events, is decorated

---

[27] http://www.podripsko.cz/menuId-1-strankaId-28-stranka-hora_rip.html

Fig. 4.13 Frame of stage, dancing hall, Ctiněves, copyright author, 2018

with carved wood motifs and a painting representing the hill (Figs. 4.13 and 4.14[28]). In other words, the hill itself has become an ornamental motif (Valsiner, 2019).

On the other side of the hill, in Krabčice, the pub is equally called Hostinec Pod Řípem – the pub under the hill – and has a stylised shape of the hill on its sign, and recently a statue of Praotec Čech facing Říp was built on the village's road crossing (Fig. 4.15). Similar paintings can be found in the restaurants and hotels in the other villages around Říp (Fig. 4.16), and even in the bus stops (Fig. 4.17).

An association was officially created in 2008 to "promote the Podřipsko region (…) which is administratively defined by the Lower Territories Act of 2003 and corresponds to the region of the municipality with extended competence Roudnice n. L.".[29]

4.2.4   The Myth Reactivated: Říp Celebrated in the Arts

The mythical-historical role of Říp is also reminded by more or less formal events and happenings. It thus became the theme of a series of paintings commissioned by the modern art gallery in Roudnice nad Labem in 2011 for its centennial birthday. For this exhibition, the Czech artist Mariana Alasseur painted a series of

---

[28] One old belief or rumor was also that Praotec Čech was buried in Ctiněves, but archeological researches have disproved that hypothesis.

[29] http://www.podripsko.cz/menuId-96-strankaId-65-stranka-spolek_rip.html

Fig. 4.14 Framed painting, dancing hall, Ctiněves, copyright author, 2018

Fig. 4.15 Praotec Čech and pub in Krabčice, copyright author, 2018

representations of the hill, including one playing precisely with the fact that Říp is so interconnected with nation building (Fig. 4.18, and see cover).

These paintings were also exhibited, with many other representations of the country and the hill, in the exhibition "Where is my home?" at the contemporary art

Fig. 4.16 Wall painting, Pension Amálka, Straškov, copyright author, 2018

Fig. 4.17 Back of bus stop, Mnetěš, copyright author, 2018

gallery Dox in Prague at the end of 2013,[30] a title actually reflecting the first words of the surprising Czech anthem. Adopting a more critical stance, Mariana Alasseur also built a recycling bin with the shape of Říp and the colours of the Czech nation, to denounce the lack of support to cultural institutions in the country; here, Říp is

---

[30] http://www.dox.cz/en/exhibitions/where-is-my-home

Fig. 4.18 Mariana Alasseur, Říp 2010 (courtesy of artist)

used critically as a as symbol against the state. More recently, in 2018, the gallery in Roudnice nad Labem celebrated the 200 years of the creation of the First Republic under the title "Genius Loci",[31] and especially, the grounding of the National Theatre with a stone from Říp; the whole gallery was filled with paintings of the hill of the eighteenth and nineteenth centuries (see Fig. 4.19).

4.2.5   Current Uses of Říp

Currently, there are three types of uses of Říp, which are deeply related and also follow the history just retraced. They draw on the material reality of the hill – its properties and its location – and its historical past.

First, because of its location and constitution, Říp has specific magnetic and natural properties. As indicated above, the composition of the stone it is made of implies that compasses do not work (the north cannot be shown). Also, its elevation on a flat land has interesting meteorological implications; for instance, it is not uncommon to be on Říp and to observe impressive rains, thunders and lightening all around the hill, yet to see then the clouds part and avoid the hill itself, or to appear diverted and just contour it. Finally, these geological and geographical properties imply that the hill hosts rare plants, some in risk of disappearance, some unusual in the region (e.g., Mediterranean plants) and some others having found a unique biotope (Jaroš, 2009).[32]

---

[31] http://www.galerieroudnice.cz/narod-sobe.html

[32] http://www.usteckykraj-priroda.cz/14

Fig. 4.19 Julius Marak, Říp (1882–1883) – public domain (wiki)

Growing from these three facts, and probably supported by its mythical past, various stories circulate around Říp about its magnetic properties. Hence, it is said that walking anticlockwise around the hill makes people younger; others say that, when people feel "low" in energy, Říp will recharge them, and conversely, if people are too excited, the hill will calm them down. Also, because of these alleged magnetic effects, the spring on the side of Říp was supposed to be one of the purest in the country, and people were coming to fill bottles with water for their babies or themselves (unfortunately analysis has shown that pollution has touched the spring and it had been declared improper for consuming in 2017). Finally, all these magnetic properties attract druids and other occult masters, who come there for retreats or to capture these properties.[33]

Second, the most banal use of the hill is of course touristic. If there has always been a tradition of visiting Říp – for schools in Prague to bring children on excursion, or for many people from the Říp region to do what they call a "pilgrimage" twice a year on Říp, after Christmas and at the annual spring fair (*Řipska pout'*) (see below and Chap. 6) – what is new is the more entrepreneurial regional tourism which is currently developing[34] and recently promoted in Roudnice (Fig. 4.20).

---

[33] See, for instance, a druid association: https://www.druidi.cz/hora-rip/.

[34] With endless advertising – here for instance https://cestovani.idnes.cz/co-mohamedu-mekka-to-cechu-rip-d2e-/po-cesku.aspx?c=A071230_175522_igcechy_tom.

Fig. 4.20 Model of Říp, tourist office, Roudnice nad Labem, copyright author, 2018

Fig. 4.21 Advertisement for Nativity under Říp, copyright author, 2018

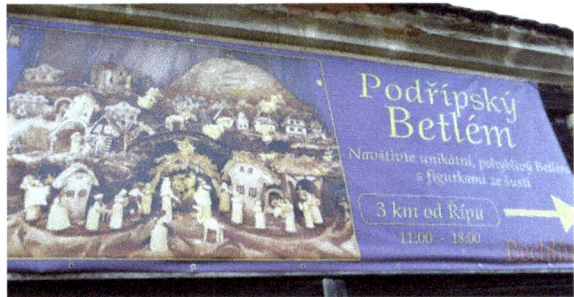

The freshly created "microregion"[35] has also new cyclo-touristic routes, with their pubs and local microbreweries on the way (see Figs. 4.21 and 4.22[36]). Pensions and bed and breakfasts are developing. On weekends, the walk to the top of Říp is covered with thousands of people from the region, Prague and beyond, who happily climb the few hundred meters, visit the chapel and have a beer or lemonade from the restaurant. Some days, uses full of tourists come from Prague and park below the hill; school classes do their trips there; and at times, weddings are organised at the bottom of the hill.

Third, and finally, the nationalist uses are still active. Hence, during the annual spring fair (*Řipska pout'*) in 2016, normally a peaceful family event with merry-go-round, sausages and a few folk concerts, the organisers in the village of Krabčice decided to invite a highly controversial rock band, Ortel, which is known for the neo-Nazi past of its lead singer, and its strongly "anti-multiculturalist" stance (one of their most known song says "We don't want a multicultural world", and it has become a powerful logo (see Fig. 4.23), where the main argument against immigration is to prevent the Islamisation of society). As some villagers opposed to this venue, which would change the nature of the meeting, the organiser invoked freedom of speech. The concert took place in the middle of the usual family public

---

[35] http://www.podripsko.cz/

[36] E.g., http://www.podripske-pivo.cz/main.php

Fig. 4.22 Cyclotour under Říp and forefather mask in pub in Vesce, under Říp, copyright author, 2018

Fig. 4.23 Ortel jumper on the back of a fan in the public, copyright author, 2016

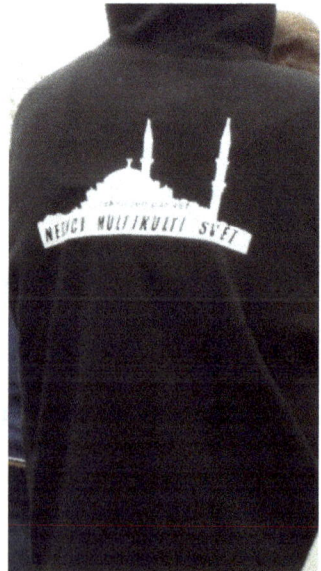

gathering of the festival – many local people actually appreciating the band – but also attracted bands of Czech nationalists, some of which went then on the top of Říp, where they waved a flag and claimed a Czech Republic for the Czechs. This event, reported by the media, obviously did not disturb the organisers much, who invited Ortel for the 2017 event again.[37]

Less dramatically, Czech Republic celebrated the centenary of its creation in 2018; public media were overflown by stories about the creation of the First Czechoslovak Republic in 1918, about Tomaš G. Masaryk, its first president, and many other related events; on that occasion, the theme of Říp came back in the press. Hence the July-August issue of the magazine *Živé Historie* (living history) proposed a four-page document on "forefather Czech on the holy mountain Říp" (*Praotec na posvátném Řípu* [Kacer, 2018]).

Hence, Říp is both a material and geographical reality, and a mythical place; both have marked, together, the history of the region and the nation. Nowadays, these two streams – material and symbolic – are deeply interrelated. If one can imagine that a tourist hiking the hill is, like any touristic place, both physically climbing the few meters of an old hill and symbolically meeting the origin of the country (see for instance Gillespie, 2006), how does this material and symbolic reality affect people living there? This we will see in the next chapters. Before this, we need to move back a little from these facts and stories.

4.3 A Preliminary Analysis of Sociogenetic Movements on and Around Říp

One way or another, Říp is a strong attractor. As a material reality, it operates at least at two levels. First, because of its location on a flat plain, not far from major rivers and from what would become a capital city, it has been visually an attractor for tribes and armies, traveling from north and east to the west and the south (e.g., Slavs), as well as for armies expanding from the south up to the north. Visible from all the main roads (including the current Prague-Dresden highway), it keeps catching the gaze and being a landmark for anyone who would cross the landscapes, from the Dresden line down to Prague, or leaving Prague towards the north. As we have seen, its geological and geographical properties have materially turned it into a magnetic attractor.

On a more symbolic level, its very presence has marked the whole history of the nation: since the twelfth century, it has been one of the anchoring points of a national narrative in the making, and every attempt to re-found the nation or a collective identity – before the creation of the First Republic, after World War I – has implied a return to Říp – either symbolically, by drawing on its story and visual representations,

---

[37] Apparently, the nationalists did not see the irony of climbing the hill for their claims, when the very logo on the hill compares them to pilgrims going to the Mecca.

or physically, as place to gather – on the *Řispka pout'*, or to ascent in pilgrimage. Finally, as was only partly addressed in these pages – but will be more precisely – Říp plays the role of an attractor for the region, now claimed as "microregion", holding together the villages that border it, and for its deep connection with the castle in Roudnice, as both are still owned by the Lobkowicz family.

Hence, Říp appears as an attractor on a complex field, and its very shape and location seem even to constitute it as an attractor in a wide centripetal movement – tribes, people, things and stories tend to be attracted from far away, in time and space, and coalesce in that small symbolic place. Of course, as any strong attractor, this place will also have repellent properties, and so centrifugal forces – as we have seen with the clouds, but may happen at other levels – may be the consequence.

At the junction of the social and symbolic, Říp is also a place and a landscape; its specific shape has become the object of many representations, and these, in their naïve or more stylised forms, are themselves part of the redundant ornaments of the region. In the hill region, the landscape thus contains both the hill and its representations, and both have acquired a symbolic value.

In the next chapters, we will consider these two forces, centripetal and centrifugal, unfolding along the axis of the core of Říp, in their material and symbolic actualisations. In addition to these circular or cyclical forces, Říp has created a redundant symbolic and material space. How then, lives can unfold around the hill, is what we will examine.

References

Bažant, J., Bažantova, N., & Starn, F. (Eds.). (2010). *The Czech Reader. History, culture, politics.* Durham/London: Duke University Press.

Beneš, E. (1954). *Memoirs of Eduard Beneš. From Munich to new war and new victory.* (G. Lias, Trans.). London: George Allen & Unwin Ltd.

Binet, L. (2010). *HHhH.* Paris: Grasset & Fasquelle.

Birčiaková, N., Stávková, J., & Antošová, V. (2014). The impact of economic development in the Czech Republic on the income inequality between groups of households. *Procedia Economics and Finance, 12,* 57–65. https://doi.org/10.1016/S2212-5671(14)00320-7

Bren, P. (2010). *The greengrocer and his TV: The culture of communism after the 1968 Prague spring.* Ithaca, NY: Cornell University Press.

Cornej, P., & Pokorny, P. C. and J. (2004). *Brief history of the Czech Lands to 2004.* (First edition). Prague, Czech Republic: Prah.

Cosmos of Prague. (2010). Bohemian chronicle. In J. Bažant, N. Bažantova, & F. Starn (Eds.), *The Czech Reader. History, culture, politics.* (Original 12th century, pp. 20–25). Durham/London: Duke University Press.

Czech Republic. (2016). In *Wikipedia, the free encyclopedia.* Retrieved from https://en.wikipedia.org/w/index.php?title=Czech_Republic&oldid=707492676

Gillespie, A. (2006). *Becoming other: From social interaction to self-reflection.* Greenwich, CT: Information Age Publishing.

Heimann, M. (2009). *Czechoslovakia. The State that failed.* New Haven/London: Yale University Press.

Holý, L. (1996). *The little Czech and the Great Czech Nation.* Cambridge: Cambridge University Press.

Jaroš, P. (2009). Botanický inventarizační průzkum. EVL Hora říp. Retrieved from http://www.usteckykraj-priroda.cz/files/files/Rip_botanika.pdf

Jilík, J. (2008). Říp. Vlastenecké putování krajinou praotce a praděda. Uhersi Hrad (CZ): Nakladeství JJ.

Kacer, J. (2018). Praotec na posvátném Rípu. *Zivá Historie, 7–8*, 20–23.

Kahanec, M., Guzi, M., Martišková, M., Paleník, M., Pertold, F., & Siebertová, Z. (2012). *GINI Country Report: Growing Inequalities and their Impacts in the Czech Republic and Slovakia* (GINI Country Reports No. czech_slovak). Retrieved from AIAS, Amsterdam Institute for Advanced Labour Studies website: https://ideas.repec.org/p/aia/ginicr/czech_slovak.html

Kopeček, L. (2017). Czech Republic. Retrieved from Freedom House website: https://freedomhouse.org/report/nations-transit/2017/czech-republic

Koudelka, J. (2008). *Invasion 68*. (I. Sorfov, J. Cuhra, J. Hoppe, & J. Suk, Eds.). New York: Aperture.

Krejčí, J. (1972). *Social change and stratification in postwar Czechoslovakia*. London: Palgrave Macmillan.

Linskey, H. (2017). *Hunting the hangman*. Harpenden, UK: No Exit Press.

Luža, R. (1964). *The transfer of the Sudeten Germans. A study of Czech-German relations, 1933–1962*. New York: New York University Press.

Luža, R., & Vella, C. (2002). *The Hitler Kiss. A Memoir of the Czech resistance*. Baton Rouge: Lousiana State University Press.

MacDonald, C. (2011). *The assassination of Reinhard Heydrich* (Original 1989) Edinburgh: Birlinn Limited.

Mamatey, V. S. (1973). The development of Czechoslovak democracy 1920–1938. In V. S. Mamatey & R. Luža (Eds.), *A history of the Czechoslovak Republic 1918–1948* (pp. 99–166). Princeton, NJ: Princeton University Press.

Mastny, V. (1971). *The Czechs under nazi rule. The failure of national resistance 1939–1942*. New York and London: Columbia University Press.

Matějka, O. (2010). *Tragická místa paměti: Průvodce po historii jednoho regionu. Tragische Erinnerungsorte: Ein Führer durch die Geschichte einer Region: 1938–1945*. Prague: Pro Collegium Bohemicum, o.p.s., vydal Antikomplex.

McDermott, K. (2015). *Communist Czechoslovakia, 1945–1989. A political and social history*. London: Palgrave Macmillan.

Mlčoch, L. (2000). Restructuring of property rights: An institutional view. In L. Mlčoch, P. Machonin, & M. Sojka (Eds.), *Economic and social changes in Czech society after 1989. An alternative view* (pp. 71–102). Charles University in Prague: The Karolinum Press.

Moravec, F. (1975). *Master of spies. The Memoirs of General Frantisek Moravec*. New York: Doubleday & Company.

Nejedlý, P. (2015, April 20). Říp: Nevypadala by posvátná hora českého národa lépe odlesněná? - CESTOMILA - cestování, tipy na výlety, turistika. Retrieved 4 February 2018, from Cestomila.cz website: http://www.cestomila.cz/clanek/1384-rip-nevypadala-by-posvatna-hora-ceskeho-naroda-lepe-odlesnena

Podripske muzeum. (2007). *Atentát. 1942 a perzekuce roudnických studentu*. Roudnice nad Labem: Publikace k vystave Podripskeho muzea.

Pospec, M. (2003). *Verifik 1*. Kostelec: Verifik.

Skvorecky, J. (2010). *The cowards*. London: Penguin.

Smetana, V. (2008). *In the shadow of Munich. British policy towards Czechoslovakia from the endorsement to the renunciation of the Munich agreement (1938–1942)*. Charles University in Prague: The Karolinum Press.

Sojka, M. (2000). The years of transformation in the Czech way: Transformation, inequality and integration. In L. Mlčoch, P. Machonin, & M. Sojka (Eds.), *Economic and social changes in Czech society after 1989. An alternative view* (pp. 227–279). Charles University in Prague: The Karolinum Press.

Soubigou, A. (2002). *Thomas Masaryk*. Paris: Fayard.

Tlustá, Z., Pařez, J., & Michovská, Z. (2006). *Mnetěš 1226-2006*. Hostivice: Petr Prášil & Eduarda Marie Doležalová.

Ulrych, J., Pivec, E., Langrova, A., Jelinek, E., Arva-Sos, E., Hohndorf, et al. (1998). Geochemically anomalous olivine-poor nephelinite of Rip Hill, Czech Republic. *Journal of GEOsciences, 43*(4), 299–311.

Valsiner, J. (2019). *Ornamented lives*. Charlotte, NC: Information Age Publishing.

Zittoun, T. (2017). Imagining self in a changing world – An exploration of 'studies of marriage'. In M. Han & C. Cunha (Eds.), *The subjectified and subjectifying mind* (pp. 85–116). Charlotte, NC: Information Age Publishing.

Zittoun, T. (2018). The Velvet revolution of land and minds. In B. Wagoner, F. M. Moghaddam, & J. Valsiner (Eds.), *The psychology of radical social change: From rage to revolution* (pp. 140–158). Cambridge: Cambridge University Press.

Chapter 5
Ontogenesis: Two Lifecourses Around Říp

> *On the definition of psychology as the science of mental life. 1.*
> *Life not in the biological sense. After all, it is not breathing and*
> *blood circulation that form the topic of a biography, of one's*
> *existence, of a drama, of a novel, but the events of a human life,*
> *i.e., the problem of the psychologie concrète comes first.*
>
> —(Vygotsky, around 1933, in Zavereshneva
> & van der Veer, 2018, p. 368)

Looking at the hill from the sky, one sees an island in the fields, a landmark, an attractor point; and, thus, the Říp region can become a home for people from faraway places, because of historico-cultural dynamics and undercurrents much stronger than them, which somehow, move towards the hill, accompanied by waves breaking down and dissolving around the shores of that island. In this chapter, after a short methodological introduction (Sect. 5.1), I retrace and analyse the courses of lives of two women in their 90s, both living in the same village under the hill since at least past 50 years, and who have experienced very comparable ruptures, due to collective events shaping the contours of lives (Sect. 5.2). The parallel analysis allows me to show, first, how the history of the region of Říp is embedded in people's lives; and second, how people still have a marge of freedom, the capacity to create their own lives, and how, as a result, they give a very unique sense to their life (Sect. 5.3).

5.1 Constructing Cultural Lifecourses

Methodologically, these two lifecourses were collected by repeated interviews, with each woman separately, in 2016 and 2017. Although I knew them through informal network, and had heard about their lives before, I announced them that I was interested in collecting their lives for a book about the region, and so I repeatedly came for coffee at their house with them, and interrogated them chronologically about their life story, in recorded slices that lasted about 1 h (between 45 min and 1 h 30 min). As a whole, the material considered here has about 6 h of recording with

© The Author(s), under exclusive license to Springer Nature Switzerland AG 2019
T. Zittoun, *Sociocultural Psychology on the Regional Scale*, SpringerBriefs in Psychology, https://doi.org/10.1007/978-3-030-33066-8_5

Sandra and 3 h with Zdenka. As we talked, Sandra showed me documents, family papers and various records. We also took a walk around the village, during which she could show me places which were relevant for her narration (places where she had lived, where her network was living, or where socially significant events were happening). From Zdenka, I had seen family pictures to which she sometimes referred, and I have visited and photographed the places in which she spent her childhood. The interviews were led in German, which was the mother tongue of the two women, and that I master well enough; as none of us spoke perfect German – Zdenka spoke mainly German as second language as a child and did not have many occasions to use it since she retired 40 years earlier, although she tried to teach it to her grandchildren; Sandra's German was more fluent and she used to communicate with some members of her family – we easily mutually forgave our linguistic idiosyncrasies. The fact that we spoke German facilitated these interviews, and especially, remembering the women's childhood, time during which they mainly spoke German. I also felt that both women were at phases of their lives during which they were happy to remember and share their life experiences, with their family and beyond. Hence, Zdenka had recently been approached by an oral historian who was interested in the life of her uncle, and so part of her narration was linked to this specific range of memory work;[1] Sandra was also asking to visit places in which her family used to live. Finally, it is clear that the personal relationship I had established with Zdenka and Sandra was playing an important part in the fact that they engaged in remembering their past with me.

The interviews were roughly following a chronological structure, that is, I started the first interview with an opening question about childhood, and each interview with the decade or the life period with which the previous interview finished. Each interview, however, was not strictly chronological; engaged in memory work, it was often emotional associations that brought the two women to jump back and forth through time. Some events were, thus, repeatedly narrated, while other probably ignored, even though I tried to come back to blank chronological spaces at the next interview. Along the narration, my questions aimed at having a sense of the diversity of spheres of experiences in which each woman was engaged, how these evolved through time, as well as what events were experienced as ruptures (as in for instance Zittoun, 2007; Zittoun & de Saint-Laurent, 2015; Zittoun & Gillespie, 2015). Given the timespan of the interviews, I was not so much interested in transition processes, but I tried to have a sense of the resources on which each woman could draw. I paid attention to their close and extended social networks, their possible symbolic resources and the knowledge or experiences they could laterally use from one sphere of experience to the other, as well as more vertical generalisations they made across experiences. I was of course following the narration of the person, and questioning any elements I could not clearly enough visualise, either because of lack of knowledge of my part, or because of the too-scarce information the women

---

[1] More specifically, the historian was interested in Zdenka for a book about the history of fish farming in South Bohemia (Hule & Kotyza, 2012).

mentioned. Finally, with both Zdenka and Sandra, we naturally stopped the interviewing dynamic at a period located in the 1970s or late 1980s, as if not so many significant events occurred anymore from these years to the present. I transcribed all the interviews in German.

Analytically, I first organised each interview into a chronological narration, using for this my knowledge of the historical background (see also Chap. 4), but also, previously defined analytical concepts (see Chap. 2). In the second step, I built the parallel reading of the two stories. For this, I was interested in ruptures more or less explicitly reported as such (as life-changing or difficult events), but I was also sensitive to more implicit expressions of difficulties. Hence, some events were reported with tears, others were told in a very fragmentary way, or repetitive and irruptive, which I interpreted as an indication of emotionally significant events, or "vital memories" (Brown & Reavey, 2015). Other events were reported so to say at children's height, or from the remembered perspective of the narrator at the time of the event, at times followed by sudden changes of perspectives, and could equally be considered as vital memories. In what is presented here, I tried to reflect these in the choice of typical quotes from the two women. For example, the first quote by Sandra, who breaks down the quasi-theatrical narration of her father sending her, aged about 4, to Konrad for her birthday, with a comment on the fact that she did not know it was her brother, reflects the emotional intensity of the discovery that came more than 10 years later. I consider this discovery as a vital memory: she still narrates it repetitively, with intensity, often as irruption in a different narrative line. And indeed, that discovery invited her to revise the memories of her childhood, and opened up new possibilities in her life, as we will see. Just below, with a contrasting style of expression, Zdenka describes how the moment in which she remained at home with a housemaid during her mother's burial "staid in her head", as she was aged 4. The intensity of the image, the insistence on the "having it in the head", I believe, reflects the strength of that vital memory, and the need to express it with the German Zdenka mastered. Hence, as my role here was to collect the narration, I did not want to go deeper into events that could have been considered as traumatic, but I was attentive in my reconstruction to account for such indications, highly personal, of the relative importance of events.

Finally, something needs to be said about the status of these narrations. The courses of life I base this analysis on are reconstructions, based on retrospective interviews. Some of the events narrated by Sandra and Zdenka had been told many times before and were, therefore, narrativised and polished; others were perhaps being said for the first time. In any case, these are narrative constructions taking place in a dialogical, trusting relationship, and addressed to me, thus co-constructed. On my side, I felt trusted and, also, I was genuinely interested in knowing about their lives. On a more personal note, I do not have any living grandmother anymore, and German was the language of communication I had with my maternal grandmother – who lived in very different circumstances, even though at the same period than Sandra and Zdenka. It is, therefore, clear that I was emotionally engaged and responsive to these discourses. Beyond the sometimes dramatic quality of the stories, the narration was often amusing, and anecdotes were told with humour – I, therefore, tried to indicate the moment in which the narrator, or both of us, burst into laughter. However, this subjective, unique nature of these narrations is in no way a problem or difficulty. First, in what concerns factual precision, as indicated, most events could be backed up by complementary material or historical documents – this is the goal of the additional third-person perspective. Second, it is precisely sense-making, which is relevant here: the object of the analysis is how people interpret their lives, and, thus, the contradictions and the gaps in the narration are as meaningful as what is said. In that sense, the analysis is not a narrative analysis; it is what Vygotsky called as semic or semantic analysis, an analysis of how sense of living experiences is built (Zavereshneva & van der Veer, 2018, pp. 291–309). Even more, as we will see, as I have the chance to have been told the lives of two women who went through surprising similar events, it is precisely the unique sense-making which becomes fundamentally important here.

In what follows, I narrate the two stories in parallel, according to a series of temporal sequences which correspond to what Tatsuya Sato and colleagues (Sato, 2017) call obligatory passage points, and bifurcation points in their life stories. I try to present a choice of quotes that reflect the quality of stories and present most meaningful events, as indicated above; quotes are in my English translation, but the German is in the footnote.

5.2   Introducing Sandra and Zdenka

Sandra and Zdenka both live in the same village around Říp, alone, as widows. They have various physical problems due to age, but they take active care of their houses, which are both nicely decorated, with paintings, pictures of their deceased husband, their children and mainly many grandchildren and great-grandchildren. Their independent living is made possible by the relative cooperation of their family and network, and financially, by their modest retirement money and widow's pension. But both, in different ways, express that they do not need much, and they are both generous with their family, that they always welcome with coffee, cakes, food and little presents.

Sandra and Zdenka were both born in typical Czech-German families in the Czechoslovakian border regions in the 1930s. Sandra was born in 1927 in northwest Bohemia, in Ustí nad Labem, a large town. Her father, a Czech craftsman, came from a small town nearby and was a wood turner with his own company. He married twice, with German women. He had two sons with his first wife, and married much later in a second wedding to Sandra's mother, 20 years younger to him, with whom he had two other children, a boy and Sandra, almost 15 years younger to him. Zdenka is slightly younger; she was born in 1930 in Southern Bohemia, in a house outside of a small village, in the fields close to a forest, and especially, to the pounds. Her father was a fish farmer (or more precisely, a "pond hunter"), a state employee in a region where carp farming was extremely developed and which was one of the main resources. A Czech man, he had been a soldier in World War I at the

Italian front from where he brought quite traumatic memories and malaria.[2] The family was living in a duty house: the father, his German wife, and four children, born between 1924 and 1932, with the oldest being a boy, and Zdenka, the third child, born in 1930. The family spoke Czech; they had animals, and a female employee to support the household.

5.2.1   Childhood: Becoming an Orphan, Developing Significant Relationships

Zdenka and Sandra grew up at a time where medical presence was what it was and, thus, both lost their mothers at a very young age. Sandra's mother was sick and sent to the hospital when Sandra was aged 4, where she could not visit her. At this point, her father, whose two eldest sons were already adults, seems to have decided not to raise his two younger children himself. The family could not take care of her either: Sandra's aunt, the sister of her mother, was living in Germany, and the grandparents, who still had a son to look after, were not willing to take her in. She was sent to a public institution, and her younger brother, aged 18, was placed under youth care until his legal majority at 21. The institution had planned that a sister would bring her to a convent where she would become a nun.

However, Sandra's mother had a couple of friends, the Schubert, from whom she was close – the children were in the same kindergarten; when they heard about this, they took steps to adopt Sandra, deciding to raise her with their two daughters, which were about the same age. Sandra joined the family Schubert in 1937, aged 10, when she also was told about her mother's death.

During this time, Sandra maintained episodic meetings with her two older half-brothers, not knowing, however, about her family tie to these two nice men – because of their age difference, they were "uncles" to her. Initially trained in woodwork, they had made their way in blue-collar jobs, one being a chemist in a large factory, and the second an economist. Both were living in accommodation provided by their employers, and the chemist had a house built for him; they, thus, lived in relative comfort for the time. Sandra explains:

> At birthdays or so, when my father celebrated, he said, go to Konrad, and so I would bring a cake, here is Konrad – at that time I didn't know it was my brother. And the other, the older one, Ludwig, had a daughter almost as old as me.[3] (Sandra, 26.04.17)

---

[2] *T und sie sagten, der Vater war im Krieg? Z Er war im ersten Krieg. Er hat da viel mitgemacht. (..) in Italien, auf der Front, jo jo. Er hat viel mitgemacht, sagt er. In 14-18 (…) Er hat uns immer erklärt, er hat das im Kopf, die Bomben sind zu ihm gefallen. Die Männer sind…pfui.. haben nur geschaut, schreckig. Nicht ist es ihn passiert. Glück hat er gehabt. Er hat auch eine Krankheit bekommen… Malarie. (..) War schon zu Hause, hat er viel Fieber gehabt.*

[3] *Beim Geburtstag oder so, wenn der Vater gefeiert hat, sage er, gehst zum Konrad, und von dort habe ich dann den Gugelhopf gebracht, das ist der Konrad, ja, aber das es mein Bruder war wusste ich nicht. Und der andere, der ältere, Ludwig, er hatte eine Tochter fast so alt wie ich.* (Sandra, 26.04.17)

Almost symmetrically, Zdenka also lost her mother when she was four; she died from tuberculosis. She remembers the day of the burial:

> I still have it in my head, what clothes she [my aunt] put me on, - - when she died. She put me clothes on, and then I went to my uncle, I was 4 years old. (…) I still know it, I still have in my head, how when the mother died, my aunt and my grandmother went to the funerals. And I wanted to go with them. I know that. It was about walking from the village to the nearby town – at that time we were always walking, there was nothing else to do. And I wanted to go, too. So the housemaid looked after me, she stayed at home, and she played with me, I liked that so much, I know that, and she read stories to me, I still have it my head, how it was at that time. I have that moment in my head.[4] (Zdenka, 8.03.2016)

At this point, aged 4, Zdenka was sent to live with her maternal uncle, a renowned fish farmer, with wide responsibilities over the region's ponds. Her older siblings were already going to school, and the youngest was considered too small to be separated from the family. The uncle lived with his wife and her parents, in a beautiful house in the forest in the hills, about 7 km from their house. The uncle and his wife did not have children of their own, and so were happy to host Zdenka; in their household, German was spoken. In that house was also a maid to help with the two cows, chicken and attached were fields. Zdenka stayed there for about 2 years, after which her father came to pick her up, apparently so that she could attend a Czech-speaking school. By then, she had forgotten Czech:

> [laughing] I know that! So I arrive home, and I could not speak Czech anymore! [we laugh]. And so we.. my brother who was older, well, about six years older than me or so, he was about 12, he scorned me! Eh.. *Niemka!* German *prase*.. German pig… that's how it was! But then I learned it [Czech] all back.[5] (Zdenka, 8.03.2016)

The paternal grandparents were helping the family, until the father remarried to a woman Zdenka calls her "second mother". The modest Church wedding gave Zdenka not many memories, unlike the return drive in the uncle's duty car (rare are that time). The father then called the children, "brothers and sister, and he told us: now you have her here – a mother, a new mother he said, and you have to obey her! This I got in my head at once"[6] (Zdenka, 8.03.2016). The "second mother" was a bit

---

[4] *Das habe noch im Kopf, wie sie mich angezogen hat, - - wenn sie gestorben ist. Hat sie mich angezogen, und ich bin zum Onkel gegangen, mit 4 Jahren. (…) Dass weiss ich noch, das habe ich noch im Kopf, wen die Mutter gestorben ist, sind die Tante und die Grossmutter und alle auf das Begräbnis gegangen, nicht, und ich möchte auch mitgehen. Das weiss ich. Und dass war.. zu Fuss nach [town] gehen von.. (..) alles war zu Fuss. Die Grossmutter, alle sind zu Fuss gegangen, das war damals nichts anders. Und ich möchte auch. So musste mir die Hausfrau besorgen, die war mit mir zu Hause, und da hat sie mit mir gespielt, das war ich so gerne, das weichweiss ich, und sie hat mit mir Geschichten gelesen, das habe ich noch im Kopf, wie das war damals. So ein Moment habe ich in dem Kopf.* (Zdenka, 8.03.2016)

[5] *[lacht] das weiss ich! Und ich komme nach Haus, und habe nicht Tschechisch sprächen können! [beide lachen]! Und so haben wir, der Bruder, no er war älter, um 6 Jahren wie ich, no, er war schon 12 Jahren, und er hat mich geschimpft! Eh.. Niemka!!.. Deutsche… Deutsche prace.. deutsche Schweine .. es war so! aber haben alles wieder gelernt. (Zdenka, 8.03.2016).*

[6] *Der Vater hat uns alle zusammen genehmen, Bruder und Schwestern, und hat uns gesagt: jetzt haben sie hier – die Mutter, neue Mutter hat er gesagt, und die müssen sie.. folgen! Das hab ich im Kopf gehabt gleich.* (Zdenka, 8.03.2016)

older than Zdenka's father, and her older sister did not like her. Zdenka learnt later that her real mother, who was apparently popular and friendly, had asked one friend of hers, also German, still single, to marry her husband after her death. He himself would have had preferred to marry his wife's sister – who, when she heard about that, took her bike to come to tell him that she did not want to marry him, and a short time after in 1935, went to a convent in Vienna, where she died during the war from an illness. Nevertheless, the "second mother", also a German, took pain to teach German to Zdenka and her brothers and sisters: "when we would sit at the table, she would say, this is a fork! This is a knife! And so we learned it (...). She always spoke German with us, and our father Czech. So we could speak both. And this was very good! German was for us not difficult, and [when] I was [at school] I learned better than the Germans!".[7]

Hence, as a child, Zdenka grew up in a German-Czech mixed family, in the region that would become the Sudetenland. In the family, and in the life of children, the two languages co-existed, although the echoes of the growing political tensions could be heard in the brother's mockery. Zdenka also reports memories of visiting the ponds with her uncle and with her father, walking across the forest with them, or being on a boat on the pond to check on carps, and also experiencing the respect both men received from their employees.

During their childhood, Sandra and Zdenka grew up in Czech-German families; they both lost their mother aged 4, and both were quickly brought to become bilingual, Czech and German. Where Sandra's father could not take care of her and was ready to abandon her to a convent, if it was not for the intervention of the Schubert family, Zdenka was temporarily placed at the home of loving uncle and aunt. Hence, we can here observe a comparable rupture, the loss of a mother at a young age due to the medical capacities of a certain time and space, as well as a first bifurcation (Sato, Yasuda, Kanzaki, & Valsiner, 2013). Sandra has the experience of having been rejected and abandoned, as well as kept in relative ignorance about her mother, her past and her family, which let some painful memories; while Zdenka grew up in a close and loving family, in which she felt supported and developed positive and strong memories, notably related to her father and especially her uncle's figure.[8]

---

[7] *Sie hat uns gelernt Deutsch, beim Tisch wenn wir sitzen, und hat so gesagt, das ist die Gabel! Das ist das Messer! Und so hat sie uns das gelernt, dass wir das besser können. Und sie hat auf uns immer Deutsch gesprochen, und der Vater Tschechisch. So könnten wir alles. Das ist sehr gut gewesen, freilich! Das Deutsch lernen macht uns keine Schwierigkeit, ich habe vielleicht besser gelernt wie die Deutschen.* (Zdenka, 8.03.2016)

[8] To the reader who needs a mnemonic trick to differentiate the two women: SAnDra is the one with the SADer childhood.

5.2.2   Experiencing the Munich Agreement, 1938: Being Positioned

Sandra and Zdenka grew up in regions bordering Germany, on the north of Czechoslovakia, and Germany and Austria, in the south. For historical reasons, these regions had large proportions of German-speaking inhabitants. In the mid-1930s, with the growth of the Nazi movement in Austria and Germany, political agitation took place in these two regions, with some growing pro-Nazi movements notably led by Konrad Henlein. This politician used the fact that the German population had lost privileges, if not had been relatively politically marginalised since the creation of the first Czechoslovak republic, to stir separatist feelings. Sandra remembers this period of tensions, during which violence was committed in town within a Czech-German mixed population. In parallel, Hitler made more direct demands to Czechoslovakia, requiring the so-called Sudetenland to be given "back" to Germany. With the threat of a European war, a meeting took place in Munich reuniting the allied countries, who, in the absence of a Czech representative, signed the "Munich agreement" which allowed these Sudeten territories to be annexed by Germany, as an attempt to maintain peace in Europe (see Sect. 4.1.3).[9] Hence, from one day to the other, the annexation took place – both regions, where Sandra and Zdenka lived, became German. The birth certificate of Sandra, for instance, reissued a few month after, was produced on a Czechoslovak bilingual document, from which all Czech inscriptions were barred out, and stamped with a Third Reich sign. The consequences of the annexation were immediate for people living in the region. In effect, Czechs citizens were forced to leave it to move inland, and mixed Czech-German families had a difficult decision to make.

Here again, the lives of Sandra and Zdenka took different courses. On the side of Sandra, Mr Schubert was quite sensitive to the growing tension: he had fought in World War I as part of the Czechoslovak Legion in Russia (for instance, G. F. Kennan, 1957 and 1958), was a railway employee – with privileged information about the border politics; his family was also mixed – he was Czech and his wife was German. Feeling that the tension was unsafe and the events were about to blow, he looked for a place to live inland. His family came from one of the villages under Říp, which gave him a right to resettle; the family, thus, moved in September 1938. And even Mr Schubert could not foresee the whole takeover of the republic: Sandra remembers him trying to convince her brother, who, as half German, would be conscripted in the Wehrmacht, to come with them:

> Mr Schubert said to my youngest brother, they can't lay a hand on you, come with us, by the time they will be at the border they won't have any right upon you. And at that time he told him: "Sir, I shall not come with you, because before the spring starts, Hitler will have taken the whole republic". And Mr Schubert then replied back: "this is out of question, the

---

[9] Chamberlain, who led that meeting, then famously declared 'the settlement of the Czechoslovakian problem, which has now been achieved is, in my view, only the prelude to a larger settlement in which all Europe may find peace' (Neville Chamberlain, 30 September 1938, Wikicommons). See also Smetana, 2008.

republic remains ours". And that how it was. In March came the order – he had taken over the whole republic.[10] (Sandra, 28.02.2016)

And so, while, in March 1939, the family Schubert and Sandra were already in one of the villages under Říp, her younger brother was enrolled in the German army. He had wanted, like many young men, to escape to England and become a soldier for the Czechoslovak republic from there; but he did not have the money to travel and was not helped by the father, who, according to Sandra, did not see the danger coming. He later died as a German soldier on the Russian front.

The move to the Říp village was not so easy at the beginning; Mr Schubert had first arranged a flat, in which the five of them had to share two rooms, a bed filled with hey, and the water to be taken from the spring. The children cried, "we want to go back, we want to go back!" (Sandra, 28.02.2016)[11] and Ms Schubert refused to take the water from the spring. Mr Schubert, then, was looking for another flat, but as he was bound by his work at the train station, he could not join other settlers who moved to nearby villages or Prague. They eventually had the possibility to rent half of a house at the corner of the village, with a garden – the owner was in South Bohemia – the condition being that Mr Schubert would take care of his disabled sister remaining in the house. Hence, Mr Schubert found himself as only men in a household with five women – Sandra comments humorously that it must have not been easy![12] The arrangement was also that Mr Schubert would buy the house; he therefore saved money for it, but the money was eventually lost in 1946 with the currency change – he nevertheless lived there until the end of his life.

As said, Sandra was bilingual; she had followed the German school in Ustí, and was anyway meant to move to a Czech school in September 1939 – bilingualism being at that time seen as an asset for many professions and the two types of schools co-existed. In the village under Říp, she was naturally sent to the Czech school; she was easily integrated in the local life – yet her origin came to the fore at two later occasions. Note, finally, that with this move with the Schubert, Sandra was now one step more distant from her family of origin: she had lost contact with her father and grandparents, her brother was sent to war, and, at that time, she did not know yet that she had two older brothers.

On the other side, Zdenka's family took different decisions. After the annexation, as a Czech man, Zdenka's father was asked to leave his house, to be relocated in a house within the new Czech borders. The family went to see that house:

> I also have that moment in front of me. We went to that small village in the hills, to that house... I went with my father, this time with a horse, we didn't walk to that place [we

---

[10] *der Herr [Schubert hat] meinen jüngeren Bruder gesagt, (…) Sie haben an dich keine Finger, komm mit uns, bis sie schon an die Grenze sind haben sie kein Recht an dich. Und so hat er damals gesagt: "Herr [Schubert], ich komme nicht mit, weil bevor der Frühling kommt, nimmt er [NB: Hitler] die ganze Republik ein". Und er hat noch festgestellt, der Herr [Schubert], "das kommt nicht in Frage, das bleibt unseres, die Republik". Und war es so. In März war da ein Befehl – hat her die ganze Republik genommen. (Sandra, 28.02.2016)*

[11] *Wir haben geweint, Wir wollen zurück, wir wollen zurück! (Sandra, 28.02.2016).*

[12] *"Weil da waren wir drei Mädel, und da hat es der Schubert auch nicht leicht gehabt, weil das waren fünf Weiber und ein Mann!" (Sandra, 28.02.2016).*

laugh]. He wanted to see where they would send us. There was a room, a bit bigger that this living room, and we should have moved in that room, the four children and our parents... Well... So my uncle worked something out again. He was the brother of my mother and had promised her that he would look after us! So he convinced my father to turn himself to the Germans. [So he became German]. And so we could stay there [at our house].[13] (Zdenka, 8.03.2016)

Hence, with the help and advice of the uncle, Zdenka's father took the German nationality, and so he could keep his house and job; hence, Zdenka could maintain her everyday life in South Bohemia.

The Munich agreement, nowadays considered as an important historical event, was, at time, a major collective rupture; in the lives of Sandra and Zdenka, it also had immediate consequences. For both, the events were object of discourses in the families, probably also causing anxieties and uncertainties about the future; for both families, mixed German and Czech and located in the Sudeten, it would have immediate consequences. The families had to take life-changing decisions, and had to draw on all possible resources to identify the best and safest options – at a time where all certitudes about the world and its course were shaking (the unexpected "betrayal" of Europe let a durable political trace in Czech Republic). Mr Schubert and Zdenka's father had both been soldiers during World War I, knew about the war and the game of politics; they both had solid social and family networks which they could mobilise. Their trades, however, seem to have weighted in their decision: as a railway employee, Mr Schubert could work anywhere; as responsible for a fishing farm, Zdenka's father was attached to the land. However, the drastically contrasting decisions made – be mobile, move the family and go inland, and remain Czech, or stay in the Sudeten, with the support of one's family, and become German – would, of course, have consequences for the years to come and the development of Sandra and Zdenka.

5.2.3 Growing Up During the War: Learning to Resist Discretely to Politics

Growing up as young girls and then teenagers during the war, Sandra and Zdenka were relatively protected from its immediate effects. Of course, some aspects of it were visible in everyday life: food was rationed, yet one could always cultivate potatoes or keep an egg or two from one's chicken; clothes were scarce, so to be used during the whole year, and people learnt to mend and sew clothes themselves.

---

[13] *Und habe ich auch den Moment von mir. Und sind wir nach [the small village in the hills] in ein Dorf, in ein Haus... Und der Vater, und ich bin mit ihm gefahren, mit dem Pferde, da sind wir nicht zu Fuss gegangen, [lachen] Und hat er das dort, anschauen wo sie ihn ausziehen sollen. Das war ein Zimmer, ein bisschen grösser wie das Wohnzimmer, in das Zimmer, alle vier Kindern und auch noch die Eltern in dort ausziehen. Na.. hat wieder der Onkel eingearbeitet (…). Das war der Onkel, Bruder der Mutter, und her hat ihr versprochen das er für uns besorgt! Und hat er den Vater überbesprochen, das er sich zu Deutschen geben soll. So hat er sich zu den Deutschen gegeben. So sind wir dort geblieben.* (Zdenka, 8.03.2016)

Zdenka narrates a diet mainly of potatoes, milk and butter, with the exceptional egg, fish or piece of meat on Sunday. Also, she mentions Polish prisoners of war now working in the ponds. War irrupted, however, here or there more directly in Sandra and Zdenka's lives, also giving space for little acts of resistance, at times shared with the community.

Sandra settled down in the village under Říp and the Schubert family soon was part of the community. In 1941, Sandra's aunt from Germany did, in her words, "remember" that she had a niece, and engaged in a procedure to get her custody. In other words, a claim for a German girl came to the village from Germany, and it appeared that Sandra was somehow still under the responsibility of youth care. So one day, a member of the Gestapo came to school, and picked up Sandra; the project was to send her to a German school in a nearby town. The Gestapo also came to control the living condition of Sandra at the Schubert's. Eventually, the village supported her, and as she was already 14 at that time and about to finish school, these claims were dropped and so she could stay with the Schubert.

Soon after, aged 15, Sandra stopped her education: she had finished compulsory school, and secondary school was in Roudnice; the family could apparently not afford the expenses of the daily commute and her support, so she started working at the button factory in Roudnice, Butonia, which had been "aryanised" in 1941. There she also was asked by the new director, an Italian man married to a German wife, to look after their child. She did, but not without discrete resistance to the new regime:

> S: When I was working there (...) some Austrian, a major or so, worked there as director; he was so *Heil! Heil!* (…) when I first entered the room: *Heil!*
> T: And what did you do?
> S: Well, *Guten Tag*! (Good day!) [we laugh][14] (Sandra, 26.04.2017)

Sandra worked there first to unload the trucks, but soon was moved to the office, where she worked as an accountant, served by her very good mathematical skills.

During these years of war, other events happened. In the village, Mr Schubert had a discretely resistant posture. He thus had a radio; braving the interdiction – every radio had a sticker saying that the foreign broadcasts were forbidden – he would catch the broadcast from the Czech government in exile. Sandra describes these evenings, family and neighbours gathered around the radio, listening to the broken sound: "tididi tididi tididi *tady* [here] London! Well, so it was kh kh kh kh pababababa kh kh kh!" [we laugh][15] (Sandra, 28.02.2016)

---

[14] *Zur meine Zeit, wie ich in der Butonka war, da bin ich Angestellt geworden, und der Besitzer war vorher Jude, aber das ist im Dings gefallen, und hat das ein, nicht ein Deutscher übernommen, aber er war Italiener. Und er hatte wieder eine Tochter, und sie hatte wieder Österreicher Mann; er war schon Major oder so, er war bei der Armee. Und denn – nicht der Besitzer, aber der wer hat gearbeitet da als Direktor, er war also Heil! Heil! Die wollte mit dem Mann irgendwo hinfahren, und sie hat ein Jungen, xxx sie hat sich angesprochen das ich sollte hin behüten. Das war das erste, wie ich eingetreten bin, Heil! T Und was haben Sie gemacht? S Na, Guten Tag! [wir lachen]. (Sandra, 26.04.2017)*

[15] *Weil man dürfte doch das Radio Fremde Linien nicht, das war verboten. (…) Weil war es erst spät Abend, zu fangen, und auf jeden Radio war so ein Zettel angehängt, "Höre nicht Fremdland!" (..) (weil jeder) Radio nicht hatte, dann sie viele Familien zusammen.. weil es war sehr gestört.. "tididi tididi tididi tady London!" Na ja, da war kh kh kh kh pababababa kh kh kh! [wir lachen].* (Sandra, 28.02.2016)

Also, at that time, food was rationed and farm products confiscated, yet most people, including Mr Schubert, were hiding some for themselves, which prevented hunger.

> Everybody helped each other. In wartime, they hid the flour, because we had to give everything up. Cereals, eggs, fat, fruit. It was not so safe… (…) there was a mill down there. In the fields were left over cereals, and so we waited until the miller had some free space, and also the patience, and when he had the possibility, we would take the cereals and he grinded it black, because if the Gestapo control would have come, and had discovered, then we would be sent straight to the concentration camp. It was not so simple to undertake such things. At home we also had five chickens more than we were entitled to. So people would tell each other: "Today they [the control] are in this or that village!" So everybody took care to hide that what should not be the case. We put our chicken in a bag… we had a goose in the garden behind the house. So we put them in a bag and bounded it, we brought it by the river, in a big bag so that they don't suffocate. So you could see the bag moving here and back [we laugh]. And so we could say: "we don't know who left that bag!" Because this was out of our house. These were crazy times. (Sandra, 19.05.17)[16].

Finally, Mr Schubert had family behind the border. As the food was rationed everywhere, but they had some, he organised trips with Sandra to the border region – by train, and then hiking through the hills and forest, with a bag pack full of goods, to deliver it to relatives. Hence, from Mr Schubert, Sandra learnt how to resist discretely, to protect one's community and one's beliefs, and to discretely circumvent absurd laws.

Here, Zdenka was in a more delicate position, as her family was living in German territories. The new Czech-German border was just on the road behind their house, and they now had to change school, and move from the Czech school, where she had been for the first 2 years, to the German school, from the third grade to the eighth grade. Zdenka remembers *Sieg heils*, how she could perceive that the new version of history they were taught was absurd, and how she was keeping an inner distance from that; she thus once told that she and her sister were crossing their fingers in their back while saying these Nazi salute. At the end of the compulsory school, Zdenka wanted to become a tailor; she had interest for it, and had sewn herself some clothes. However, the government imposed 1 year of compulsory inland service for

---

[16] *Jeden hat der andere ausgeholfen, weil zu Kriegszeit, haben das Getreide versteckt, weil man musste es alles abgeben. Getreide, Eier, Fett, Obst. Es ist sicher, jeder sucht Hilfe. (..) Dort war die Mille. In die Wiese war alles verwachsen, Sträucher und so, haben wir gewartet, bis der Miller erstens reine Luft hatte, und auch dazu Geduld, und hat nach Möglichkeit das Getreide angenommen, und wieder im Schwarzen gemalt, weil die Gestapo Kontrolle gekommen ist oder sowas, und hätte das entdeckt, dann werden wir gerade angewesen in der Konzentrationslager. Das war nicht einfach sowas unternehmen. Mir zu Hause hatten selber auch fünf Hühner mehr, als was gemeldet war. Und das haben sich die Leute schon gesagt, "Heute sind sie in [anderes Dorf]! Dann jede hatte Vorsicht, das was nicht sein dürfe musste man verstecken. Mir haben die Hühner im Sack eingelegt, .. im Garten hatten wir eine Ganz, mit dem Haus. Dann haben wir den Zaum gewegt, das war bei der Bach, das musste einen grossen sack sein, dass sie nicht ersticken. (Der Sack ist so hin und her..) (wir lachen) und so konnten wir sagen, "wir weissen nicht, wer das da gelassen hat". Weil das war Ausserhaus. So Verrückte Zeiten waren das. (Sandra, 19.05.17)*

all Germans after school, and so she was sent to another farmer. She had a very bad experience:

> I was a weak child… I was 14 years old, in 44 (…). It was a big farmer, with two children, a boy and a girl, and they had horses, it was a big exploitation. There were a man and a woman from Poland. The old man, he took care of the farm, the young man was in the army. German people had to go to the army. They were scared... And we had to wake up at 4. At 4 o'clock! All of us! They took care of feeding the cows, the horses, and me, as I was the youngest, I had to peel potatoes. The whole day, not only early morning. Such a big container of potatoes, I had to peel. At 6 o'clock we were already going to the field, to work. With the horse, and we walked behind. Collect potatoes, collect and throw away stone so that they don't stay on the field, various things… I was there – July was holiday, so I spent there August, September, October.[17] (Zdenka, 8.03.2016)

Her work also consisted in washing the dishes and working in the kitchen. As food they only had potatoes for breakfast and potato soup for lunch made out of water and potatoes accompanied by one piece of bread, white coffee with bread for tea and potatoes for dinner.[18] Although Zdenka lived all her life in a farm and was used to take care of animals and fields, she had been so far quite protected from the hard work she experienced there. Also, she describes herself as a "weak" child, a weakness that can perhaps be explained by the years of relatively low nutrition for growing children during the war. Although she was used to a diet mainly based on potatoes, with salt and butter or with milk, at home it had been completed by occasional eggs, meat or fish, while she apparently received no source of protein during her time in the farm.

---

[17] *Ich war ein schwaches Kind.. ich war 14 Jahre alt, das war in 44. (..) und so ist ein grosser Bauer, haben zwei Kindern gehaben, ein Mädchen und ein Jungen, und dort waren Pferden, ein grosses Wirtschaft war das. Ein Polack ist dort gewesen, und eine Polackin. Und der Alter, der das Haus besorgt, der Alter, und die Jungen waren beim Militär. Deutsche Leute mussten zum Militär gehen. Und sie führten das. Und da müssten wir früh um 4 Uhr aufstehen! Um 4 Uhr! Alle! (..) die haben.. die Kühen das Füttern besorgt, die Pferde alles besorgt, und ich, ich bin die jüngste gewesen, ich müsste Erdäpfel schälen. (..) den ganzen Tag nicht, nur früh Morgens. So ein Kübel Kartoffeln müsste ich schälen. Und um 6 Uhr sind wir schon auf das Feld gefahren, arbeiten. (..) mit dem Pferden und zu Fuss gegangen, das war hinten. (..) Erdäpfel klauben, Steine klauben dass sie nicht auf den Feld sind, verschiedene Sachen… und damals – ich war dort schon- Juli ist es Ferien, ich war da August, September, Oktober.* (Zdenka, 8.03.2016)

[18] *Damals war die Kartoffeln ausnehmen, und damals das. Jittoh zusammengeben .. von 6 Uhr bis 11, dann sind wir wieder nach Hause gegangen, zum Mittagessen, sie haben wieder die Kühe gefüttert, no, und ich müsste das Geschirr waschen und so etwas in der Küche machen, und das Mittagessen. Das war - - [wir lachen]. Sie sagten das war Kartoffeln suppe. Kartoffeln waren auch zum Frühstück. Aber das war nur Wasser mit Kartoffeln gekocht. Und mich schmeckt das gar nicht.. und geben sie Brot dazu, können wir Brot dazu nehmen. So ich habe mir das Brot mit der Suppe gegessen. Und möchte mir noch ein Stück Brot nehmen, so hat sie die Frau gesagt: das ist auf Zetteln das Brot, nur eins! Mehr darf ich nicht nehmen. T (..) und kein Fleisch, keine Käse, keine Milch? Z: Nein. Aber zum (Dessert?) haben wir weisses Kaffee gehabt mit trockenen Brot [gehabt]. Aber auch nur. So eine Sorte wo sie geben.. nicht viel! Hunger haben wir nicht gehabt, aber war nicht genug, für mich. Ich möchte mehr, aber das dürfte ich nicht. T und dann, abgewaschen und wieder auf das Feld? Z: Wieder auf das Feld. Wir arbeiten, sind zurückgekommen so um 6 Uhr, und wieder füttern, alles ausraumen, und das Nachtmahl war.. das war wieder Kartoffeln oder so. T: wirklich, kein Ei dazu? Z: kein Ei, bubec! Gar nicht (…).* (Zdenka, 8.03.2016)

Anyway, Zdenka spoke to her uncle in 1944 and described her work conditions. He seemed to have been in a social and political position that enabled him to intervene again; he, thus, took her out of her post and had her service reassigned at his own house. Needless to say, this was in far better conditions than at the farmer's.

> I could sleep as much as I wanted, and the food was good; I helped as well, I worked, but it was not so hard. I just brought food to the cow, and took care of her. This was in the morning, once I was rested and after eating, I took care of the cow. So I did that until 11, then maybe I helped a bit with the dishes, but I don't know, it was the grandmother or my aunt who cooked. I also helped in the fields when I didn't want to stay home alone. It was good, at my uncle's. It was better than home. I didn't want to go back home! [laughs][19] (Zdenka, 8.03.2016)

Zdenka had much less space than Sandra to clearly oppose to the new forces in power. However, her way to avoid most difficult options was to rely on her uncle: as he did encourage her father to change nationality before the war, he was now able to modify her year of service and turn a chore into an extremely pleasant and memorable stay at his house.

If we now reflect on the childhoods at war of the two women, we can guess that they were both exposed to the discourses and propaganda of the Nazi power in place. Under Říp, in the Czech lands, life was going on relatively normally; the occupying rules were strict, but there was space to circumvent them. The German presence was mainly felt through the awareness of the rules and the irruption of the occasional Gestapo control. However, the village seemed to have developed a network of solidarity and complicity, which allowed people to find small spaces of resistance, fed by individual initiatives, amplified and supported by the group, and, therefore, allowing these local actions. It is thus that Mr Schubert could have a radio around which the village gathered, or that people could save food. Sandra seemed thus to have learnt, on the one hand, the critical stance of Mr Schubert, but also, on the other hand, the experience of being part of a community that creates a relative space of freedom. In more psychological terms, it is possible that she internalised these two social aspects: the critical analytic posture of Mr Schubert; the experience of being held in a trusting network with its positive emotional tonality balancing the overall fear. Hence, these years may have allowed her to develop distancing and reflexive means, based on this double internalisation. Zdenka had a different experience, being directly in a part of the country having become German, and submitted to these rules; here, survival was much more dependent on blending in and obeying

---

[19] *Und damals habe ich mit dem Onkel gesprochen, -- ich habe ihn besucht, nicht, und er fragte mir, wie (..) geht es mir dort. Ich habe ihm das erzählt pffff! So hat er sich dafür genommen, und hat mich von dort genommen, zu ihm. Ich werde der Dienst bei ihm. (...) Dort konnte ich schlafen wie ich wollte, und essen alles gut, habe auch geholfen, habe auch gearbeitet, aber nicht schwer. Ich habe nur die Kühe zum fressen geführt, ich habe sie gehalten.(...) Das war Vormittag, wann ich ausgeschlafen war, gegessen, so die Kühe genommen. So haben wir die Kühen bis 11 Uhr, und dann habe ich vielleicht das Geschirr ein bisschen gewaschen, aber.. ich weiss nicht. (..) da hat die Grossmutter gekocht, oder die Tante. (..) Habe auch mit ihr gearbeitet [auf die Feldern], wen ich nicht mochte allein zu Hause. (..) Das was gut, beim Onkel. Das war besser wie daheim. Ich mochte nicht daheim gehen! [Lacht].* (Zdenka, 8.03.2016)

the rules, if not turning them to one's advantage. Even in the discourses at home may have been critical of politics, this was not overt. Correspondingly, resistance seems much more internal: Zdenka knew enough through her family's history and was a bright enough young woman to critically assess the dumbness of the new history teaching. Difficult memories have been silenced in the interview – such as the fact that her brother was enrolled in the Wehrmacht. Rather, the gloominess of these years seems concentrated in the memories of the forced labour in the fields, which, for having lasted only 3 months, is described with darkness and despair. The life of Zdenka and her family is, however, greatly protected by the advices, action and power of the uncle: it is he who suggests what to do, and has the power to move people and arrange things in his way. This protective wing is also doubled by very positive feelings: again, in her teenage years, Sandra seems to have had the best years of her youth at this house. In more psychological terms, Zdenka learns to support her critical thinking and modulate her obedience by following, and being supported by, a highly invested authority figure. It, thus, seems that Sandra and Zdenka develop two contrasting ways to dialogue with the world, two ways of handling the war and the social discourses that go with it: on the one hand, by drawing on a horizontal network, and on the other hand, by drawing on a vertical relationship. How will this further develop?

5.2.4   End of War: 1945, Being Repositioned

The war ended in 1945. This had all kind of consequences for the people living in the Sudeten or of German origin. In effect, from the moment of the truce, a period of about 6 months took place during which the population retaliated in an uncontrollable way against Germans. In the villages inland, the hunt for collaborators started, and retreating soldiers were assassinated in total impunity. In the Sudeten, things where more violent, with direct attacks to Germans and the organisation of a massive deportation of German families. Hence, both women were touched by these anti-German measures, with different consequences.

In 1945–1946, under Říp, Sandra had to prove, as many other people of German origin, that she had not been a Nazi or a collaborator during the war. As that time, she had no official papers, as they seemed to have been kept by her aunt. Some people wanted to single her out as German – one of the measures of retaliation and stigmatisation, corresponding to the shaved heads in France:

> They sort of had started with the politics, and because I had no papers, and they knew that I came from the borderland, there was this one "important" man and he was adamant that I, who didn't have papers and had a German mother, he was adamant that I should walk with a white armband.[20] (Sandra, 21.03.16)

---

[20] *Das war irgendwann mit der Politik schon angefangen, und weil ich nicht die Papiere hatte, und sie wusste dass ich von Grenzgebiet bin, da war einer so "wichtig" und er wollte absolut dass ich, wenn ich keine Papiere habe und die Mutter war Deutsch, dann wollte er absolut dass ich mit weissen Bändel, laufe. (Sandra, 21.03.16)*

The community was supportive; people spoke in her favour and silenced these demands; she also obtained a certificate from Butonia stating that she was not a collaborator. She finally had to go to the castle in Prague – the government – to obtain these papers proving her origin – a very impressive trip. It is through these papers that she actually discovered that these kind men she often met as a child were her brothers. Sandra learnt later that during the war, the brothers had to demonstrate through their genealogy that they were not Jews. Sandra's older brothers, who escaped conscriptions, still met some troubles. One of them spoke his mind about the likely failure of the German troops in Stalingrad to his grandfather; he was overheard by a younger relative – a "Nazi enthusiast" – and was reported and arrested; he spent the end of the war as a political prisoner in Theresienstadt.[21] Another brother became ill and spent the end of the war in a hospital in Morava – they eventually both survived the war, unlike the youngest brother who died on the Russian front as a soldier.

Things were more complicated at that time for Zdenka, who was still at her uncle's at the end of the war. In effect, in 1945, the Sudeten region was given back to Czechoslovakia; one of the first Czech reactions was to organise the deportation of the German residents. The transfer of Germans started as a spontaneous and often chaotic movement, and progressively became a more systematic expropriation of the German families. In Zdenka's region, the movement was orchestrated by the leaders of groups of Czech resistance (Kovařík, 2005) – before becoming regulated by the state (Luža, 1964, p. 275). As soon as the order to evacuate came to Zdenka's family, her father came to pick her up at her uncle, and they walked back home through the woods, as the first families started to leave their houses to go to Austria and Germany.

Z When the father came for me, some people had already moved out. [He came], so that we are all together, when they ask us to leave. So where we… but I cried again – ah! Nobody cried, but I cried, that we have to move out! I was so sad! But we could not go back.
T And could you take many things with you?
Z Only 50 kg per person, we could take. The father had been at war, so he told us, each of us takes a bread, at that time we were still cooking it, so what we each have a large bread, so that we don't get hungry. And some things, a few things. And then we took a wheelbarrow, we put our things on it, and the mother pushed it.
T And where did you go with it? To the train station?

---

[21] Theresienstadt, or Terezin in Czech, is a town located 25 km from the hill. A former Napoleonic army fortress, beautifully star shaped, it was used by the German army during World War II for a part as a prison for mainly Czech political prisoners, and for the rest, as a transit camp for the deportation of Jews from West Europe to the East, as well as ghetto or camp for a selection of mainly Czech Jews, relatively rich and educated. It is this "model camp" that was shown by the Nazis to an international red-cross delegation. Terezin has inspired many important studies and documentaries (for instance Adler, 2017; Lanzmann, 2013). The town is now a poor peripheral city, but attracts crowds of daily tourists and visitors who can see the rest of a camp, a museum and visit various buildings of the city and the fortress that were used in these times. https://www.pamatnik-terezin.cz/visit-of-terezin-memorial

Z No, we went from the house, to the next village to which the road goes, there we had to wait until all the people from the village would gather, and we had to wait, until the order would come, that we have to go. All together.[22] (Zdenka, 8.03.2016)

Once assembled there, the families received orders to leave, and so they went, through the next village, pass the border and to Austria, where they survived in more or less difficult conditions. However, while already waiting on this square, Zdenka's family suddenly obtained the right to stay at the last minute – again, "der Onkle hat auch geholfen", the uncle helped again.[23] The uncle intervened again towards the authorities in charge, reminding them that Zdenka's father was a Czech, and that he did not commit any bad action during the war. His position was thus examined and enough people, his employees and others, spoke in his favour; the family could thus go back home. However, the father eventually lost his job as a state of employee for having been a German during the war, and so the family had to leave the house. The father, who had been quite foreseeing, had bought another farmhouse in the village nearby for his retirement, where the family could move.

The uncle himself, a German, had enough Czech employees that he treated well and who spoke for him, so that he could remain for some time after the war. However, pressure was made upon his German wife and her family. Not wanting to separate, after having arranged the fishery of which he was in charge, he eventually left the country a few months later through an epic escape with wife, mother-in-law

---

[22] Z *Wenn der Vater für mich gekommen ist,(..) da sind schon welsch Menschen ausgezogen (???) das wir allen zusammen sind, wen sie uns ausziehen lassen. So sind wir auch.. so habe ich wieder geweint – ah! – niemand hat geweint, und ich habe geweint, dass wir ausziehen müssen. Mir war das so leidig! Aber dann können wir zurückgehen. T Und sie sind gegangen, mit viele Sachen? Z Nur 50 Kilos, auf Person – dürften wir nehmen. Der Vater, der war im Krieg, so hat er gesagt, jeder nimmt ein Brot, damals haben wir noch gebackt, dass wir jeden allein ein grosses Brot haben, dass wir nicht Hunger haben. Und Sachen, ein bisschen Sachen. Und dann haben wir – ich weiss nicht wie man sagt trackar – so in Holz, und da haben wir die Sachen drauf gelegen und die Mutter ist mit hm gefahren. T (…) So sind sie gegangen, mit dem Holtz. wo sind sie gegangen? Zum Bahnhof? Z Nein, wir sind gegangen, von dem Haus, nach [next village] wo die Strasse hingeht, so dort müssten wir warten, alle Leute aus dem Dorf hin, und dort müssten wir warten, bis sie Befehl geben, dass sie gehen müssen. Alle zusammen. (Zdenka, 8.03.2016)*

[23] *Hat der Onkel auch geholfen. Die Tschechische Leute auch, die Arbeitern, die zu ihm – er hat Tschechische Leute auch gehabt; und sie haben ihm geholfen, das er war nicht so gut Deutscher. [wir lachen – kein guter Deutscher] so können wir zurückgehen, in das Haus. So sind wir dort geblieben. Aber nach dem Krieg [lacht], war er Deutsch, so haben sie ihn aus der Staatlichen Arbeit ausgeschmissen. Darf er nicht mehr der Teichjäger machen. Und das Haus, (…) das hat er gekauft. Er wusste, dass er alt wird, dass er nicht dort bleiben kann. So hat er das Haus gekauft! So können wir dorthin ausziehen. Wenn er die Arbeit nicht mehr dort hat. (..) So sind wir dort gegangen. Das war leer, und war da nur die Hausfrau – er hat das im Krieg gekauft – und war nur die alte Frau dort, und sie sollte bis sie stirbt dort sein. Das war gesprochen. Die ist dort geblieben, sie war Österreicherin, und sie könnte auch dort bleiben, sie hat ein Zimmer dort gehabt. Sie hatte ein Sohn in Österreich, und das war dort sehr schlecht, und so hat er sie mit ihm genommen. So waren wir alleine dort. Ohne sie. Das war besser. [lacht]. (Zdenka, 8.03.2016)*

and chicken in a small car.[24] Extremely respected in his trade, he was offered a prestigious position in nearby Austria, where he played an important role in the development of the fish ponds.

Finally, a last element (learnt off-record) is that Zdenka's brother, who had been conscripted as a German soldier, had been missing as he was on the front in Norway; the family had been informed of it during the war, but it was just after the war that the uncle tried to enquire about it, in vain. He was, thus, considered dead; Zdenka hardly speaks of him.

In summary, the end of the war was again an even of collective importance and a turning point in the country's and Europe's history. It also had direct consequences in the everyday life of Sandra and Zdenka. In both cases, their origins were again pinpointed and stigmatised, together with that of millions of others; both also learnt the loss of a brother. In Sandra's case, the end of the war was marking, but the aggression came from a minority in the village and she found the support of her community to avoid it. More remarkably, the doubt on her origin had as consequence the more important research for official papers, by which she discovered her family history and realised that the two nice uncles were two older brothers. On Zdenka's side, she had to be parted from her uncle, and, then, the family experienced the traumatic mass deportation and was expecting to lose everything – until the last-minute intervention of the uncle, creating conditions of exception for the family. Although the family could remain in the village, its situation changed radically, as the father lost his job, the family had to move and the uncle eventually left

---

[24] Here one of the narration of the epic escape by Zdenka: *"Er ist hier geblieben, er ist nach dem Krieg nicht gleichgegangen. Er war Direktor der Fleischfischerei, so haben sie ihm das Haus gelassen, er sollte das übergeben. In 45 musste alle Deutsche aussiedeln, er ist erst in 46. Er hat das übergegeben; sie wollten dass er hier bleibt, aber die Frau und die Mutter, sie musste ausziehen. Und die sagten, er soll scheiden lassen. Das sagte er, das ist unmöglich, das will ich nicht. So wollte er auch ausziehen. Aber sie geben ihm nicht die Bewilligung. So – das weiss ich noch nicht, er hat der [niece] gesagt, wir haben uns nicht gesprochen, und der war bei der [niece], uns dort war eine Frau, sie hat die sied(?) gemacht, um die Fischen zu fangen, fischen. Und er hat sich dort gestellt bei der Frau, sie geben ihm nicht die Bewilligung geben das er wegzieht, so wird er schwarz gehen. So hat er Auto bestellt, noch in [the village], bei eine Bäckerei – er hat bekannte gehabt – der mit dem Auto haben sie alles eingeladet, und die Frau und die Grossmutter, und da sagten sie, die Grossmutter hat auch Hühnern mittegenommen in einen Kasten, aber über die Grenze dürften nicht, so haben sie die Hühner ausgelassen, und sind sie über die Grenze gefahren, und dann hat sie die Grossmutter gerufen, Piii, piiiii, und die sie gekommen! Das kann man gar nicht glauben das es war ist! So hatten sie die Hühner. Am Anfang war auch schwer, in Osterreich, hat der Onkel auch nicht gleich Arbeit gehabt. Und har er eine Arbeit bekommen bei einen Teichjäger, dann ihm jemand gesagt – er hat auch Bekannte gehabt. Und hat gearbeitet, und hat keine Zahlung bekommen. Und er har gefragt, wieso bekomme ich keine Zahlung? Das hat verboten, von Wien, einen. No. Das war ein Mann der etwas mit Onkel etwas gemacht hat, vielleicht im Krieg. Und der Onkel ist zu ihm gefahren, er weiss wo es das war, und hat ihm gesprochen, und hat ihm gesagt, Wenn du mir die Auszahlung einhält, so sage ich alles über dich, was du im Krieg gemacht hast! Und war schon fertig. Er hat wieder die Anzahlung bekommen. Und das war wieder gut. Dann hat er Arbeit bekommen. Er hat viel Ordnung gebracht zu der Fischerei, es war Unordnung, Er hat Teiche gebaut. Es war seine Arbeit und noch sein Hobby. Er hat keine andern, nicht Gasthaus.."* . (Zdenka, 25.05.2016)

the country. Finally, two points can be highlighted. First, following the analysis started above, we can see a similar pattern happening: facing danger, Sandra finds the support of a strong inclusive community; Zdenka and her family, in face of danger, is protected – a last time – by the powerful wing of the uncle, as a sort of vertical authority. Second, this end of war has consequences for the two women's experience of being part of a family: on the one side, for Sandra, the end of the war was paradoxically an expansion of her family; for Zdenka, with the departure of the uncle and the end of access to the fishery, it was an important loss, for the family and for herself.

5.2.5   1946: After the War, Being a Young Woman, Meeting a Man

The next section is defined by a combination of personal and political events. After the end of war, the country was in a relatively unstable situation: liberated by the USSR army as well as the United States in the South West, the country entered under communist influence; however, the first government was moderately communist, democratically elected by the population. It is only 3 years later, in 1948, that the USSR imposed a real communist governance (see Sect. 4.1.4). Hence, in the immediate after-war, for a couple of years, life in villages and small towns started to take a more normal taste – even though food and goods were still rationed – with a young generation discovering freedom at the same time as adulthood.

For Sandra, a new and happy period began. Immediately after the war, she met the man to become her husband, Roman. Roman was born in one of the village under Říp in a family of musicians – himself a drummer, next to his work as a railway employee. Like every man under the age of 24 at the beginning of the war, he had been sent to compulsory work to Germany during the war, and spent these years fixing railways tracks all around the German-occupied territories. Sandra and Roman met right upon his return – and the return of all young men in the village. This period must have been joyful – Sandra calls it "lustig", funny: all the young women had been without young men their age during the war; they had learnt to dance in women-only dance classes but had not been to balls, and then could attend these dancehalls only after the war, but chaperoned by their mothers – here Ms Schubert.[25] In contrast, the end of the war was marked by an intense period of parties and dances in the villages around Říp; Roman and his family were musicians, playing in one of the bands that were making dance everybody. Roman was 8 years older than Sandra; they started to date, and so together they went dancing everywhere, in all the villages in the Říp region and beyond, to parties, events and festivals,

---

[25] *Zu der Zeit waren alle sehr lustig, weil jede war sehr froh, das schon der krieg geändert hat, und dann war keine Not, das wir bei der Bevölkerung.. überall war das Saal voll, weil überall Jungen und auch die älteren, und zu der Zeit war es noch Mode, wenn eine noch einzeln war, es war Pflichtig, die Mutter musste uns begleiten.* (Sandra 19.05.17)

in the summer as well as in the winter.[26] Soon after, Sandra was pregnant. The couple married in 1946.

Political events were still active in the background and having consequences in Sandra's life. Hence, because of the massive devaluation in 1946, the dowry that Mr Schubert had saved for her vanished; the young couple had to start their life with no money at all. Sandra started to work again soon after the birth of her first child, this time at a chemical company. The couple first moved into two rooms in a farm, with the water pump in the courtyard, in relatively difficult conditions with their first baby. In parallel, after the evacuation of the Germans from the Sudetenland, two dynamics took place; on the one hand, many people from the villages around Říp started to move to the Sudeten to take empty flats and abandoned houses. On the other hand, in 1946, some of the Sudeten houses were given back to the Czech families expelled in 1938. Now that Sandra's family ties had been clarified, Sandra obtained the legal right to recover one of the flats of her brothers in Ústí. Although this would have solved the family's housing problem, Roman did not want to move away from the Podřipsko region, precisely because he had his whole family there, and he played with his family band in the region. Sandra tells that story quite flatly, but at time wonders what happened to these family properties; whether she regretted the choices made then is unknown. Anyway, having stayed in one village under Říp, the living conditions were quite harsh, and Sandra's family had to move houses a few times. Eventually, they rented the house of a musician friend who had moved to the next village, and who later was ready to sell the house to the young couple. They did buy it after having borrowed small amounts of money to a group of friends. From there on, Sandra was very carefully counting all the earned money, making sure that they could pay their friends back, and living with the absolute minimum.

Life, however, seem to have been extremely colourful. Every week was punctuated by endless dancing parties in the villages around, in which Roman and his brothers would play. Sandra and her new sisters-in-law – the wives of the other musicians – would join them. They would first go by train, while Roman would have his drum kit on his bike, and later on a motorbike:

> The husband had to go by bike. He had the bass drum on the back, and the second box and the snare drum were in the front. It was not so easy, when it was windy or raining... Later he had a moped, but that was similar. And with my sister in law, we went to work by motorbike, so that we then both could go straight to the place where they were playing[27]. (Sandra, 19.05.17).

---

[26] *Mit der Mann war ich immer alle – da war ich in Krabčice, Kostomlaty, Mnetěš, Černouček, Cernous, Beřkovice, und auch tanzen waren auch in Leitmeritz (Litoměřice), im Msceno, weil im Msceno hatten wir jedes Jahr so wie Sommerfest, haben auch dort gespielt..* (Sandra 19.05.17)

[27] *Der Mann musste auf dem Fahrrad. Die grosse Trommel hat er auf dem Rücken gehabt, und der zweite Koffer und kleine Trommel waren vorne. Es war nicht einfach, weil wenn Wind war, oder Regen... Und nachher hat er ein... nicht Pionier aber so was endliches gehabt. Und mir sind, mit der Schwägerin, weil sie ist mit Motorrad in die Arbeit gefahren, da konnten wir zweie dann zu der Musik kommen.* (Sandra, 19.05.17)

Fig. 5.1 Zdenka (left) with a self-made dress, 1945, with relative, reproduced with courtesy of family

In the winter, they would sled to villages, and dance the whole might. The children were kept by the other women in the village. And Sandra, who did not have much of a youth before, had her happiest year, dancing all night long with all kind of men, while her husband, Roman, was playing the drums on stage with an eye on her:

> And so, I finally experienced dancing, with my husband – because when an unknown young woman arrives in a village, it stirs interests, and so, where do you come from, and this and that. And it was good, that my husband was not so jealous. He told me, I am happy that you dance, speak how much you want, do promise what you want, but don't go out![28] (Sandra, 9.03.16)

On Zdenka's side, life also had to take over after the war. Once back home from the uncle, the future of Zdenka had to be decided; she wanted to become a tailor – and had done very nice handwork on her own, which she learnt at school. She proudly tells how good she was at it and got the best grades at school in knitting and handwork, and also continued doing such work at home; she made herself a nice dress when she was aged 10 – a dress immortalised by a photographer in 1945 (Fig. 5.1). But her father objected to it, arguing that she was too weak ("dass Ich schwach bin"), and that she could get tuberculosis. The uncle, still there, was

---

[28] *Und da habe ich erst eigentlich das Tanzen erlebt, eben, mit meinen Mann, weil im einen anderen Dorf ein fremdes Mädel kommt, dann ist es erst Interesse zu holen, und wovon kommst zu her, und das und das. Und das war Gut, dass mein Mann nicht so Eifersüchtig war. Er sagte, ich bin froh, dass Du tanzt, rede was Du willst, verspricht was Du willst, aber geh nicht raus!* (Sandra, 9.03.16).

informed, and according to Zdenka was very upset, but he was probably just about to leave and could this time not intervene anymore.[29]

Zdenka had no choice but to obey her father, and she started to work in a knitting factory in the nearby town, which meant that she had to take a very early morning bus, at half past five, and could come back home at half past five in the evening.[30] Whether she liked it or not – after all, one has to work ("Damals musste man arbeiten, das geht nicht anders") – she learned fast, and she declared quite proudly that she was good at it. She worked in the factory for 2 years, until she married.

In Zdenka's life, the meeting with her husband reflects some of the background political forces still active, and people's strategies. She told me the story twice, in two slightly different ways – the first one explaining how she met her husband on a bus trip organised by the church to which she belonged, to visit a famous church. Her mother had offered her the ticket of a woman who had planned to go, and finally could not make it; the husband happened to be in the same bus with his family, and so they spent time together and sympathised during the visit.[31] The second time, she actually told me the background of the possibility of their meeting:

> We took the bus for this daytrip, organized by the church, to that [famous town]. And then a woman, Miss Gross was her name, she escaped and passed the border – she had bought a

---

[29] *Weil der Vater möchte nicht, dass ich auf die Schneiderin gehe! (..) Das ich schwach bin, und kann Tuberkulose bekommen, und so. Und der Onkel, wenn ich ihm das gesagt habe, hat er sich sehr geärgert! Weil ich möchte das machen! Sehr gerne! Und ich habe nicht gelernt! Sehr.. ich habe mich schon ein Kittel gemacht, wen ich 10 Jahren gehabt. Ich möchte die Schneiderin machen, aber der Vater sagt, ich bin zu schwach. (Zdenka, 8.03.2016). Ja, das nähen möchte ich. .. das haben wir auch in der Schule, in 6ter Klasse haben kochen gelernt, und nähen auch. Das erste bei Nähen, war das Hemd für das kleine Kindlein. Das habe ich noch irgendwo, oder ist vielleicht schon weg… Und ich habe das beste gemacht!! [wir lachen] Ich habe das beste.. ich habe sehr schön ausgenäht, damals war das gut, und ich habe auch das gut gekonnt. Das Nähen, das geht mir auch gut. Wir haben gestrickt, auch, Fussocken (ja, diese), das kann ich alles, Pullover haben wir gemacht. Ja, den habe ich gemacht.* (Zdenka, 25.05.2016)

[30] *Ich bin in der Fabrik gegangen, in [town] Dort war, das war eine Maschine, da muss man machen den Faden auf die Spulki, und da machen sie die Schallen. (..) jenelkovi shala! Damals hat man das viel getragen. (..) Damals musste man arbeiten, das geht nicht anders. Aber das habe ich gut gemacht… Und dann – dann bin ich nach Haus, zu Hause gewesen. Ja, lange bin ich die Fabrik gewesen. Vielleicht zwei Jahren. (..) Damals sind wir schon mit der Autobus in der Arbeit gefahren. Früh um halb sechs, und halb sechs wieder daheim. (..) wir haben eine Stunde Mittag, von 12 bis 13, da könnte man sich etwas zum essen kaufen, und dann wieder zu Arbeit, bis 17. (…) das war gut, man gewöhnt sich. (..) Sie zeigen mir und ich mache. Und da ich habe das bald gelernt, sie geben mir wieder andere Arbeit. Wir haben Stoff gemacht, und wo es falsch gemacht, musste man wieder gut machen. (Baumwolle und Leinen). (Zdenka, 8.03.2016)*

[31] *Na ja, das war so, wir sind auf einen Ausflug gefahren nach.. von einem Autobus, die -ich weiss nicht.. nach [a known church]. Das war von der Kirsche ein Ausflug. Und die Mutter hat mich doch hingestellt. Nein, damals war eine andere Frau bestellt, und sie könnte nicht fahren, so hat sie mich… dass ich fahren soll. (..) und mein Mann ist auch gefahren, auf den Ausflug, auch mit einem Freund, von wo sie die Fleischhackerei haben. Die Frau ist auch gefahren, und die Schwester, und sind wir viele Leute, no ein ganzes Autobus sind wir gefahren. Und, dort haben wir und bekannt. Im Ausflug. Und im Autobus her hier gesiezten und ich bin hier vorne gesiezten. (…) so haben wir uns kennengelernt. Wir waren einen ganzen Tag draussen, und dort war eine Kirsche, und draussen war ein Wahlmarkt, so mit Geschäfte, wir sind nicht so viel in der Kirche gewesen, wir sind draussen gegangen. (Zdenka, 8.03.2016)*

ticket for that trip, and they wanted to escape through the border to Austria. Hence my mother, who knew her well, gave me the ticket to that trip... so that nobody notices that she was missing and gone. (…) This woman's husband was a hunter, and they lived in a hunter's lodge 2 km from the village. (…) She had bought the ticket for the daytrip, and then the men organized their escape. They [the communists] had taken everything from them, and it was bad for them – it was in 1948, it was already bad.[32] (Zdenka, 25.05.2016)

Hence, the meeting of Sandra with her husband results from a cover-up of an escape. The two young people started to date for a couple of years as he was doing his military service; he came back in 1951 and they married in 1952:

He was doing his military service in Prague, so he was coming once every 14 days. Then he was posted in [the north of country], and he could not come so often. So maybe we didn't see each other for one month, maybe two. But we wrote to each other… [we laugh]. In 51 he came back home where he belonged, and we married in April 1952. At that time we were living [in my village, with my parents], in one room, I was happy, I didn't mind; and he was working in town, in his sister's butchery.[33] (Zdenka, 25.05.2016)

This short section was defined to show how, at the end of the war, life took its course and youth had to happen. Political forces work in the background, and the two young women feel the muffled resonances of these in their daily life. The most important events, however, are the meetings with the men to be their husbands. Both meetings are actually strongly channelled by political forces. The intensity of the meeting of Sandra with her husband is linked to the return of the forced labour to which he was sent, and the end of the war embargo on parties and dances: suddenly, and ocean of happy possibilities seems to have opened. In a less explosive way, Zdenka meets her husband as the result of a community arrangement to hide the escape of one of its members; the meeting seems coincidental, yet in an occasion created precisely in these specific post-war conditions, in the small spaces of free action people could find. Anyway, Sandra seems to have lived her happiest years, compensating for her more difficult childhood, finding a community, and enlarged

---

[32] *Wir sind auf den Ausflug gefahren, mit der Kirche in [a town], mit dem Autobus. Und eine Frau, die Frau Gross hat sie geheisst, sie sind über die Grenze – sie hat einen Zettel gekauft, und dann wollten sie weggehen über die Grenze nach Österreich. Und so hat meine Mutter, sie kennten sich gut, so hat sie den Zettel meine Mutter geben dass ich fahre. . . Dass niemand wisst – weil sie weggegangen sind. Aber dürfen sie nicht! Aber sie sind über die Grenze gegangen. (in 1948). Das war die Frau – er war Jäger, und sie sind auf dem Jägerhaus gewohnt, dort bei [the village] und dort waren sie im Wald, ein Haus nur der Jäger! Sind zwei Kilometer in das Dorf, wie wir, so haben wir uns bekannt, wir kannten damals alle. Und mein Vater hat sich auch mit ihnen gekannt. No, und sie wollte auf den Ausflug fahren, hat sie den Zettel gekauft, aber nachher die Männer haben das gemacht, dass sie weglaufen. Sie haben mit ihnen… sie haben ihnen alles genommen, und nicht gut war es. In 48 war das schlecht, schon.* (Zdenka, 25.05.2016)

[33] *Er war beim Militär in Prag, so kommte er in 14 Tage ein Mal. Er war auch übergelegt in Olomouc. Dort war er auch im Militär. Da konnte er nicht so oft; das war längere Trace. So haben wir vielleicht Monat nicht gesehen, zwei Monaten. Aber haben wir uns geschrieben.. [wir lachen]. In 51 kam er im Herbst nach wo er gehört Hause, und 52 haben wir im April geheiratet. Da wohnten wir in [village] (mit den Eltern), in ein Zimmer, ich war zufrieden, mir ist das Egal; und er hat gearbeitet in [town] bei der Schwester in den Geschäft, in die Fleischheckerei.* (Zdenka, 25.05.2016)

family, warmth and support, which largely balanced a difficult working life. Zdenka had to make compromises with her ambitions, for the first time without the protection of her uncle, and start a normal working life, while eventually meeting a life partner and starting a happy family of her own.

5.2.6   1948–1953 and a Bit More: Starting a Family in Times of Hardship

The USSR takeover of Czechoslovakia in 1948 had growing consequences, with the progressive nationalisation of means of production, and "re-education" of people suspected of being capitalist or bourgeois. A real Stalinist style of governance was installed, with a second devaluation, random arrests and torture, mock trials, persecutions and forced labour and concentration camps. Both Sandra and Zdenka saw the effects of this politics, and this time it is Zdenka who was most hardly directly hit; thus, the family had to move to Říp.

Here is how Sandra describes the situation in the village under Říp, where, from 1948 onward, every small farmer or craftsperson had to give over their means of production and did not receive rationing cards:

> When they started with the communism, in the village were only small businesses. Opposite our house, there was a baker; under that small house was a small shop; in the first house of the other street was a shop; here was a pub; there was a pub – these people were not rich. If they didn't have goats or chicken at home, they would have died of hunger! Indeed, as they had small businesses, they were not allowed to receive rationing cards. This was the worst – because who was working at the factory would get them without problems. Crazy world.[34]. (Sandra, 19.05.2017). So Roman's brother had nothing big, but because he was a house painter, he didn't receive the ration tickets. That was a crazy world. (…) The tailor, he was lucky to have a goat and a pair of chicken so that he could live, but because he had his shop, he could not have the ration tickets. He was already a capitalist. It was… The baker, because he had a bakery, was already a capitalist. Because they wanted to nationalize everything. That was crazy. That was in the 50s, these were the worst years. Now it is crazy again, with the return from state to the private sector. Crazy world[35] (31.03.2016).

---

[34] *Ja, aber bis sie angefangen haben mit dem Kommunismus, da waren eben viele nur solche Kleinbetriebe. Das gegen uns, das Haus war Bäckerei; unten das Häuschen war Kaufladen; im erstes Haus der zweite Strasse war Kaufladen; da war Gasthaus; da war Gasthaus; das waren keine reiche Leute. Wenn sie noch nicht die Ziege zu Hause hätten, die Hühner, dann würden sie verhungern! Und so ist es so passiert eben, weil wer der Kleinbetrieb hatte, dann hatte er keine Nährmittelkarte bekommen. Das war das schlimmste, weil wer in der Fabrik war, bekomme es ohne Schwierigkeiten. Verrückte Welt.* (Sandra, 19.05.2017)

[35] *Darum hatte [Romans'brother] nichts grosses, aber die Nährmittelzetteln hat er nicht bekommen weil er eben Mahlermeister war. Das war immer verrückte Welt. Da waren viele.. er hat sich zu Hause.. wie Schneider, der war glücklich das er hatte Ziege und paar Hühner und etwas das er überhaupt leben kann, aber war er Schneidermeister war, hat er keine Nährmittelkarten bekommen. Da war er schon Kapitalist. Das war schon.. der Bäcker, weil er Bäckerei hatte, war er schon Kapitalist. Will sie wollten doch alles Verstaatlichen. Das war verrückt, das waren die 50ten Jahren, das waren die Schlimmsten. Jetzt ist es wieder verrückt, vom Staat aufs Privat.. Verrückte Welt.. (31.03.2016)*

At that time, precisely, Sandra was working for a factory and was therefore in a relatively more comfortable situation than some neighbours. However, she had troubles there as well; in 1948 and especially the 1950s, the communist life was taking more and more space at the factory; people had to participate in the 1 May demonstration and other events. Sandra had her child looked after by her husband's mother; pretexting that this lady was not available, she did not attend these meetings of which she disapproved. She was reported by a colleague; yet, before becoming really in trouble, she deliberately quit the job. In 1953, there was another massive devaluation when the government took all people's saving; the period was dark.

On Zdenka's side, who was now living with her family at her father's house while the husband worked at the family's large butchery, 1953 brought an important rupture, resulting from the accumulation of two facts. First, the family butchery was a large company, with 14 employees. With the communist policies, this was of course intolerable; the factory was confiscated,[36] and two members of the family had to be sent to "educative treatment". So Zdenka's husband, as the youngest man, was sent to work in uranium mines. He could come home only once in a fortnight. Second, at home, Zdenka's father had bought a few animals to make a living out of farming after he lost his state job in the fish farm. He was requested to join the collective farm, which he refused. As retaliation, the whole family lost their right to food coupons.

At this point, thus, Zdenka, her husband and a baby had no means to obtain food beyond the few father's animals. Zdenka's husband decided to bring the family in his own village, under Říp, where they could claim for these tickets:

> So goes my husband: we will move [back to my village under Říp] and there we will get the food tickets! So that was immediately arranged, that we would get these tickets, so we moved there by car; we took the furniture, we took everything we had, isn't it and – this was in May or June, I don't remember exactly, we arrived here, and still in the same very week at which we arrived, the food tickets were abolished! So we didn't get any, nobody did! (..) And the value of the money collapsed, with the money exchange, in 1953. The same week! One week we came, and this was immediately so.[37] (Zdenka, 25.05.2016)

Asked whether she agreed with the decision, she explains not having had much choice:

> T: In 53 your husband said you had to go to [his village under Říp]; did you agree with that or not?
> Z: Well, these were bad times. If we didn't get food tickets... to buy food. We had to eat, didn't we? For these who didn't have tickets, there was a free market, but we couldn't afford

---

[36] *Sie haben eine grosse Fleischhackerei dort gehabt, 14 Leute arbeiten da, und machen alles. Aber nachher haben sie ihn den Geschäft auch genommen, das war alles weg.* (Zdenka, 8.03.2016)

[37] *So mein Mann: so werden wir uns herziehen und dort bekommen wie es!! Na das war gerade eingerichtet, das wir das Nährmittelkitte bekommen soll, und sind wir hergezogen mit dem Auto, haben wir die Nabytek, alles haben wir uns mitgenommen, nicht, und – das war im Mai, oder Juni, ich weiss nicht mehr genau, sind wir hergekommen, und noch diese Woche wir gekommen sind, so ist Nährmittel Karte gefallen! So bekomme wir auch keine, Niemand! (Brauchte man nicht mehr). Nein. Und das Geld ist gefallen, Umtauschen, in 1953. Die gleiche Woche! Eine Woche sind wir gekommen und gleich war wieder das.* (Zdenka, 25.05.2016)

it. At that time my [child] was 8 or 9 months and I was not working. I didn't have money; and when the [baby] was born we didn't receive any support either. So I thought, if we get the food tickets, and he can have work there, after he finishes [the time in the Uranium mines].[38] (Zdenka, 25.05.2016)

Thus, in 1953, the family moved hastily to Říp in hope to have coupons. The same week, the system of coupons was cancelled and the money lost its value. They did not have money so did not lose it, yet still she recalls it as a difficult moment for everyone. Another difficulty awaited them. In the village under Říp, they moved in the husband's family house – a traditional U-shaped house, with a side on the street, where there was a small workshop and butcher shop, a main building, and the second aisle with workshop and fridge. The house, however, was in bad shape, occupied by the husband's father and his sister with her husband:

Z: But... I didn't like it, here [laughs]
T: Why?
Z: I didn't want to come.. well, but... (..) Nothing was fixed. Nothing at all [in the house]! Here [she shows the living room] was totally empty, up to the roof, it had burned down, and they didn't do anything to fix it, that was the husband's sister and her husband (…). We slept upstairs with the baby, and the sister slept here [in the kitchen where we sit]. We cooked together. There was a shop [in the courtyard], a butchery, and my sister-in-law was selling there. Her husband worked in the factory by the train station[39]. (Zdenka, 25.05.2016)

Zdenka arrived in this worn-out place, in a family that had lost its trade. In effect, the small family butchery had been taken over by the communists in 1952, too, who confiscated and destroyed the meat machines, and turned the butchery into a resell shop for the cooperative larger meat factory in the nearby town. The butchers, that is, her husband's father as well as later her husband, were thus obliged to work for the meat factory.

In order to overcome what appears to have been difficult beginnings, Zdenka started to work as an aid in the in-law's shop (while she was having a second child).

---

[38] T: In 53 sag den Mann, wir sollen nach [das Dorf]; waren Sie einverstanden oder wollten Sie nicht? Z: Na ja, es war eine schlechte Zeit... so wenn wir nicht Nährmittelkarten bekommen.. das Essen zu kaufen.. . Musste man essen, nicht? Und wenn wir nicht Nährmittelkarten bekommen, so war auch ein freier Verkauf, aber der war sehr teuer. Und das könnten wir nicht leisten. (Damals war [unser Kind] 8 oder 9 Monaten alt, ich habe nicht mehr gearbeitet). Damals habe ich kein Geld bekommen, nichts. Wenn das Kind geboren ist haben wir nichts bekommen. So meinte ich, wenn wir die Nährmittelkarten haben, und er wird hier Arbeit haben, oder wird er noch nach Pribram fahren – das musste er noch zu Ende machen, es war noch nicht fertig. (Zdenka, 25.05.2016)

[39] Z. Aber.. mir gefällt es nicht, hier. [lacht] T: Wieso? Z: Ich wollte nicht hier gehen.. na ja, aber. (…) Hier war nichts eingerichtet. Nichts..(im Haus?) Gar nichts!! Hier war das leer, bis zum Dach, das ist ausgebrannt, und sie haben das nicht besser gemacht, und war noch die Schwester hier mit ihren Mann, sie wollte wieder nicht zu der Mutter gehen, zu seinem Mann, die Mutter war im [nächsten Dorf], er war auch nur Einziger und er wollte nach Hause gehen, aber sie Schwester meinem Mann wollte nicht hingehen auch! Dass war so. (..) Wir haben oben geschlafen mit die Kleine, und die Schwester hat hier geschlafen. Und gekocht haben wir zusammen. Es war hier Geschäft, die Fleischerei, und die Schwägerin, meiner Mann die Schwester, hat hier verkauft. Ihr Ehemann hat in der Fabrik gearbeitet, hier war auch eine Fabrik im [Dorf], beim Bahnhof. (Zdenka, 25.05.2016)

She started to save on her husband's salary in order to be able to refurbish the house. She also explains how she decided to replace the single-glazed windows with double-glazed ones, as she was about to have a second baby during the winter; she ordered them from the craftsman, imposed that decision against the will of her father-in-law who thought that it was not useful, and saved that money on her husband's salary – which corresponded to a full month's salary. Waiting for these windows, after the departure of the in-laws who eventually moved out, they finally were starting to have a home[40]:

> We were living in the living room. We slept there and cooked there and did everything in there. I often think about it. But we were all together! And it was good. We were already alone, our youngest [child] was small, it was January, and we had simple-glazed windows! (Zdenka, 25.05.2016).

She refused to take a loan, and exerted a strong control on the young family's expenses. Asked about how she learnt to save and make such financial planning:

> Z: Well. My husband gave me his salary, and I gave him money for beer; he was not allowed to have more.
> T: How come did you know how to do that?
> Z: I don't know… At home it was also like that… Well no, my father was in charge of the money. Perhaps I got it from with my father, to keep the accounts. (…) Yes, I learned from him, that one needs to save; one has to work it out and plan so that one has no debts, I learned it from my father. And my husband, he was ready to borrow money, no, this I didn't like. I didn't want it, at the end you pay much more! It's a bad calculation. We had to save money, we had to calculate.. (…) Eat potatoes, and so on. No, we weren't hungry, we had meat, but that costs also money…[41] (Zdenka, 25.05.2016)

---

[40] *Wir wohnten im Wohnzimmer. Wir haben dort geschlafen und gekocht und alles gemacht. Ich denke oft darauf. Aber waren wir alle zusammen! Und es war gut. Weil wir schon allein waren, die [jüngste Tochter] war klein er war im Januar, da war es kalt, hier waren nur einfache Fenster! Keine zwei Fenster. Ich habe noch den Fenstern gelassen machen wen sie geboren ist. Weil das kann man doch nicht aufheizten! Sie haben so schlecht Wirtschaft gemacht. Und ich möchte gerade ein so grosses Fenster hingeben. Aber der Vater sagt Nein! Fenster bleiben wie sie sind! So bin ich wieder nach [stadt] gefahren, dort war ein Tischler, wer die Fenster gemacht hat, habe ich ihm das bestellt, er hat das gebracht, und sagte auch, Hier war gleich ein grosses Fenster machen! Ja, aber der Vater will das nicht. (T: Wieso wollte der Vater nicht?) Seinen Kopf! (…)Dort haben wir alles gemacht, gekocht gebadet, geschlafen, alles. Da war einen grosses Bett, hier war den Ottoman – den Gautsch, und hier war ein kleines Bett. Und in der Mitte war den Tisch, und dort war wieder der Kredenz wo oben ist. Der Kredenz war auf der Seite, und der Offen, zum heizten, und kochen… na ja… Ich habe das alles.. gemacht.. Aber zuerst musste man die Fenster zahlen, und die Fenstern die kosten (..) damals 1200 Kronen, das war der ganze verdienst für ein Monat. Ich musste sparen.* (Zdenka, 25.05.2016)

[41] *Z: Na ja. Mein Mann hat mich die Auszahlung gegeben, und ich habe ihm auf das Bier gegeben, und mehr dürfte er nicht haben. T: So wieso haben sie das gewusst, wie das zu machen? Z: Ich weiss nicht.. Zu Hause war es auch so. Aber nein, mein Vater hat das Geld gehabt. Ich habe vielleicht etwas von den Vater gehabt, dass ich rechnen musste. (.) Ja ich habe von ihm gelernt, dass man must Hospodarit – man muss wirtschaften, keinen Schulden machen und nichts, das habe ich schon von den Vater gelernt. Und mein Mann – er wollte Geld ausleihen, nein, das habe ich nicht gerne gehabt. Das wollte ich nicht, weil dann zählt man viel mehr! Das ist schlechte Rechnung. Wir mussten immer sparen, man musste zählen… (..) Kartoffeln gegessen, und so. Nein, Hunger hatten wir nicht. Wir haben auch Fleisch gehabt, aber das kostet auch…* (Zdenka, 25.05.2016)

Asked about what the difficult years, Zdenka replies that it was 1954 onwards; hence, if the politics harshened in 1953, we can think that the subjective cost of the transition to her new living conditions was quite high, until some stability could be achieved again.

In this section, we focused on the year 1953 and its consequences for the lives of Sandra and Zdenka. The year 1953 and the years around were marked by harsh communist policies in Czechoslovakia. It affected directly everyday life, and both women, who were living in families of small craftsmen, were violently hit by the consequences of nationalisation. Sandra saw her family members and neighbours finding themselves in trouble, with more difficulty to survive than during the war; paradoxically, being an untrained factory worker, she found herself in a better position. Zdenka experienced a major rupture: she now left Southern Bohemia, where she had spent her whole childhood and youth and where she had her family, to settle in the village under Říp with her husband and baby with the hope to find better living conditions. However, this time, the odds were against them: they were faced with very bad living conditions (a burnt-down house); in addition, the distribution of food tickets was abolished the same week – the very reason for which they came. This move, which she accepted to follow, trusting her husband's decision, must have been quite a distressing experience. Anyway, Zdenka seemed to have quickly learnt to take things in control again. By now, let us simply note that Sandra is quite affected by the policy that is not touching so much herself, than the members of the network to which she belongs. She also, with distance, critically reflects on the absurdity of these policies. Zdenka finds herself for the first time without her father or her uncle; trusting her husband for this one decision to move, she very soon learns to change position, and using some of the resources she learnt from these older men, to take things in control, as can already be seen with the window incident.

5.2.7 1953–1980s, Onwards: Being a Woman, Living and Working in Times of Hardship

In the following years, life had to go on, as communism was there, yet progressively softening. In historical accounts about the period, 1968 is often remembered as the Prague spring, with its artistic and cultural freedom in the Czech capital. It was followed by harsh politics – the so-called normalisation – until a progressive weakening that would lead to the end of communism in 1989. Around Říp, 30 km from that, the Prague spring and its consequences were hardly felt; however, small openings to the West were experienced. Sandra and Zdenka, who now lived in the same village, tell less stories about their families than about their working lives in these condition under communism.

In 1954, Sandra found a job in a large food and agriculture factory (owned by the communists) in Roudnice, where she worked from 1954 to her retirement in 1991. Working conditions were quite harsh; she had to leave the house and take the

4:30 a.m. train for a working day starting at 6:00 am and lasting 8 h, with just a lunch break at the factory. She started to work in the production; under the heavy communist atmosphere, Sandra expressed her discrete resistance again, denouncing the hypocrisy of some:

> S There was also one who was totally eaten by it [communism] in our factory, we were working by the noodle machine, she would always come, *Cest! Cest!* [NB: Cest, as Communist greetings, means honour, or pride]
> T So what did you do?
> S Because she always came like this, I told her: "Listen: you always repeat *Cest! Cest!* But you don't act upon it". She became red. [Then summarises how she discovered that she was falsifying the reports and stealing some of the flower and eggs]. That's why I say: Holy belongs only to the church! Well, every person is different, but the worst is when one is fanatic[42].

Sandra worked later in the same company as an accountant; then, for one week a month, during salary calculation, she had to stay for longer hours and would come back home at 10:30 p.m. Later, when the company started to have exchanges with the West, she was called upon to translate German-Czech discussions and documents.

In parallel, her husband was still working at the railway and playing music, which often make him arrive back home at 4 o'clock or 5 o'clock in the morning after a night in the pub, and before his 6 o'clock morning shift. He would take care of the children after his shift, ending at 5:00 p.m. Later, he became a painter and had easier working time. As she was working in a factory, she was entitled to 14 days of yearly holidays, and access to holiday resorts such as chalets in skiing regions.

Probably in the late 1950s, Sandra started to receive small amounts of money regularly from her older brothers in Germany; she could not use or exchange them for Czech money, but for coupons, with which she could have access to small goods and building materials, and could also progressively refurbish their house. Eventually, the brothers started to visit them. Finally, around 1968, Sandra and her two teenage children could also travel to Germany to visit with their rich uncles. In other terms, life seemed to have relaxed a bit.

On Zdenka's side, work was less stable. Three years after the birth of her second child, in 1955, Zdenka started to work in a small grocery in the village nearby; a few years later, as her sister-in-law had, in the meanwhile, moved out and started working

---

[42] S *da war auch so eine Verfressene aber KSC, da waren wir Angestellte an der Nudelding, und sie ist immer gekommen Cest! Cest! T Und was haben Sie gemacht? E Weil sie immer so gekommen ist, ich hab's gemacht: "Hörst mahl: Du bist immer Cest! Cest! Aber handelst nicht danach". War sie rot. Weil wir mussten Streifen machen, wieviel Mahle wir müssten Mehl eingeschüttet haben, das die Übersicht hat, wieviel Eier und so zu bestellen. Und zu der Zeit wollte sie von mir, ich sollte zwei Schichten machen, ohne Eier; das war für die Hunde gerechnet, nur Mehl und Wasser. Und ich bin am nächsten Tag gekommen, und einer der Striche war weg, die ist dann gekommen: "Frau Y, ich wollte doch zwei Schichten!" Ich hab's gemacht: "Es waren auch zwei Schichten"... na dann wusste ich, sie hatten solche... ja, und dann sind sie gekommen, Cest! Ich hab's gemacht, Ja.... Deswegen sag ich immer: Heilig ist nur die Kirche! Na ja, jeder Mensch ist anders, aber das schlimmste ist, wenn man fanatisch ist.*

in the next village, she took over the work at the butcher's shop in the house, as a second job in the afternoon. But the work was physically demanding:

> Work was hard in the shop, because one had to carry the meat out of the fridge to the shop, and then back to the shop, where it could be cut... this was not light.[43] (Zdenka, 25.05.2016)

In effect, the factory would deliver half animals, and she had to carry them from the fridge – a deep refrigerating room at one side of the courtyard – to the other side of the courtyard. Zdenka worked in the butcher shop for 3 years, until she started to have heart problems in 1961:

> Then I became so ill. With the heart. So we had to close the shop down, nobody could sell. I was at the hospital for three weeks, I was heavily sick. The heart (...) ... My sister-in-law looked after the [children]. The doctor said that I could not work in the shop anymore, that it was too hard work for me. So it stayed closed, and I had to find an easier job. So I found this easier job at the restaurant.[44] (Zdenka, 25.05.2016)

Then, for the eight following years, she worked to the nearby restaurant, located a few kilometers from the village, on what was then the main Dresden-Prague road; she would go there on her small red motorbike, by bus in the winter. She was selling small grocery items from a counter:

> I worked there from 64 to 72. It was not a hard work (...) It was better. I was by the coun- ter – where you would sell things. I sold sausages, sweets, fruits, everything. I had to be standing, but it was not hard, I just had to cut (?). After some time there, when they needed, I had to help with the service, but not always, not every day. (..) We started at 6, and closed at 21 h30. It was closed at night. Every other day was free. So 12 hours long shifts, with one day free.[45] (Zdenka, 25.05.2016)

Zdenka enjoyed the work; two interesting things have to be noted from that time. The first one is that the German language, which had such ambiguous status in her childhood, was now a valorised skill:

> I was happy there, but it was long working hours. (...) I liked the work. And many German people came, and nobody could speak German! So I translated the menu. The menu was

---

[43] *Die Arbeit war schwer in der Geschäft, weil das Fleisch musste man aus dem Kühlschrank im Geschäft tragen, wieder im Kühlschrank, hacken.. das war nicht leicht.* (Zdenka, 25.05.2016)

[44] *Hier in die Fleischhackerei verkauft – 3 Jahre. Und dann war ich so krank. Mit dem Herz. So war es zu das Geschäft, und niemand hat verkauft. Ich war lange im Krankenhaus, (drei Wochen) ich war schwer krank. Vor den Herz; die Ärzten... Die Schwägerin besorgt die [Kindern]. Und (...) der Arzt sagt das ich darf nicht mehr das Geschäft machen, das ist schwere Arbeit für mich. Das ist zugeblieben, und ich sollte leichte Arbeit bekommen. Und so haben sie mir leichte Arbeit mir bestellt im Gasthaus.* (Zdenka, 25.05.2016)

[45] *War ich von 64 bis 72. Das war nicht schwere Arbeit. (...) Dort war es besser. Ich war beim Puld – wo man das verkauft, da habe ich Wurst, Zuckerle, Obst, alles habe ich verkauft. Muss man auch stehen, aber nicht schwer, muss man nur schneiden. Wenn ich lange schon war, und brauchen sie, dann musste ich helfen (zu servieren), aber nicht immer, nicht jeden Tag. Damals haben wir früh um 6 Uhr eintritt, um halb zehn haben wir zugeschlossen. War nicht über die Nacht offen. Jeden zweiten Tag hatte ich Frei. 12 Stunden Schiften mit ein Freies Tag. (..) Das Geschäft hatte ich auf mein Uzet, ich musste schreiben was ich verkauf habe, und das kann man nicht nach 8 Stunden, das waren 16 Stunden.. ja zwei Dienste Tag. (...) Aber im Winter musste ich mit dem Autobus, und führte von hier um 5...* (Zdenka, 25.05.2016)

only in Czech. There were many German auto-bus trips, they ordered their food, I translated, so that was something that I could do! [we laugh]. The Chef was happy, that I can
translate. That was a big business – it was the road to Prague, every bus made a 10 minutes
break – people came for a sausage, a sweet or a fruit. It was good business. Alone I made
3000 a day. That was a lot of money! Today is everything more expensive. That was good![46]
(Zdenka, 25.05.2016)

Second, during that time, her capacity to take charge of issues was manifested
again, when she felt she was unjustly paid a lower salary than others, while she had
such extra skills:

At that time I was selling there, in 69 or 70… The girls had a bigger salary than me! So I
was not happy with that. Young women still at school, who were working in the kitchen, and
had a bigger salary than me! So I phoned the company where they had their accountants,
and I said, How come do I have a smaller salary, and I am also translating German, I said,
and the young women have a bigger salary? Well, he was a good man, there, and he
increased my salary at once. (…) Then I was happy. But this was only for two years, then I
went to pension. But it was good that I get this bigger salary, so I had a bigger pension. It
was also not that much. That was not that much money – 600, 700, 800. My husband had as
man in the factory only 900 crowns. At that time we had to be two to work, one could not
stay at home.[47] (Zdenka, 25.05.2016)

In effect, Zdenka's heart condition started to be threatening; she became quite ill
again, unable to move the day when she was not working, until she was put on early
retirement in 1972, aged 42:

I felt very bad, worse than now. I was lying here, and the [children] cooked, as I instructed
them (…). There one cannot think, not read, not reflect, just lie down. The husband was at
work, the [children] helped me (…) By 72 I was often ill, with my heart. The doctor put me
on sick leave; with every cold I had to lie down. But at work, they didn't like it, that I was
so often ill. Then I learned that the doctor said I should absolutely not work. In 72, I had

---

[46] Ich war dort zufrieden, aber es waren lange Stunden. (…) Die Arbeit hatte ich gerne. Und viele
Deutsche sind hingekommen. Und dort kann niemand Deutsch! Ich habe die Karte übergelegt. Die
Karte war nur in Tschechisch. Und sind Ausfluge gewesen damals, Deutsche Leute ein ganzes
Autobus, haben dort bestellt das Essen, und so habe ich das essen übergelegt, so war ich etwas, das
ich das kann!!! [wir lachen] Der Chef war zufrieden, das ich das Überlegen kann, und der Kellner.
Und dort was viel Geschäft – auf diese Strecke nach Prag, jeder Bus hat Haltestelle gemacht, 10
Minuten – Leute haben Wurst Zuckerle, Obst.. Geschäft war gut. Ich habe allein 3000 am Tag
gemacht. Das war viel Geld! Heute ist teuer alles! Das war gut. (Zdenka, 25.05.2016)

[47] Und damals habe ich dort verkauft, das war in 69 oder 70, und ich habe.. die Mädchen haben
grössere Zahlung gehabt wie ich! Und das war ich nicht zufrieden. Junge Mädchen noch in der
Schule und haben in der Küche gearbeitet, und haben grössere Zahlung wie ich. So habe ich in der
Firme, wo sie die Rechnungen machen für die Zahlungen, angerufen, und sage ich, Wieso habe ich
so ein kleines Dienstgeld, und überlege noch Deutsch, habe ich gesagt, und jüngere Mädchen
haben grössere Zahlung wie ich. Na, aber war ein guter Mensch, dort, und hat mir gleich die
Zahlung grösser gemacht. (..) Dann bin ich zufrieden gewesen. Aber nur 2 Jahre, dann bin ich in
der Rente. Aber war Gut das ich grössere Zahlung, so hatte ich grössere Rente. Aber war auch
nicht viel. Aber auch nicht viel Geld war das – 600, 700, 800. Mein Mann hat als Mann in der
Fabrik nur 900 Kronen. Damals sollte viele zu Zwei arbeiten, könnte man nicht zu Hause bleiben.
(Zdenka, 25.05.2016)

been already ill for a long time, and I was put on invalidity pension because I could not work anymore.[48] (Zdenka, 25.05.2016)

Asked about her leisure and holidays all these years, Zdenka mentions family's yearly trips to the Southern Bohemia, where she came from:

Every year we went to [our village], at home, for a 14 days holidays. Often we could not make it, it was expensive for us. The train was expensive for us, and the parents did not have much either, so we had to buy the food; but we were happy to be together. My father died in 80, my mother in 87.[49] (Zdenka, 25.05.2016)

Finally, asked about the political contexts during these years, and especially 1968, Zdenka does not remember.[50] It must be said, however, that in previous, unrecorded communication, Zdenka mentioned the shaking grounds when, in 1968, the USSR forces sent their tanks to Prague to break down the Prague spring – the tanks passed indeed over the main road crossing the village. In any case, the main consequence of these political transformations was that Zdenka and her family could, for the first time, restore her relationship with her uncle in Austria and travel to see him in 1968. Asked if they had contact with him the preceding years, she tells how the uncle was talking to his brother over the border. She herself did not have contact with him:

Nothing. In 1968 we could travel there for the first time. That's the time where we obtained the right to go. But we could not go there all at once, I went with the [children], the husband had to stay here. We went there for the first time in 68, and then again in 72.[51] (Zdenka, 25.05.2016)

The uncle also sent a bit of money regularly, which could be exchanged in authorised shops in Prague, and also that allowed them to travel – they could not afford

---

[48] *Mir war es nicht gut, schlechter wie jetzt. Ich habe hier geliegt, und die Mädchen habe gekocht, was ich ihn sage. (....) Da kann man nichts denken, nichts lese, nicht überdenken, nur liegen. Der Mann war in der Arbeit, die [Kindern] haben mir geholfen. (…) Es war nicht gut schon auf der Arbeit, eine Tag habe ich gearbeitet, der andere tag habe ich geliegt. Der Mann hat im Haus geholfen, die [Kindern] gekocht. (…) In 72 war ich oft krank, mit dem Herz. Die Doktor hier hat meine Gesundheit geschrieben.. (…) mit jeder Grippe muss ich zum Bett. Im Geschäft gefällt das nicht, das ich so oft Krank bin. Später habe ich gewusst dass der Doktor sagte, ich soll überhaupt nicht arbeiten. Nachher in 1972 war ich schon lange krank gewesen und haben sie die Rente gegeben, weil ich nicht arbeiten kann. (Zdenka, 25.05.2016)*

[49] *Nur sind wir jedes Jahr nach [unser Dorf] gefahren, und nach Hause, auf 14 Tage Urlaub. Aber mehr mahl könnte man nicht, das war auch teuer für uns fahren, Der Zug war nicht billig, und dort die Eltern hatten auch nicht viel, so musste man etwas kaufen zu essen aber wir waren zufrieden das wir zusammen sein. (..) in 80 ist der Vater gestorben, und 87 die Mutter war 78 (Zdenka, 25.05.2016)*

[50] *T 68 war ein bisschen besser. Und dann sind die Russer gekommen? Z: Ich weiss nicht mehr, nach 4 Jahren konnten wir wieder gehen. Die Bewilligung war teuer, aber wir haben gespart. (Zdenka, 25.05.2016)*

[51] *Nichts. 68 könnten wir für das erste Mal dort hinfahren. War die Zeiten wo die Bewilligung bekommen. Aber konnten wir nicht alle Fahren, bin ich mit der Mädchen, der Mann musste hier bleiben. In 68 war das erste Mal, dann sie wir in 72. (Zdenka, 25.05.2016)*

the trip otherwise.[52] In the later years, they also met the uncle in the South, or he came on visit. The family thus had gifts from the West:

> He always brought us something, clothes or something. He offered us the machine to make noodles. And clothes for the [children]; at that time I didn't have time to make them, so I was having them made by the tailor. So people looked at us, how come they have such nice clothes. Because we could not find such nice fabric here. (…). Of course we had to pay something at the border.[53] (Zdenka, 25.05.2016)

Later, Zdenka's husband was diagnosed with a rare illness (due to his profession, or more likely, to his work in the uranium mines) and had to stop working in 1980. From there on, he had to rest a lot and go to the spa once a year. He also helped their children's family to build their house in the village, and took care of dogs, with which he went for long walks. The young retired couple did mincemeat once a month that they could sell and with which they could get a bit of money.

Hence, Sandra and Zdenka lived most of their adult lives under communism. Living in the same village under Říp and in comparable family situation, their lives seem again to be surprising similar. Both women took care of their children, and worked very hard to earn money to complete their husbands' salaries. They both became in charge of the budget of the household, being able to save enough money to arrange and refurbish their houses. Professionally, they were committed employees; without being educated beyond primary school, they could use their counting and German skills at work. For both, paradoxically, their German skills, which were once stigmatised, were eventually valorised. Both had a fair sense of justice, and were able to speak for themselves. Perhaps, here things differ a bit: Sandra was sensitive to political absurdities and able to maintain a critical distance to it, while denouncing the hypocrisy of others; Zdenka was more directly suffering from its consequences without a political analysis, yet able to defend herself when she felt unfairly treated.

Under the changing politics, the liberalisation of the late 1968, the soviet intervention and the normalisation of the 1970s have no saliency at all in the two women's discourses. The only main consequences for their lives was the opening to the

---

[52] *Wir mussten! Wir mussten, das war teuer für uns hinfahren, wir musste über 1000 Kronen umtauschen. Das war viel sparen. Aber der Onkel hat uns etwas gegeben, wir brauchten dort nichts zahlen. Wir sind mit dem Zug, und [at the border] ist er für uns mit dem Auto gekommen, das haben wir geschrieben. Früher durften wir nicht. Auf der Grenze har er sich mit der Bruder getroffen, durften sie eine Stunde dort sitzen auf den Grass, ein bisschen mit der Mutter, der Bruder der Kommunist hat Bewilligung bekommen. Politisch.. er meinte er hat recht, und her auch, so streiten sie. Die Frauen sagen geben sie Ruhe von der Politik! Geht nicht. Er hat andere Sache gemacht, er war gesperrt – der Kommunisten – im Krieg. (….) (Zdenka, 25.05.2016).*

[53] *Da hat er uns immer etwas eingekauft, auf Kleider oder etwas mitgenommen. Ja, die Maschine für die Nudeln hat er auch gekauft. Und die Kleidern für die Kinder, damals hatte ich keine Zeit zu nähen so habe ich bei der Näherin die Kleider nähen lassen. So haben sie die Leute hier geschaut, dass sie so schöne Kleidung haben. Weil hier bekommt man das nicht! Haben wir viel immer von dem Onkel bekommen. Die Kindern sagten sie – wieso hast ein so schönes Kleid. Sie haben das nicht, und ihr haben. Hier war sehr wenig Stoff.. (..) Haben wir auf der Grenze auch etwas zahlen.* (Zdenka, 25.05.2016)

West, that is, for them, the possibility to restore the relation with their German family – Sandra's older brothers and their families, and Zdenka's uncle. They could both travel abroad to visit them with their children and receive small financial support, which made their life slightly easier and gave small advantages over other people.

Finally, the main difference is perhaps that Sandra could still count on the network around her; the extended family was present, and the musical family was still often celebrating – life could be fun, even with just a bit of beer and bread rubbed with garlic. Zdenka seem to live slightly more isolated; taking a great deal on her shoulders, years of hard work, pressure and perhaps deprivation brought her to become very ill and retire early.

5.2.8   And Since 1989…: Learning from Life, Cultivating One's Life Creativity

Communism in Czechoslovakia ended up in 1989, with the so-called Velvet revolution (Zittoun, 2018). Life went on, children grew up, Sandra and Zdenka became grandmothers, retired and became widows. Although they do tell a few events after the 1980s, such as the death of relatives, neither of them even mentions the end of communism. However, both kept reading newspaper and books, listening to the radio, watching the news, visiting friends and relatives, taking care of their houses and their gardens and reflect about life and their experiences.

Sandra maintained a social life in the limits of her capacity, but also constrained by the progressive death of many of her acquaintances and network members. In her daily life, she maintains her beautifully decorated flat – her husband having been a painter, each room has a dominant colour, and the wall have patterned motives, an old craft in the region using sculpted rolls, which she maintained alive by refreshing these painting with the help of the few craftsmen still able to use them. Sandra developed a very critical sense of the evolution of events. Reflecting on her experience, she said:

> Every period was hard for somebody. With the Nazis, the politics were bad and it was very bad for the Jews, as well as for the mixed families – [with the yellow stars, and the concentration camps]. Then with the communists, the big farmers and entrepreneur were sent to Moravia. (…) Each period has its bloody mess. But it is always the small people who suffer. The big ones, they escape first, [and] they have the money. This is still the same today – many hide their money in Switzerland…

Sandra learnt from experience, but developed a reflective, distance and abstract way of understanding her life in history. Her experience became generalised into an analysis of patterns of oppression – the strong and nasty one change, but what is constant is that they find a weaker group that has to pay – and the nasties end up saving their interest.

Zdenka kept active all these years, adjusting her level of activity to her health. She maintained the habit of preparing minced meat, organising for this the members of her family. She also continued other activities. First, Zdenka was a very good cook, especially proud of her fish soup, a Southern-Bohemian specialty which she learnt from her father, and that she was also happy to teach to her grandchildren. Most of her other cooking practices she remembered from him – making noodles for the soup and the meat preparation; she had seen it at home, learnt it at school and, then, kept self-teaching herself with cooking books:

> T: How did you learn to cook?
> Z: I learned alone. My mother didn't cook much. I have books, and I learned from the books alone. I actually had cooked at home! I cooked early. And my father used to say, Well, the food you prepare is so good! [we laugh].[54] (Zdenka, 25.05.2016)

Second, she kept on enjoying sewing clothes, and mending things for her family and network. When I admired her white, handmade jumper, she said:

> Z: Do you know how long I have it – it is from the 70s; I was retired in 1972 and I knitted it. It's a beautiful wool, to wash by hand - I can do this from school.
> T: But it was already 30 years since school!
> Z: Yes, but I still had it in my head how to do that, I knew how to do it, and I learned something as well later. (…) So I made it myself. (…) Sewing that's good for me.[55] (Zdenka, 25.05.2016)

Zdenka's two preferred activities, developed especially after her retirement and now that she had more time for herself, are in straight continuation to her childhood

---

[54] *T: Und das Kochen, wie haben Sie das gelernt? Z: Das habe ich alleine gelernt. Meine Mutter har nicht viel gekocht. Ich habe Bücher, und aus den Büchern habe ich selber gelernt. Und ich habe schon zu Hause gekocht! Bald habe ich gekocht. Und mein Vater hat wieder gesagt, No, du machst das Essen so gut! [wir lachen!] T: wieso haben sie so einfach gekocht? Sie hatten gerne.. Z: Wir haben alle gekocht… Mir machte keine Arbeit schlecht, ich kann alles machen. Mir ist das egal, Hauptsache, dass es geht! Und wenn man es weist, wie das soll sein, so geht es. Muss man auch lernen. Ist auch nicht auf dem ersten Mal so gegangen, wie ich will. Aber das lernt man, das lernt man. Ich habe viel gekocht, zu Hause. Ich habe immer gekocht, meine Schwestern nicht. Die ältere möchte gar nichts machen in der Küche, und die jüngere sehr wenig. Aber ich wollte kochen, so kann ich kochen. Da war damals.. ich habe damals Kartoffelsuppe, und Sonntag, hat der Vater die Fleischsuppe gekocht, das habe ich auch von ihm gelernt. Er hat das Fleisch gekauft, jede Woche, kaufte sich Rindfleisch auf der Suppe, und er hat gekocht, die Mutter war auf der Kirsche, er hat die Suppe gekocht. Und Nudeln hat er selber gemacht. Eingemacht, und geschnitten klein, das habe ich auch von ihm gesehen. Jeden Sonntag hat er Nudeln gemacht. (…) Die Mutter war in die Kirche, und ich mit der Schwester waren zu Hause, die ältere weiss ich nicht… sie war mit den Freundinnen, und für die Küche war sie gar nicht. Geschirre wachen wollte sie nie, das habe ich viel gemacht. Das musste man nach jeden essen musste man das Geschirr waschen, damals waren nicht so viele Tellern und alles. Ich habe das immer gewaschen. Aber der Ofen, war immer heisses Wasser. Heizt man, so hat man das Wasser… und die Heizung, das habe ich auch schon allein eingeheizt in den Ofen. Das weiss ich! Der Vater hat uns das Holz gemacht, da haben wir Holtz immer gehabt. Genug Holtz haben wir zum einheizen, musste man kleinen Holtz haben das hat er uns gelernt… Das war gut, alles. (Zdenka, 25.05.2016)*

[55] *Z Wissen sie wie alt es ist schon der habe ich schon von Jahre 70; 1972 bin ich schon in der Pension gegangen, und so habe ich gestrickt. Das ist schöne Wolle, das muss man nur Handwaschen.. Ja das kann ich, schon von der Schule kann ich. T Aber das waren schon 30 Jahre seit der Schule. Z Ja aber das hatte ich immer im Kopf wie man das macht, das wusste ich wie man das macht, und etwas habe ich mich zugelernt. Aber den habe ich sehr gerne getrogen. (…) das war Mohair – und das habe ich mich selber gemacht. (…) Nähen das geht mir.* (Zdenka, 25.05.2016)

attachments and dreams: cooking fish, which comes from her father and uncle's trade and reflect the respecting and loving relationship she had with these men, and sewing – her childhood dream and project, which was impeded by her father. Hence, in some ways, one could say that she managed to restore a sense of continuity far beyond the ruptures caused by war, migration and communism, by cultivating and maintaining these spheres of experiences.

Hence, in the last part of their lives under Říp, Sandra and Zdenka developed modes of life in the everyday fabric of village and home life, with each of their own daily creativity. Both reflect on the lives that brought them where they are. Sandra, on the one's hand, spontaneously and repeatedly makes meta-commentaries about the course of history, and how things did evolve. Sensitive and critical about political games all her life, she keeps observing current politics; she sees patterns and continuity across time, such as the move from private property to state, and back from state to private companies, or the game of dominant power discriminating a minority while protecting its interests in places like Switzerland. Zdenka, on the other hand, is more focused on her daily activities; she easily confess that she does not know much about politics, but she actually proudly cultivated and enriched the memories and know-how connecting her to her childhood, and especially her father and uncle, in what regards directing a household and cooking, and her own personal creativity, related to sewing and handcraft. In some ways, thus, one could see a generalisation of the dynamics that started to emerge in both woman's childhood and youth. Sandra learnt to count on a community, and discuss with her group and network, worrying and carrying for the others, being also supported by them in the face of absurd political events. These community dialogical dynamics, thus, appear generalised in her way to apprehend the course of things, beyond her personal case. Zdenka, in contrast, who was much more dependent on intergenerational ties, and especially to the vertical relationship to father figures from which she found inspiration and support, became also much more focused on issues of learning and transmitting – teaching German, telling about the uncle, and so on. Her generalised dialogue is less with the world, in general, than with her family's past, and perhaps its future.

5.3   One's Life Around Říp: Personal Life Philosophies

In this chapter, I have tried to retrace and analyse the lives of two women in their 90s, who both were born at the periphery of the country, and because of the hazard of life and especially the detour of history, were pushed or pulled to settle down in a village down Říp. Both hardly mention the hill itself; asked about it, they would say that of course, like everybody, they used to go for walks there, and bring their children to the annual fair. The hill region was, however, part of their daily life: in Sandra's life, it is particularly salient during her happy dancing years, where the musical profession of her husband made her visit and dance in every village hall around the hill; in Zdenka's life, it is more as a professional that she was brought to work in one or the other village where there was a free position. For both, family, relatives and friends extended, however, in the neighbouring villages and in the main town of Roudnice.

The parallel reading of their life stories aimed at showing how their courses of life were quasi similarly shaped by history, because, mainly, they happened to be both born from Czech and German families in regions that became the heart of an important political controversy, not far from Říp, and because Říp itself was on the road connecting Germany with Prague. My reading highlighted the comparable turning points: the death of a mother at age four, the position taken by the family in 1938, the effects of 1945 on half-German citizens, marriage immediately after the war, the difficulty of starting a family in the years around the Stalinisation of 1953 and the arrangements one could find when living in the Říp region under communism, and finally, the reestablishment of relationships with a German relative abroad after 1968, with the possibility to travel and have some small advantages. The two main factual differences in their courses of life are consequences of decision made by others: the decision made by their fathers in 1938 – staying in the Sudeten or moving inland – and the consequent period of the move to Říp region – in 1938, or when life became impossible in 1953.

My analysis then tried to show, keeping an attention to sociocultural and sense-making dynamics, the different ways in which both women came to handle ruptures and learnt to confer meaning to events, with whom, and with what sorts of outcomes. On the one hand, Sandra soon learnt to be part of, and count on an extended family and community, that were creating a protective space from the outside world, finding collective solutions, and allowing to develop a critical stance over political discourses. On the other hand, Zdenka developed as quite a protected and supported girl by two strong father figures, who had power – a power actually never critically examined – and could thus fix problems, give directions and propose solutions. She, therefore, developed a more vertical relation to things, relying on, then accommodating with authority, until she could herself take such an authority position, and continue, in her creative way, some of what she learnt from these men. These contrasting forms of dialogical engagement with the world, I suggest, expanded and generalised along the lifecourse, and, thus, allowed very different positions and comments on the course of the world and their location in them – on what they learnt from life. Hence, although the two women went through the same events and learnt from others and their personal life experience, they developed very different styles of dealing with life – different melodies of living (Zittoun et al., 2013) – and generalisation from life.

Finally, to highlight this, we can characterise these contrasting life philosophies with the two woman's recurring verbal expressions. I identified the most common formula that each of them used, and that I tried to maintain along the examples. Hence, Sandra is using the expression "Das war verrückte Zeit": "these were crazy times", alternatively "crazy world". She at times also says: "All this is already not true anymore". Zdenka is using expressions around "Hauptsache, dass es geht!", "The most important things, is that it goes!", with variations on what can be done, or one has to do it. I understand these expressions as highly synthesised generalisation from experience, using ready-made cultural forms to be expressed. In that sense, they can be understood as life philosophies, that is, learning about life and the world, which are both the distillation from a life's experience, expressed in the most easily available culturally available sentences. More specifically, one may differentiate between Sandra's "personal world philosophy" (de Saint-Laurent, 2017a, 2017b) – she generalised her understanding of the course of history into an understanding of "crazy world", and Zdenka develop a more "personal life-philosophy" (Zittoun et al., 2013) where the most important thing is to make things go.

Thus, to come back to our point of departure, if the movements and streams of history and life have brought Sandra and Zdenka to live under and around Říp, the waves of time and event have polished their lifecourses in different ways; and at the crest of these waves, slowly have emerged these specific patterns of seafoam.

References

Adler, H. G. (2017). *Theresienstadt 1941–1945. The face of a coerced community* (B. Cooper, Trans.). Cambridge: Cambridge University Press. https://doi.org/10.1017/9781139017053.

Brown, S. D., & Reavey, P. (2015). *Vital memory and affect: Living with a difficult past.* London: Routledge.

de Saint-Laurent, C. (2017a). Personal trajectories, collective memories: Remembering and the life-course. *Culture & Psychology, 23*(2), 263–279. https://doi.org/10.1177/1354067X17695758

de Saint-Laurent, C. (2017b). Trajectories of resistance and historical reflections. In N. Chaudhary, P. Hviid, G. Marsico, & J. W. Villadsen (Eds.), *Resistance in everyday life: Constructing cultural experiences* (pp. 49–63). Singapore: Springer https://doi.org/10.1007/978-981-10-3581-4_5

Hule, M., & Kotyza, M. (2012). *Rybníkářství na Jindřichohradecku.* Třeboň, Czech Republic: Carpio.

Kennan, G. F. (1957). The Czechoslovak Legion. *The Russian Review, 16*(4), 3–16. https://doi.org/10.2307/125745

Kennan, G. F. (1958). The Czechoslovak Legion II. *The Russian Review, 17*(1), 11–28. https://doi.org/10.2307/125722

Kovařík, D. (2005). Vysídlení Němců z okresu Jindřichův Hradec 1945 – 1948. *Jihočeský Sborník Historický, 74,* 219–234.

Lanzmann, C. (2013). *Le dernier des injustes* [Documentary, History]. Retrieved from http://www.imdb.com/title/tt2340784/

Luža, R. (1964). *The transfer of the Sudeten Germans. A study of Czech-German relations, 1933–1962.* New York: New York University Press.

Sato, T. (2017). *Collected papers on trajectory equifinalty approach.* Japan: Chitose Press.

Sato, T., Yasuda, Y., Kanzaki, M., & Valsiner, J. (2013). From describing to reconstructing life trajectories: How the TEA (trajectory equifinality approach) explicates context-dependent human phenomena. In B. Wagoner, N. Chaudhary, & P. Hviid (Eds.), *Cultural psychology and its future: Complementarity in a new key* (pp. 93–105). Charlotte, NC: Information Age Publishing.

Smetana, V. (2008). *In the shadow of Munich. British policy towards Czechoslovakia from the endorsement to the renunciation of the Munich agreement (1938–1942).* Charles University in Prague: Karolinum Press, Charles University.

Zavereshneva, E., & van der Veer, R. (2018). *Vygotsky's notebooks. A selection.* Singapore: Springer.

Zittoun, T. (2007). Dynamics of interiority. Ruptures and transitions in the self development. In L. M. Simão & J. Valsiner (Eds.), *Otherness in question: Development of the self* (pp. 187–214). Greenwich, CT: Information Age Publishing.

Zittoun, T. (2018). The Velvet revolution of land and minds. In B. Wagoner, F. M. Moghaddam, & J. Valsiner (Eds.), *The psychology of radical social change: From rage to revolution* (pp. 140–158). Cambridge, UK: Cambridge University Press.

Zittoun, T., & de Saint-Laurent, C. (2015). Life-creativity: Imagining one's life. In V. P. Glǎveanu, A. Gillespie, & J. Valsiner (Eds.), *Rethinking creativity: Contributions from cultural psychology* (pp. 58–75). Hove, England/New York: Routledge.

Zittoun, T., & Gillespie, A. (2015). Integrating experiences: Body and mind moving between contexts. In B. Wagoner, N. Chaudhary, & P. Hviid (Eds.), *Integrating experiences: Body and mind moving between contexts* (pp. 3–49). Charlotte, NC: Information Age Publishing.

Zittoun, T., Valsiner, J., Vedeler, D., Salgado, J., Gonçalves, M., & Ferring, D. (2013). *Human development in the lifecourse. Melodies of living*. Cambridge, UK: Cambridge University Press.

Chapter 6
Microgenesis: Everyday Life Around Říp

> *Wherever a process of life communicates eagerness to him who lives it, there the life becomes genuinely significant. Sometimes the eagerness is more knit up with the motor activities, sometimes with the perceptions, sometimes with imagination, sometimes with reflective thought. But, wherever it is found, there is the zest, the tingle, the excitement of reality; and there is "importance" in the only real and positive sense in which importance ever can be.*
>
> —(James, 2009, p. 5)

How is daily life organised around the hill? In this chapter, I adopt a more synchronic perspective to try to retrace the everyday life of people living under Říp. I thus emphasise the microgenesis of these forms of living: the actual organisation of life, intergroup dynamics and people's daily errands.

After a short methodological introduction (Sect. 6.1), the analysis progresses in three steps. The first part describes the context, that is, the villages around Říp and their population (Sect. 6.2). To move beyond this static depiction, the second step aims at retracing the dynamics observable around the hill, in terms of the organisation of time (Sect. 6.3), actual geographical circulation (Sect. 6.4) and emerging group dynamics (Sect. 6.5). Then, to understand more specifically how the life on Říp is experienced, I move at the level of two contrasting case studies (Sect. 6.6). Here, I identify how people came to live in the region under the hill, and how their life is organised both geographically and symbolically – that is, their geographic and semantic, or symbolic, movements. I especially examine their spheres of experiences – the distal and the proximal ones – and show in what respects these overlap (Zittoun, Levitan, & Cangiá, 2018), and are integrated or not (Gillespie, Kadianaki, & O'Sullivan-Lago, 2012; Zittoun & Gillespie, 2015). This eventually brings me to identify four patterns of modes of life around the hill (Sect. 6.7). I conclude this chapter by starting to highlight the further implication of these findings both in link with the other analysis – the sociogenetic and the ontogenetic – and in terms of theory (Sect. 6.8).

© The Author(s), under exclusive license to Springer Nature Switzerland AG 2019   115
T. Zittoun, *Sociocultural Psychology on the Regional Scale*, SpringerBriefs in
Psychology, https://doi.org/10.1007/978-3-030-33066-8_6

6.1 Methodology

This chapter is based on my fieldwork in Podřipsko region – or more exactly, is an attempt to account for some of the observations I made, first as I was getting familiar with a universe very foreign to me, and second, after I had decided to write this book, and therefore, developing a more deliberate observational stance. It is thus based on my peripheral participation to, and observation of the life of the hill – family and friendly gatherings, pub sitting, walking, shopping and partying, with some observations simply recalled, other written down and some discussed with various friends and colleagues visiting me in Czech republic over the years – which helped me to recover my first initial naivety and surprise. Second, some factual information is gathered via the webpages of the villages around Říp, which often allows backing up and completing my partial access to the village life. Third, it is based on a modest series of five interviews I made with people living in the villages around Říp – people that I interviewed "about life around Říp". These people were met mostly in villages' local pubs, with the exception on one person I contacted by mail. Two were men, three women, all between their mid-30s and mid-40s.

The interviews were led at people's place, except one, at my place. They were informally accompanied of followed by a drink, at times a dinner. Four were led in English (by me) and Czech, translated in vivo by a bilingual speaker (male, born in the region); one was led in French and a last in German by me. Because of the semi-informality of the procedure, I promised anonymity and discussed the condition of participation orally, and these agreements were recorded.[1] In any case, to protect the people interviewed, I decided to not analyse them as closely as I did with the case of Sandra and Zdenka. Transcriptions are made by me; for the interviews led in Czech, only the English parts were transcribed, completed by a few missing information from the Czech original, later edited by a bilingual reader.

Again, the data gathered are not exhaustive and the collected interviews do not reach the classically expected saturation (see Chap. 3). Here, as elsewhere in this book, I count on the multiplication of perspectives and layers of analysis to bring depth to the case, rather than covering all the varieties of lifecourses and villages. In effect, as we will see, what this analysis brings about is a proposition to articulate sociogenetic and ontogenetic dynamics, through an analysis of the microgenetic ones.

---

[1] The translator knew informally some of these persons and would have occasions to meet them again in public occasions. We made the promise that the content of these interviews would never be mentioned by me or the translator in other circumstances unless mentioned by the person interviewed.

6.2 Villages

The six villages around Říp are all about 3 km from each other; they are connected to each other by the road as well by pathways in the fields, at the bottom of Říp; most can also be joined by the pathway at midheight of the hill. From all of these villages, Říp is in the landscape, and for many houses, Říp is the main feature of the view. In addition, Říp is celebrated in the villages: Říp, or under Říp, or the forefather Czech (Praotec Cech) are in the names of the pubs, the theme of local wall paints (in pubs, at bus stops), the themes of sculptures or present on a few advertisements and on touristic signs (see Chaps. 1 and 4). Říp is part of the ornamentation of life and as such is absolutely redundant.

Most villages are built along one or two main roads, with a perpendicular or two, and then smaller streets. In this region of Northern Bohemia, these villages are not built around a central square (unlike in the South), but most have a pond or two, surrounded by trees and grass, a school building, one or two pubs, a church, a small shop and a bus stop. Most villages have also old protected trees – an oak, a chestnut or a linden – on their square, with often a bench where older people can meet and discuss in the shadow (Fig. 6.1).

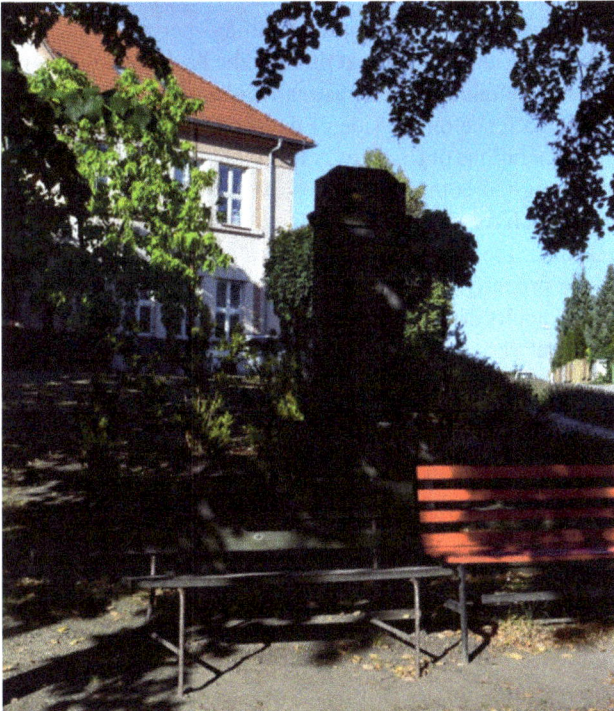

Fig. 6.1 Bench under the protected trees, Mnetěš, copyright author, 2018

Fig. 6.2 Typical backstreet in a village around Říp – Vodochody, copyright author, 2018

Meeting points are thus diverse: for adults, the pub; for teenagers, the bus stop, in some places, benches along the pond. In the villages, most housing are family houses; some are old farms with two main buildings perpendicular to the road with a courtyard in between and a garden, at times at the back, and a main portal towards the street; a growing number of the houses are quite classical houses with V shaped roofs, a garden and a fence on the side of the road. Many of these houses still host the two or three generations of a family. A few villages have "bittovka", three-storey building built during the communist times, with two or three staircases, and two flats per floor, which have now been mostly sold as individual flats. To the walker-by, the villages under the Říp are peaceful; trees and flowery bushes decorate street and spill over the property walls, cats are running their errands, dogs are barking, children bike, and adults drink a beer on benches in front of pubs. The humming of the highway is never very far, but in the summer birds chirp louder (see Fig. 6.2).

The villages group between 300 and 1000 people and the population is relatively homogeneous (see Chap. 1). In Mnetěš, for instance, there are 565 inhabitants for an average age of 38.2, which is slightly younger than the median age in Czech Republic (41.4 in 2015).[2] Such average hides the fact that there is a good proportion of older persons, and especially women, in the villages; there are also many children growing up in the villages, and an important group of persons in working age. Unemployment is currently very low in the country (2.9% in July 2018),[3] so most people are actually busy, and in many households, two adults are working.[4] In terms

---

[2] https://www.statista.com/statistics/369760/average-age-of-the-population-in-czech-republic/

[3] https://fr.tradingeconomics.com/czech-republic/unemployment-rate

[4] Unless the woman is on maternity leave, which still can be expanded up to 4 years with some small financial support.

Fig. 6.3 Train to Roudnice nad Labem arriving at Vražkov station, copyright author, 2018

of occupations, some of the inhabitants work in the village or around, as farmers, tractor drivers, craftsmen, shopkeeper, school cook or pub owner; some are employed by the state as policemen, firemen or work for the army. Some others, especially women, work in the medical sector as nurses or carers in retirement homes or centre for alcoholics, reflecting a national tendency (Heinen, 2017); some also try to work part-time from home, as hairdresser or masseur. Many people work in the nearby town of Roudnice; some work in factories and offices; others are small entrepreneur, with building companies or others. A growing part of the population commutes to Prague, where they are employee in various sectors (bank, insurance) or have liberal profession, in social work, advertisement or the media. Most households have one or two cars, yet the old train line relating villages to Roudnice nad Labem is still in function and used for instance by the teenagers who go to secondary school to Roudnice (see Fig. 6.3). There is also a bus line that relates most villages to each other, and another that connects to Prague in half an hour, and that circulates mainly at peak hours. A common view is that of tired workers, mainly women, waiting in line for the early morning bus to work in town, and coming back even more tired at the end of afternoon. During their free time, most families cultivate a bit of vegetables and flowers, if not in the courtyard or garden, in small fields that can still be rented around the villages.

6.3 Cyclical Times

In the countryside, down a hill, next to the forest, in villages surrounded by fields, the seasonal cycle is strongly felt. Temperature and the weather change from freezing winters to summers in the high 30° Celsius, and nature does its full cycle; human activity follows. This includes of course the life of those who have professions bound by nature, such as farmers, who have to prepare their fields or harvest according to the seasons, and who see their working life depending on it, but also many informal activities by local inhabitants, from swimming and hiking, biking and hunting, and making jams and conserves with garden products.

Time and seasons are formalised in three series of intermeshed events or rituals. First, there are all the calendar, Christian and traditional, probably more pagan inspired, collective or at least common events. For Christmas, families usually eat a carp, as well as various types of sausages and potato salads, with many cookies and sweets. Early spring, villages celebrate *Masopust*, or carnival, with children in costume and food and drinks in the streets. At eastern, young boys make sticks out of beaded young shoots of willow; they go across streets and hit the low back of girls, thus meaning to make them healthy and fertile – passing the vigour of the willow unto them. At the very end of April comes the burning of the witch, burned symbolically to prevent them from damaging the crops. At the same period the region celebrates the *Řípska pout'*, the hill's fair, which gather people from all the villages at the bottom of the hill, up the main tree alley. Finally, a children's party takes place in June, with parents and their costumed children gathering in the local hall. In the fall, people celebrate *posvícení* – the "illumination" – on St-Vaclav's day, in September, with a ball. To this traditional cycle, some villages have added new celebrations, such as Halloween, to create other village events for the children and their parents.

A second line of calendar or ritualised events are more personal, related to birthdays and name's days: in effect, most people's first names are still chosen in the traditional repertoire and have a saint-day in the calendar; these name's day are respected with at least as much attention than birthdays. People celebrate these with visits to relatives, coffee and cakes or the additional shot of strong plum alcohol (*slivovice*); women, mainly prepare large plates of *chlebíčky*, small breads covered with carefully arranged slices of salami and tomatoes, and a large display of cookies all most patiently crafted. Here, we may add weddings: many are celebrated at the local pub, and demand a day of celebration in an informally scripted scenario of joined lunch for the family, typically after the official ceremony, and a public party and ball with food in the evening, ideally with a roasted pig and a wedding cake. At parties in the summer, meat is grilled in gardens and courtyards, and when possible, for special occasions or sometimes at the local pub, a whole pig is grilled; when this is the case, cakes of beer are brought in and tap-beer is served and punctuated by shots of home-made plum brandy.

A third group of events are parties and events related to the local associations. Some have a very long existence, such as the football or the hockey club, the firemen or the hunters. Each have their special occasions, locally or their inter-village tournaments and their village balls. In addition, in the recent years, new associations have been created (e.g., dog-raisers or the tennis club[5]). The "tramps" have installed

---

[5] See for instance the associations on the webpages of Straškov, http://www.straskov.cz/; Mnetěš, http://www.mnetes.cz and Ctiněves, http://www.obec-ctineves.cz/zivot-v-obci/kalendar-akci-1/

a camp place next to the spring on the hill; they at times gather there and play country music; other times, groups of young people organise wild techno-parties on the same spot.

Altogether, village life is punctuated by private or public events. There is not a week without someone's name's day, and in the spring and summer, hardly a month without a party – to which are added of course all the spontaneous pub meetings, neighbour grilling and family gatherings. Of course, not everybody celebrates all these events; but I was surprised to observe how common it was, and how assumed it was, that one would celebrate the burning or the witch, of take one's children and partner to visit one's relatives on one's name's day.

Of course, this cyclical nature of time is only one aspect of everyday life, naturally maintained by older inhabitants and cultivated by younger. However, this is combined with time being linear and walking with progress, political, technological, touristic, etc. Hence, new pubs appear, villages are transformed, new houses are built and other renovated, agricultural techniques improve and with it even the shape of the haystacks, villages improve their webpages and everybody has a mobile phone, by which a good part of the hill's village social life is mediated by various electronic social networks. Life under the hill also slowly evolves with the new generation, population movements and rapid touristic changes.

My emphasis here on the cyclical time, probably usual in rural areas and less in the urban one, is not only due to an over-romantic idea of it (as discussed in the literature, see Chester, Forrester, & Forrester, 1996; Haigron, 2017); at the contrary, most of the events have been mentioned by people that I interviewed or have been manifested by people close to whom I lived during all my time under the hill. In any case, these events make both the time and the social life extremely predictable – some would say boring – and yet open to improvisation.

6.4 Dynamics: Circulations…

The very geography of the place, the fact that people feel belonging to one region, as well as the seasonality of life, brings about many circulations in and across villages, through semi-formal and informal channels. As alluded, people use the goods and services offered in other villages (such as the doctor or the shop); they may attend to associations to the next village especially when these are shared (as certain football teams), or who compete (as the fireman), and the fireman's ball from one village would attract people from beyond.

On the informal side, as mentioned, the cyclical time involves continuous meetings in and across villages. Relatives visit each other, friends meet across villages, street neighbours interact and share meals, grill, gossips and children surveillance, and people gather at their pub or the next village's where most of the social life happens; as said Vera, "Everything happens in the pub!." Young people who grew up in the villages have usually been to primary school in their village or in the neighbouring one; they then usually have done a secondary education in schools that

gather young people from the region. Consequently, most people from one generation end up knowing each other, through education, parties, social life – and there is
thus a strong generational interconnection between the villages.

As a consequence, and also, as remnants of the solidarity built in the communist
years (see Chaps. 4 and 5), people help each other, and exchanges goods, within and
across villages. Hence, people cook for more than they need for their family, and
welcome other's children or passing-by neighbours to have a portion; building
material can be "recuperated" from work or renovation and is offered or exchanged;
people who have access to tractor can carry a heavy load for someone without; men
can be called upon to put down a tree or raise a wall; villagers coordinate to reforest
the alley to Říp. Given the sudden seasonal abundance of garden goods, zucchinis
are offered around when too many, and peaches will be given back; jams and con-
serve are proposed, and cakes with berries received; wild dill will be collected, in
exchange of a bit of the grilled pig it perfumes.

6.5 Dynamics: … and Divisions

Of course, not all is pink and blue in village life, and under this joyful sociality,
many more or less active of underground divisions operate. To examine these divisions, I am attentive to indications of boundary work – in the socio-anthropological
sense of the term (Dahinden & Zittoun, 2013; Wimmer, 2013) – in people's practices or discourses, that is, indications of we/them distinctions, in everyday dialogues and practices, as well as in the interviews more formally led.

At one first level, in the villages around Říp, the population is relatively homogeneous, and I do not know of many foreigners who came to live in these villages,
besides some couples with partners from the region and others from neighbouring
countries. Villagers are more likely to have families living in the region, and some
came from Prague, either directly, or after recovering old family property, during
the restitution procedures at the end of communism. The only clearly visible minor-
ities are, on the one hand, the Vietnamese families, who are mainly the shopkeeper
of the local grocery,[6] and on the other hand, a few Roma families, usually living in
houses at the periphery of the villages, but with very little interactions with the other
inhabitants.[7]

---

[6]Vietnamese came to Czech Republic when communism invited them as guest workers; many
remained, and they now constitute the third minority in the country (after Slovak and Ukrainian)
(Wikipedia, 2018).

[7]There is in the Czech Republic a long and complex history of forced sedentarisation, segregation
and stigmatization of Roma communities, by which they lost their traditions, and have very
unequal access to education, therefore reduced to lowly qualified profession; families are often
dependent on social support. In the villages, many stories circulate about people using, if not abus-
ing the social services; whether true or not, such stereotypes feeds mistrust in Czech population;
intergroup tensions are still far being resorbed. For a situation of the Romani people in the country
see for instance http://romove.radio.cz/en/. For a recent and differentiated evolution of the status of
Roma people in Czech republic see Ruzicka (2012).

Beyond these first obvious divisions, other classical sociocultural and political ones take place. A first very obvious one, which one learns very quickly to identify, is the difference between the *prajak* (plural *prajaci*), people from Prague, and people from Říp. The term often comes at the turn of a discussion, and people who moved from the capital have all been exposed to jokes, at least in the first times. However, this does not strictly correspond to a division in the villages; in fact, some people remain "prajaks" for the villagers only because they come from the nearby town, but maintain a distant attitude towards local villagers; while other inhabitants, really coming from Prague, are treated as if they were local. Also, the divisions that can be observed, and that were reported by people that talked to me, were much more nuanced.

First, divisions can be guessed by observation: for instance, in one of the villages, there are two pubs: the local pub gathers people from the village for a couple of hours every day after work. In the summer, they often come with the blue or green working trouser and old T-shirts – from their fields or their workshop. A group of women, younger or less, join them, also after work and relatively informally dressed – shorts, simple T-shirts, open sandals; older people come with their old stray hats and stay just for one or two pints or to fill a pet bottle of tap beer for the evening. In contrast, a new pub nearby is making its own beer and is called unsurprisingly *Podrispko pivovar*, the brewery from under the hill. The clients there are more often bikers stopping on their tour; people are dressed with more care and more expensively – white trousers and assorted polo shirts, or simply more fashionable informal clothes. Hence, there is a more urban, middle class allure to that brewery, whereas the old one seems to gather the local farmers–hunters and their families and friends. If the first pub is a place where one goes "to have one after work", the second seems more of a place where ones goes "to go out".

Other more political divisions take place. One can be deduced by online information. Hence, in Krabčice, an online survey was initiated to ask the population about its readiness to have the band Ortel, a right-wing rock band promoting a nationalistic, protectionist, anti-immigration message, as main guest for the Řipska pout' – the hill's fair – in 2016 (see Chap. 4); out of 2945 respondents, 48% were strongly for, 52% strongly against, with a 1% of undecided.[8] The survey suggests a fracture in political postures and opinions, even though the message is probably more nuanced: people against the presence of the band were not necessarily against its political message, but may have found not appropriate to present that band at a family, traditional yet symbolic local event; people in favor of the presence of the band were not necessarily sharing all the ideas promoted, but would defend the band for the right of free opinion. In any case, such political polarisation was also reflected in the interviews; some persons told me they refused to attend that event that year because they could not accept the band, while others said that they were quite happy about the concert, as they thought that the band was saying things they were feeling.

---

[8] https://www.krabcice.cz/anketa/. The indicated total is actually superior to 100%.

Social and political divisions actually were spontaneously mentioned by almost all the people who talked to me; these dynamics were partly invoked, of course, in interviews addressed to me and therefore had a presentational purpose; yet they interestingly reflect some rather nuanced representations of life in the villages and its condition of possibility, themselves grounded in contrasting worldviews.

A first division that came to the fore is that between "good people" and "bad people". For Jaromir, "bad people", people with bad intentions or hidden agenda, prevent the smooth course of village life, in its activities and appearance. For instance, he said:

> The firemen competition is being held here, and the other day, a denouncement comes to the financial authority, that we're making business out of it. But we don't have any business, we're doing it for the local people. Not for ourselves, but to have something happening here. Otherwise it would be a dead village.

These people also imposed a hygiene control over the traditional grilled sausages. Such conducts, Jaromir interpreted as bad will, if not as an attempt to sabotage an old practice validated over the years – the doings of "bad people". Similarly, where he can appreciate the initiative of a mayor who proposes to replant a tree alley on the way to Říp, "bad" people propose to build a playground and a square which is useless and aesthetically not in line with the village style at all. As a consequence, comments Jaromir, "they are trying to look friendly, but because we live here for very long time, we know these people and we don't let them close. We say hello, but otherwise…". This division, Jaromir is careful not to align on a difference between "prajak" and local people difference; although he disapproves of the growing number of commuter, he can appreciate the initiative of a "prajak" if he perceives it as respectful to the village or constructive, as the tree alley mentioned above.

A second division, also perceived at the level of local life, yet slightly different, is that between "young and old" villagers, a division Ester would put at around 50 years of age – herself being still under. The mayor of her village she considers populistic, proposing measures that have short-term effects and mainly bring support from the "old people". In her analysis, they would accept the mayor's offer to transport the rubbish for free, not seeing that an important part of the village's budget would be spent on it – while it was not grieving much individual budgets – and thus preventing long-term or cultural investments; or they would attend the *posvíceni* party because the mayor offers a free grilled pig, while the younger people would attend a dancing party at the football field. Asked about the reason for "old people's" position, she answered "I think the old people live here and now; they don't think the future, they think: now I saved 1,000 crowns. But the fact of investing… [they don't understand]". Her profession brings her to know well the amount of the pension people receive, and according to her people live well enough not to have to act in such way. Of course, one may wonder if such "short-term" thinking also reflects habits developed in harsher time, such as the war and communist years, during which short-time saving was a matter of survival (see Chap. 5).

A third division, which affects both public and private life, is that between men and women. Vera mentioned it to my surprise, as I had perceived her as active and outspoken in the pub, and sitting with no inhibition at men's table. As she first jokingly said that men met every day at the pub so that they could complain about women, I asked her where women would complain about men. To this she said: "I am holding inside and one day I am going to explode. And then everything flies." She then explained that she felt she had to do a double share of work; after work, she still had to take care of the garden, the house, the chores, while eventually her husband would enjoy his hobby. She also had the impression, talking to other women, that it was the same in other couples; couples took decisions to have houses to be fixed and gardens, and the women ended up with all the house care, in addition to their day of work, while men enjoyed their hobbies or longer evenings at the pub. Such division may thus simply reflect traditional gendered role, apparently relatively uncritically reproduced. Various analysis converge in saying that communism has brought women to double careers – having a job to sustain the family and taking care of the household, the husbands taking care of their building hobbies, and that remaining inequalities since the Velvet revolution has been very little addressed and reflected upon by women, resulting in still strong inequalities (Heintzelman, 2016; Vesinova-Kalivodova, 1998).

A fourth division came to the fore, which concerns more lifestyle; it is mentioned by Jeronym, who feels a division people who, like him, would like to explore and experience the world and build relationships, and others, which he feels are simply happy with what they have and their habits, that is, sit and drink at the pub. Jeronym appears as a bit of boundary breaker; he likes to sit with girls at the pub, because they are interesting or have new stories, and to engage in conversations with people from other regions to hear different stories. As a consequence, although he is himself from the region, he feels that he is not accepted as "insider" by the villagers.

These divisions, experienced by the interviewees, interestingly reflect punctual dynamics of boundary work, around certain objects, some clearly political, in the sense that they concern the social and collective life, others more relational or existential: urban development of the village, activities that reinforce social cohesion, but also, about a general attitude towards others, the past and newness. These divisions for some part overlap with classical sociocultural categories, or boundary work shown in many other social groups and communities: insiders versus outsiders, men versus women, countryside versus urban, conservatism versus social liberalism, or intergenerational differences. However, to avoid easy reductionism, I will not collapse these differences, and I would like to maintain these idiosyncratic experiences of divisions a bit longer.

In effect, the boundaries can partly overlap: hence, Jaromir is careful not to let "inside" people who do not share his worldview, which tends to maintain the village's tradition, as we will see, but also he considers himself as an "adventurer in life", joining hence Jeronym, even though the latter feels "outside"... So how is individual experience constructed within these boundaries, and how does that reflect more general sociocultural dynamics?

6.6   Everyday Life Near Říp: Two Short Case Studies

As I have done in the previous Chap. 5, I will try to identify deeper cultural life dynamics by comparing two contrasting stories which, however, cover some elements heard in others', those of Jaromir and Ester. Jaromir, like Jeronym, for instance, was born in a village around Říp; in his mid-30s, he lives in a house that he bought to settle down with his girlfriend, thanks to a loan, and he slowly renovates it as he can afford. Most of his everyday life unfolds in interactions around Říp. Ester, like Julie and Irma, moved from Prague to settle in a village around Říp; in her 40s, she commutes to Prague where she has a creative profession, and fully enjoys the time she spends under Říp. In what follows, I retrace how they arrived or developed as persons living under Říp. I also retrace their main spheres of experiences, as well as their movements in space.

6.6.1   Jaromir: An Anchored Man

Jaromir was born in one of the Říp villages, he spent his youth in the region and now lives in a house shared with his partner in one other Říp village. His childhood memories are about farms and running in the fields and ponds, as he was living with his family at his grandfather's house. Hence, he spent all his life mainly in the Říp region, which constitutes the geographical basis of most of his spheres of experience. His professional life is also anchored in the region, both spatially and temporally; this is in effect how he presents his life:

> I wanted something in the farming, in the footprints of my father, because my father was farmer since he was 17, but I couldn't choose a lot, because I wasn't equipped enough for more, so I did the bricklayer for me, and then I told myself, well, if I couldn't do the "agricultural machines' repairman", I'll simply be trying what I can do. And if it didn't go well, the employers would have told me, but I caught up well everywhere: somehow an experiment, my life. Now I have a job in a workshop for repairs [the maintenance office], I am in charge in the factory with the maintenance of the machines… and I am happy with that.

He did his education in the local schools and then a bricklayer apprenticeship in Roudnice; after, he says,

> I was working for the council here in the village, then I travelled through life, changing jobs… (…) I was doing everything, except the bricklayer job for which I had been trained. (…) I was trying the life, what I can do, what I know (…). I lasted about four years in each job.

Hence, although his training and working experience kept him within the Říp region, Jaromir likes to present himself as an experimenter with life, "trying the life"; the limitation of the geographical space did not prevent the diversity and the creation of new spheres of professional experiences.

Among these, his longest experience was driving a small announcing car in front of a very large truck across Czech Republic and all the neighbouring countries.

He enjoyed the job that allowed him to visit other places, but eventually renounced to it after having been involved in an accident which could have had very harmful consequences; he decided it was not worth to risk one's life for work. He now works in the maintenance of farming machines, which he enjoys, and which corresponds, according to him, to his childhood dreams. Hence, although the travelling job allowed him to explore the world beyond Říp, he came back to it; his experiences of the world, now his distal experiences, have been expanded by these explorations.

Next to his work, Jaromir has both personal and social activities. One of his hobbies is to fix engines and especially an old tractor. In addition to that, he loves racing rally cars; he reads magazines and watches videos, and at times goes to see tracks. He does not have enough money to race himself but tries to arrange occasions with acquaintances. Here, these spheres of experiences seem very close to his professional duties, and we can think that his skills are horizontally transferable – what he develops in one can be used in the other.

On the social side, he is engaged as voluntary fireman and as a hunter. When I asked him to tell me more about firemen, he laughed and then said:

> My father was a fireman, my mother was a firewoman; my mother competed in the republics' championship, she went to [the capital of the region], she did well – she probably even won, so it did draw me to it. I like to do it, I am keen on it, but it is not as it used to be. In [the village] in the old days there was not much else to do and the whole village was participating, but now the young people don't want to do it anymore. I understand that this is a new era, with the internet, we would just go out in sand, but now, they stay at home, they have their mobile phones, I can see that [in my family]. So every village has a firemen team but it does not function anymore everywhere.

Fireman is an old tradition in Czech Republic, which is an extension from the legal duty for each municipality to have a voluntary fire brigade. In addition, fire sports developed apparently under the influence of Russian fire sports imported by communism in 1967,[9] and became practiced both by professional and amateurs, and this, especially in the countryside. The fire sport involves training and competition; one of the main task in the competition opposes two teams of seven, each from one village and with its distinctive T-shirts, who have each to start a pump, attach a hose, connect it to a water reservoir, unfold it running, and release the water pressure so as to touch a target at 100 meters from the pump; the first team who touches the target wins. This apparently simple task demands a very high coordination between players, and precise movements beyond the apparent clumsiness of the apparatus (Figs. 6.4 and 6.5).

During a tournament, village teams' fight by pair, age group per age group, men and women team separated. Like in football, the winner of each pair is promoted for the next round, until the finals within the category. Around Říp, villages are organised in the *Podřipská hasičská liga*, the league of the firemen from the region under

---

[9] https://en.wikipedia.org/wiki/Czech_fire_sport; http://www.hzscr.cz/hasicien/article/fire-sport-in-the-czech-republic.aspx

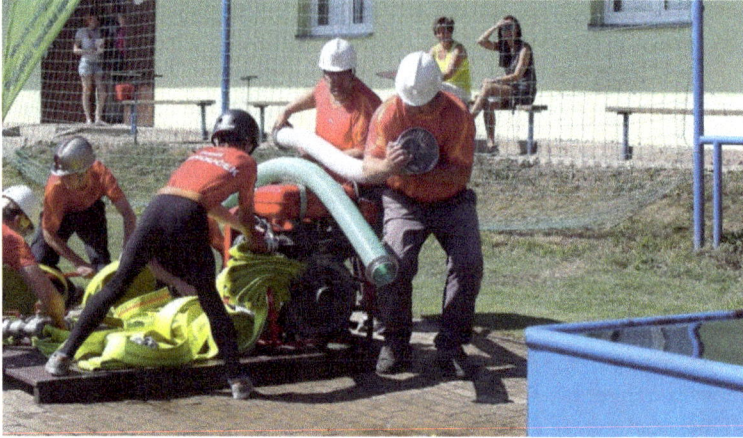

Fig. 6.4 Firefighters starting their run, Podřípska league, Hrobce, 11.8.2017, copyright Pavel Novák, 2017 (Available at: http://www.podripskaliga.cz/galerie/123-hrobce-11-8-2017-2-cast/. Reproduced with authorization of author)

Fig. 6.5 Fully deployed competing teams, Podřípska league, Hrobce, 16.7.2018, copyright Pavel Novák, 2018 (Available at http://www.podripskaliga.cz/fotky/149/fotka. Reproduced with authorization of author)

the hill; inter-village tournaments last half a day to a day, with each team having to install their material and clean the place before the next run. Families and friends and team members waiting for their run hang around, hectolitres of beer and lemonade are drunk, and sausages can be bought from small stands.

Jaromir is running for the team of men of his village, active in the training of younger people in the village, and also in the organisation of tournaments, as well as related activities, such as the firemen's ball.

Another traditional activity, widely spread in the country and also encouraged during communism, is that of the hunter's associations. Jaromir is part of the hunting men of the village, a group of 27 including two women:

> Well, I do hunting for 14 years. Since 2001. In 2001, I went to the army, and after and since that I started doing the hunter things. I like this as well very much. It is not about the killing, as everyone says, but it is about the relaxation in the nature. (…) People call us murderers because we shoot the animals, but this is not true, we actually spare wild animals, we don't really touch the population of local animals, we grow the animals, we let them free, and at the end of the year we have this chase, the pheasants. We put a lot of money in it and take care of it.

In effect, the village is attached to 750 hundreds of hectares of land, including fields, forests and part of the hill – each village having its portion of land, fixed by the cadastre. The hunter's work is for a big part that of gamekeepers; they look after the population of wild animals – deer, boars, rabbits, pheasants and others – and regulate them. Their activity thus runs all year long, with various weekly tasks attributed to the association's members, such as feeding the pheasants which are raised, or bringing water to the animals – which then will be released for the annual hunting period. The hunters also have to control the population of boars, which is extending and causing lots of damages:

> It is since the last four years, that the population of wild boars has grown, it's never been here before. There used to be lots of different smaller species, pheasants and wild hares, but they are not so many anymore, the boars eat them all. Little rabbits, everything. We call it "the vacuum cleaner" ("vysavač"). In one night, a wild pig can make 40km or more, on their way they liquidate couples of lines of potatoes, they are looking for snails, and when there's a rabbit or when there's a hen in its nest, they eat everything.

As the animals are marked, the hunters have to pay the damages made to properties and fields. The association manages to collect money for its activities – raising pheasants, paying back damages – on the one side by selling some of the killed boars, and mainly, on the other side, by renting and cultivating some fields and selling the harvest. Hence, cultivating the fields is part of the hunters' activities, and it covers the year's expenses.

In addition to cultivating, looking after the wild animals and cultivating the fields, Jaromir is also training aspirant hunters. The status of hunter is delivered after the successful passing of a test on knowledge about the alimentation of the animals, the annual cycle of activities, the recognition of animals and the mastery of the specific attached vocabulary. Jaromir currently trains a young woman:

> They will get familiar with the nature and learn everything. I go sit on one of these viewing towers (Fig. 6.6), take her with me, and explain her everything, what kinds of animals are there. Every animal has different signs, eyes are the "lights" ("světla"), ears are "slecha", the white bottom of a young fawn is a "mirror" ("zrcátko"). And so on, and so forth. There are many specific names to talk about wild animals. Roes have "větrník". The white line in the fox's tale is a flower ("kvítek"); she actually can smell through that, it is a smelling organ. It simply has some sensing devices in it and it is called "kvítek". To be a hunter is not a joke.

Fig. 6.6 Hunter's
observing tower, Říp,
copyright author, 2018

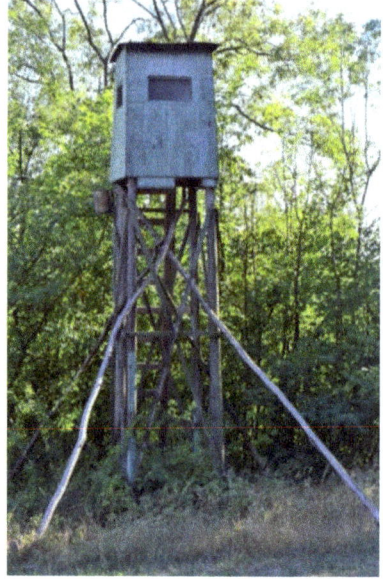

Hence, these two spheres of experience in which Jaromir is committed both cor-respond to small socially shared traditions, that is, cultural subsystems with their guided practices, rules, norms, objects, social organisation and institutions. In these cultural subsystems, his engagements are socially acknowledged and encouraged; they bring status and recognition. These spheres of experience thus allow Jaromir both to maintain old traditions that he enjoys transmitting to younger generations, and to circulate in and around the villages around Říp – with the tournament, or with the activities related to hunting. One could say that the deployment and variation of these spheres of experiences precisely take place on the geographical territory of the Říp region, and within its social networks.

Finally, asked whether he also goes on Říp itself – to the top – Jaromir explains a ritual which reflects this anchorage in an intergenerational, masculine tradition:

Sometimes we go. But we wait for the winter, because we have this tradition to go for a trip to Říp. (…) I used to go there as a child with my father… He had this tradition with his friends, they used to have a sort of camp ("osada"), men's ride only ("pánská jízda") and then Říp climb. It used to be going like this: men's drinking and ravening on Friday and the Říp climb on Saturday morning, they went on the top to bury a bottle, which we keep doing until nowadays. We renewed this tradition with my brother and we're about to do the third year. So, just for this feeling, that we climb the Říp up a dig out the treasure – we call it treasure –, drink it up and dig a new on in. So we keep changing bottles from year to year. And when climbing Říp up, we carry flags, we take ice-axes with us, pickaxes… we honour each other with medals… (…) We have our own flag, carved out of leather, with forefather Czech on it, a photo of him, there are dates as well, and all members of the trip sign up next to the year number, there are ten of us right now, we make top-pictures, and we put a record into the guest book up there – so next time you go to Říp, you can find the guest book there, and if you look every year between the 10th and 20th December, you will find our "on-the-top-writings", we would write there every year that we climbed up and we're happy, that the treasure had been found and there's satisfaction, well, and signatures. Then there's the stamp of the forefather Czech.

Here Jaromir has created a new sphere of experience which, shared with others, turned to a new social activity or quasi-institution; this one demands a geographical move on Říp, but is symbolically anchoring Jaromir and his friends to a lineage of men related directly to the imagined founder of the nation, strongly related to the collective imagination of the region – functioning quasi as a totem, treated with a mixture of irony and respect.

Asked about the future, Jaromir reveals to be very sceptical about the country's development and its politics, which he judges negatively and in front of which he feels powerless – he stopped voting – and that, he thinks, goes downhill since the time of Václav Havel, which he admired very much. On a more personal level, he imagines the same life. He adds that if he would win the lottery he would give money to his family, travel a bit abroad, come back, perhaps buy an autocross – but continue his life: "I like it here, I grew up here, and I want to stay here".

To sum up, Jaromir grew up in the region under the hill, lives there and his committed in activities that allow him to circulate in the region, both to preserve it in its natural aspects – as a hunter – and to support its social fabric – by his commitment in the associations of firemen and hunters. His spheres of experiences could be represented as all distributed around Říp, many overlapping each other, most taking place in historically and socially constituted cultural subsystems; each of them is active in the present, but connects him, on a more symbolic plan, to the generations before him and to these after him. Even if he did travel abroad, these experiences seem to feed possible imagination of future trips – if he wins the lottery – but to come back to the hill. His commitment to the region is also much stronger than to the country, and also seem to shape the horizons of his life. Hence, his spheres of experiences, both proximal and distal, seem strongly organised within the region and around Říp (Fig. 6.7).

In other words, Říp functions as very strong attractor – as a geographical space, a symbolic universe, as social network – structuring and organising Jaromir's spheres of experience, and it provides elements to confer sense, purpose and stability to his life, while allowing everyday creativity.

6.6.2   Ester: An Oscillating Life

Ester was born and grew up in Prague; she knew about the hill from school where she had learned "the classical [story], yes; the forefather Czech arriving on Říp" – and had a school trip there. She also used to come in the Říp region as teenager, and moved to live here after having met her husband to be, as she explains in her first utterance:

> I lived all my life at the [periphery] of Prague, where people live like in rabbit houses. My grandmother used to live around here, I went to discotheque as a young woman; and [I started dating Leoš]. I was coming here for weekends, but I was still going to school in Prague. We dated for a long time, and I was coming here for a long time, and I felt this region was attracting me like a magnet. As if it was pulling me here through something greater above. And then I suddenly found out that we had some roots (…). One of our family roots is here Podřipsko, which I didn't know before.

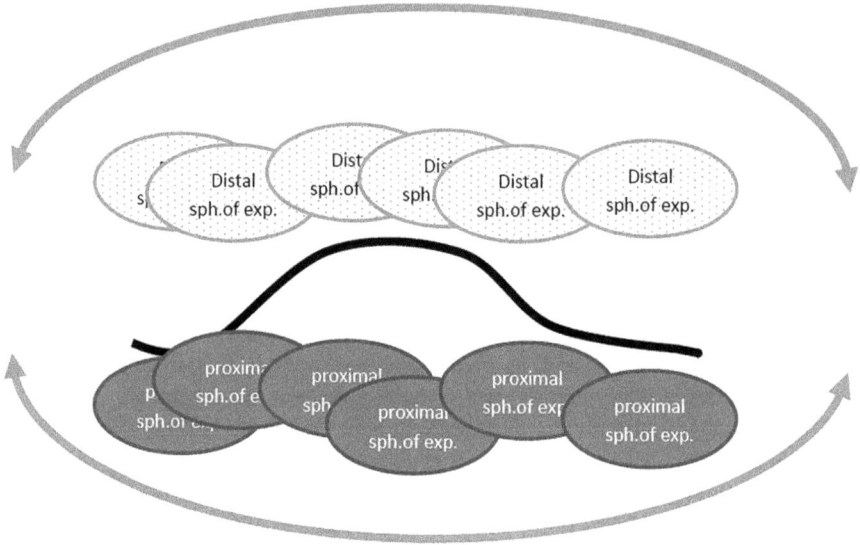

Fig. 6.7 Anchored, stable pattern

Ester thus always knew about Říp, first at a symbolic level, then experienced with the school and then taking a more personal shape as she came as teenager – her meeting with Leoš becoming an important element of rupture in her progressive transition to the life in the village. Note, however, the expression used – the region attracting her "like a magnet", and also, the identification of family roots to make sense of this feeling of attraction.

Ester and Leoš were first living at his family's house, until they later had children and had a house built in one of the Říp villages; she explains that having a view of Říp was a condition, and that she was ready to pay more for it – and indeed, their carefully decorated villa has a remarkable back view on Říp. Hence, both as a reason to move and a place to live, the Říp region seem to be experienced as much as geographical-material place, than as a symbolic and aesthetic reality; the imagination of the place seems to feed in the proximal sphere of experience of everyday home life.

After an art school, Ester made a business school, worked for a few years in marketing, and then took a second education and became an independent in Prague; with time, she also opened an agency for further professional education. She is now an active and successful professional. Hence, Ester's vocational and professional career is an active, transformative one, spheres of experience being constantly renewed and challenged.

To coordinate work and family life, Ester is a daily commuter. She explains the contrast and the moves between the two parts of her life, family under Říp and work in town:

> I go there from six to half past two, but when I come back, I pass [a village on the way] and I see the hill, and I turn off the work, and now I am home! (…) When I became pregnant, I was living here physically for a year, full time. When I then went to visit my family in

Prague, I felt physically sick each time. Because it was on the sixth floor, which started to be too much of a height for me, the metro – one could not breathe in there, and strange, grey people... Because here, when you meet people, it is, "Good day! What are you cooking?" "Today smoked meat arrived!" Then the whole village has smoked ham baked pasta! And there [in Prague], the people are strange, they don't have it in the eyes, no expression… (…) Now that I go there to work, I am used to those looks, probably. I am using the advantages of the big town, I do my shopping in town where you can buy what you want, when you want, compared to the shop here; it is open only a couple of hours a day, like from 8 to 15, cakes are there only Tuesday and Friday, yoghourts only on Wednesday.. That was difficult for me. (…) And another thing which I found very funny, is about make-up. Because I come from Prague – when we [people from Prague] go to the countryside, we don't wear make-up. [When I came to live here] I was still not wearing any make-up. (…) I had been feeling all the time as if in a chalet [in permanent vacation]. In Prague, on the contrary, I would put my make-up on even when doing litter, it was a standard. So there are for me three things [which were difficult]: shopping, public transport, and the make-up.

The contrast was even stronger when she was younger, when she was learning to drive a tractor with Leoš, or when the family had some goats and chicken:

I would wake up at 5, take care of the goat, milk it, I had to wear a scarf to be able to lean my head against it, which than stunk terribly, so I would take a full shower, put my make-up on, put a skirt on and then I went [to work in Prague]. And that was radically different and I used to be thinking to myself: "Oh girls, if you had seen me the morning with the scarf on."

In any case, Ester describes very strongly contrasting spheres of experience, the private family and social life under Říp, and her professional spheres of experience in Prague. She spontaneously highlights the differences: the directness and authenticity of Říp, against the comfort of modern shopping in Prague. She also interestingly emphasises the daily liminality (Stenner, 2017) of her experiences of moving from one sphere to the other: the necessary shower and make-up after goat-feeding before leaving the village for town, the feeling of peace when passing the village midtrip from Prague to the village. In both cases these liminal transformations seem to demand some cleansing and leaving behind the other sphere of experience: the smell of nature to wear the town's mask, the worries of the city to come back to the reality of the hill.

And in effect, Ester has an intense social life under Říp. She describes the dense relationship with the neighbours, resembling the one that took place in another village 60 years ago and described by Zdenka (Chap. 5):

We are living here, here the neighbours vis-a-vis have two children, over there is my husband's aunt, who is the mother (and the grandmother) to those neighbours, then, there is Alena with Luboš. And I, for example, don't have to think about food for children's lunch, there is always somewhere where they can eat! Either they go to Teresa's or they go to Alena's (…). So those moms say "today, I cooked this and that for my kids…", I reply to them "you know, I didn't cook anything today morning, but they're going to be fed…" and I don't have to take care of this. But then, on the other hand, when I cook, I never cook four portions only: this one comes and eats, that one comes and eats…(…) So, that's how the living here is, and when one grills, and when it starts to smell nicely around, then you take a bottle of wine, some meat or a zucchini or just anything you have, and we sit, and just eat and drink, and we do that here, or there…it's beautiful.

Ester describes as life of horizontal, spontaneous exchanges of informal social networks, at the scale of the street, which constitutes for her a supportive, warm and meaningful sphere of experience.

Her commitment to the village goes beyond the street, as she also participated for some years to the mayor's office; she left it feeling that the efforts she made for the social life – organising events and festivals, for instance – were often not sufficiently appreciated. She is however very aware of the local politics and the decisions made, of which she is also extremely critical, such as the cutting down of old trees, and she suspects corruption. She for instance says how she engaged actions to oppose the urban development plan proposed by the mayor. Here, thus, Ester creates a sphere of experience within a much more institutionalised frame, where the resistance of others brings her to stronger reaction of distancing and criticism.

In her leisure time, besides these commitments, she likes gardening in the back of her house. She did travel abroad – "to Croatia, to Greece, those classical destinations" – but mainly around the country, where she accompanies Leoš who like to collect mushroom. She does not need to travel, she says:

> But I like it here the most; I am here as if on holiday! [we laugh] We have large windows here, and also a door-window to the balcony; and I didn't even want to have too many paintings – although we have plenty in my family, my mother knows some painters – but I was saying I don't want painting in the room, because we have here a living picture [the view on Říp] which is changing all the time: it can be frosted, dropping off, springing up…

Hence, Ester grounds her leisure sphere of experience in her home and street; although she did travel abroad and in the country, these geographical experiences do not seem particularly significant. Asked about her readings, which she does while accompanying her mushroom collecting husband or in free time, she says she like books related to her profession and further education. Hence, one could say, her distal experiences from home are experiences related to the development of her professional sphere of experience.

Living under Říp, she and her family go to the Říp fair; and "since we live here, we made the promise that we go at least once a month on the top of Říp, and we doing it since that, for the past five years. We don't go by the main road, we go on the back road". Hence, if like Jaromir, Ester and her husband have tried to ritualised an annual walk to the hill, and like other local people, they take the back road, their ritual is more private – that of a couple – than anchored in a long tradition.

Finally, asked about how she sees the future of life in 5–10 years, Ester ironically answers "Some prince will come, change with the mayor, and put everything back in order." When I asked about her personal future, she more modestly says "I hope that my husband is going to finish to work on the garden, and that he will find water in the pound;" eventually she mentions her plan of attending evening classes to reorient her professional career. She comments:

> And I think one should keep advancing during one's whole life. Because for me, a day, when I don't learn any new information, has no sense (*nesmysl*). That's how life should be, always learn something new.

Interestingly thus, Ester has different modalities of imagining the future: one concerns her spheres of experience under the hill, and is about the maintenance and the development of the quality of living, at home and in the village; it is extension of the present proximal spheres into a possible better form. The second modality of imagining is related to her professional life, for which she has imagination of the future grounded in her experience and that of others that she saw taking on later educations, projects for further learning and development – a permanent learning and development which seems, for her, confer sense to her life.

To sum, Ester has two groups of quite clearly defined spheres of proximal experiences, one located around home – home with family and view on Říp, the street and its social community, and the village with its tensions, that is, all with strong emotional and aesthetic qualities – the other around work, in Prague, more learning-oriented. Ester seems engaged and committed in both, while maintaining them quite separated, geographically and symbolically. There is little overlap between the two, yet it can be found on two points. First, in her free time, she reads books which expand and nourish, as distal experiences, her professional life and that contribute to its transformation. Second, as she worked at the mayor's office, she seemed to have used some of her entrepreneurial know-how to try to create activities; it is these active propositions that have been refused by the village. Hence, one may say that she used resources from her professional life within this village sphere of experience – an attempt to horizontally integrate spheres of experience (Zittoun & Gillespie, 2015), or a horizontal transfer (Perkins & Salomon, 1994) – and that these have been invalidated. As a result, it seems, the two groups of spheres of experience need to remain distant, and the mutual enrichment can be only done at the more distal level (Fig. 6.8).

Finally, there thus seem to be two attractors in Ester's life, one around work and the other around Říp, and the balance of her life is precisely made by the commuting movement. Here, stability is more given by the oscillation in present times, and without so much relation to the past; it seems however to allow her to have two complementary engagements and to keep developing creatively.

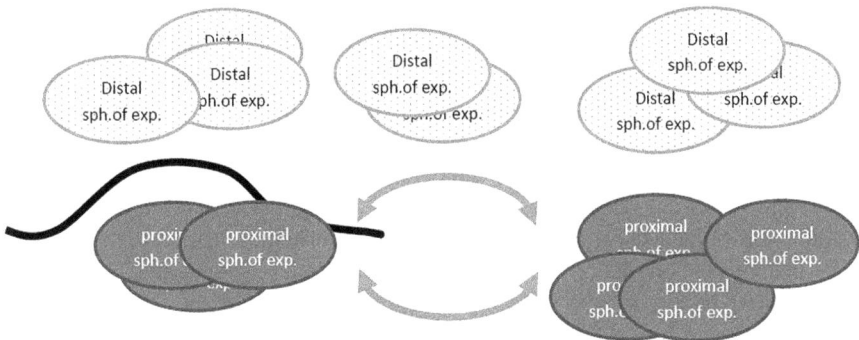

Fig. 6.8 Oscillating stable pattern

6.7 Dynamic Patterns of Everyday Life

At this stage, I would like to step back and consider what is common and what differs in the ways in which people organise their lives around Říp. For this I will propose a transversal analysis, pursuing the theme that emerged out of the two small case studies: located round Říp, their lives have specific patterns organised by what seems to be relatively clear attractors.

6.7.1 Entry Points

As first point, there is the question of how people came to live under the hill. I saw three main entry points for people's trajectories to unfold under Říp.

First is the case of people who were born there and always lived there, and whose families were established in the region for a few generations. The hill region is thus the "natural" context of living, and unless people want to leave it, this is from where things will grow.

A second entry point is that of people who were carried by social or cultural or other broader sociogenetic dynamics, diffracted in microgenetic events, to settle in. Sandra and Zdenka (Chap. 5) were thus pushed or pulled towards the region because of the political events in the borderlands, and then, through the social networks to which they belonged: the family of Sandra's adoptive father or that of Zdenka's husband.

The third case is that of people declaring having felt "attracted" to the hill and subsequently having decided to move. Interestingly, in effect, among the interviewees, half had discourses very comparable to that of Ester saying that she was attracted like "by a magnet": Julie describes a strong experience of "*déjà vu*" as she came for a walk on the hill; Irma strangely was "feeling at home" in comparable circumstances, before, like Ester, discovering some distant family connection to the hill. These feelings of "magnetic attraction" and *déjà vu* seem to put the finger on an emotional reaction, both aesthetic and embodied, beyond reasonable explanation, closer to a dreamwork.

This can be explained in two complementing ways. First, people do not approach places, and especially, landscapes, with blank minds. Landscapes are perceived through people's story of seeing, meeting, experiencing landscapes, through real experience, films, novels or hearsay. To the urban, the forest becomes a magical resourcing place or a jogging space, while the forest constitutes for the mountaineer home and resource. Landscapes are thus met through people's experience and imagination of landscape, in great part developed through a large variety of symbolic resources (Gillespie, 2006; Ingold, 2012). But then, people may be more or less sensitive to this whispering and buzzing of semiotic streams associated to a place. Our research on symbolic resources shows that people are much more likely to be reminiscing songs or films somehow relevant – often analogically, or through emotional resonance – to the present situation, if they engaged processes of transition (Zittoun, 2003, 2007, 2018), that is, experiencing liminality – which are affective and prone to transformation (Stenner, 2017). Interestingly, the persons who moved towards the hill had very different reasons to do so, but usually at times of ruptures or need for transitions (e.g., after a divorce or starting a family). As junction of these two lines of thought, then, one possible explanation for this would be that these magnetic experience or déjà vu correspond to the "a-ha" moment observed when people come to experience the synthetic creation of a solution to problem under elaboration (Stenner, 2017) – whether in science, or in the situation of parents looking for the first name for a child (Zittoun, 2004). These impressions of "strange familiarity" (Freud, 1919) would then be built on the meeting of different semiotic streams: all of these persons had heard and seen images about Říp or visited it as children; most of them also knew all the hearsay about the supposedly magic powers of the hill, that is, were exposed to social representations of the hill (see Chap. 4); and all of them were, consequently, exposed for a long time to these redundant semiotic indications. Being actually on the hill and having an agreeable walk or visit generates an aesthetic experience which is likely to create emotional resonances with these streams of available and internalised social discourses and patterns; it thus provokes a semiotic shortcut (Zittoun, 2019). In some conditions, it is very likely that that meeting creates such a personal relevant experience; it is equally possible that difficult decisions to be taken at a personal level, that is, move to the hill, can take a socially sharable shape if they wear the cloth of these collective mythical discourses. In that sense, what draws these people to live under the hill is due to ontogenetic dynamic, finding a resonance with sociogenetic dynamics.

6.7.2 Říp as Pattern and Organiser in People's Lives

For people who live on Říp, the hill appears in many different ways; it is present as a geographical and material place; it is a visual presence (or more generally, a sensorial one); and it has symbolic value, both collective and socially shared, and personal and intimate. Each person develops a unique relation to the hill, resulting from a unique and evolving configuration of meaning along these four dimensions.

On a geographical and material place, all the villages are positioned around the hill, which means that the hill is ever present in the landscape and the creation of the microclimate. Each village has a street or path going to the hill, and each village is related to the others by roads that follow the flanks of the hill. The hill is part of the ecology of the place, and thus affords various conduct (Gibson, 1986). Hence, the hill itself and its forests offer a field for possibly activities – running, hiking, dog walking, biking, hunting and mushroom picking. In addition, it imposes certain constraints: one cannot go in straight line from a village to another, the weather forecast cannot be trusted around the hill, and the hill attracts flows of tourists.

Then, the hill is offered to the senses. Although things could be said about the particular soundscape in the forests of the hill, or the smells on its flanks – and as I write these lines on a sunny morning after the rain, it is very peculiar – it is the hill as shaping the landscape that it is of primary importance. On a visual plane, the hill – as a shape in the landscape, as a presence, and so and always also, as a symbol – is absolutely redundant, under its various angles. It can be constantly seen, it is painted, often realistically, but also schematically, in nature, but also in various frames – some frames, we have seen, themselves representing the hill (Chap. 4). People who see the hill from their windows consider it as a painting (as Ester), that is, framed by the window; Mariana Alasseur, the artist whose work is presented (on the cover), also told me that she painted Říp from a window – it was framed before it became a painting. Hence, such redundancy and omnipresence of a pattern is quite likely to be participating to the shaping of people's psyche (Valsiner, 2019).

This is where the symbolic existence of the hill comes to play a role. In effect, people experience the hill as a place, but also as THE hill Říp, that is, their perception is always already mediated by the semiotic networks – historical, mythical, political – associated to the hill as symbol. As an indication of the symbolic dynamics at work, then, we can observe new creative synthesis. Not only do people live around Říp and speak about it, they also reappropriate its shared meaning; they internalise it and create a personal sense of Říp, (Valsiner, 2019); and so it becomes "ingrown" (Lawrence & Valsiner, 1993, 2003; Zavereshneva & van der Veer, 2018). I can identify two modes of constructive internalization, that is, of turning collective meaning into personal sense: first, through ritual; second, through active distantiation.

Regarding the first mode of constructive internalisation, both Jaromir and Ester anchored these symbolic discourses about the hill into actual practices: Jaromir recreated with his family a ritual of going on Říp with a flag and a bottle; Ester and her husband created a ritual of an annual climb to the hill. In both cases, distal spheres of experiences, infused by social discourses, are thus anchored into actual, relationally shared, emotionally invested, proximal experiences. The second mode of constructive internalisation appears in the case of Ester and artists using the theme of Říp: in both cases, they frame the landscape, and turn it into a work of art, that is, they recreate it by directly semiotising it; hence, they create the distance (Valsiner, 2019) to reflect, narrate, share or even criticise Říp.

A third level of redundancy could be suggested; as we have seen, time is organised in a very cyclical way, which is quite common in rural areas; but the specificity of it is that the organisation of time, that is, the rhythmicity of life, hence becomes redundant with the shape of the place. The landscape is also, in some ways, a "chronospace", or perhaps, a chronotope, if the notion designates a specific time-space (Bakhtin, 1982).

Finally, if at a theoretical level we can show that redundancy in place, time, movement and semiotic thickness is very strong, and that is seems, to some extent, to shape people's lives, we still have to ask: do such redundancies have actual, empirical implications? How do they manifest in everyday life? The next step proposed is therefore to identify patterns in people's everyday life.

6.7.3 Patterns of Living

Once living under the hill, people's daily life gets organised around certain routines that we have analysed in terms of geographical mobility, as well as more symbolic mobility at the level of both proximal and distal spheres of experiences. Looked from afar, each person's organisation of movements and spheres of experience seems to take specific shapes, or patterns. These became apparent in the two short case studies presented above, but also in the two longer life course analyses in Chap. 5. In what follows, I distinguish two types of patterns, inspired by dynamics system theory (Van Geert, 2009), one stable and one unstable one, and shortly present two further short vignettes.

6.7.3.1 Stable Patterns

Among the small group of interviewees I talked to, two were born and lived all their lives around Říp; with variations on the type of activities, and corresponding to my informal knowledge of lives of many others, the patterning of life resembles that of Jaromir: these are organised around one main attractor, proximal spheres of experience overlap partly with each other, and are at least for one part socially acknowledged; finally, their distal spheres of experience correspond to some extent to these. Hence, with such central attractor, dynamics of circulation can take place within the space and across spheres of experience, while these movements maintain the balance of the system. Experientially, people develop private and professional spheres of experience around the hill: these are partly overlapping the experiences of their social networks; and these spheres of experience correspond, more or less to socially established cultural subsystems. Hence, Eva, born not far, lives in one of the village, works in the town nearby, bikes around the hill, participates in the pub life and engages in various informal exchanges network in her street and around the pub; although she did not live all her life under Říp, Sandra's patterns of living under the hill took a comparable shape once she joined the community and the life around the family band (see Chap. 5).

A second stable pattern would be closer to that of people who came from somewhere else, or developed an important part of their spheres of experience not on Říp; their life is organised around two main attractors, and the balance is given by the oscillation between these attractors, with necessary liminal dynamics from one to the other. This could be called an oscillating pattern, as in the case of Ester. Other commuters, such as Julie, have similar patterns, for instance with challenging and creative professions in town, and a local partner, more anchored in the life around the hill, where they then develop some part of their social engagements. Also Sandra, who continued to travel every year to south Bohemia, where she had kept her family, could be said to be engaged in such a stable oscillation (see Chap. 5).

Interestingly, such patterns are also produced by two persons who actually engaged in an active recreation of the meaning of the hill – Jaromir by creating a family ritual, Ester using her window as frame for the view on the hill – an act she clearly compared to that of hanging a painting of the wall. In that sense, the anchoring power of the hill could be said to be both geographical – the hill as social and geographical place for overlapping proximal spheres of experiences to take place – and symbolic, as semantic field that has been personally internalised and created. This, double anchorage perhaps could turn the hill into an attracting point, functioning as vector, or axis, coordinating the fields of material activities and semiotic ones. To challenge this interpretation, we can now examine two cases of unstable patterns.

6.7.3.2 Unstable Patterns

Beyond people whose lives around Říp seem organised by stable patterns, other persons seem to be engaged in more instable forms. To present these forms, I will sketch the situation of two persons whose situations could be seen as following more unstable patterns.

Jeronym came to live in one of the villages as he grew up not far, and developed friendships around the pub of one of the villages; he moved in, attracted by what he felt was a rich social network and a warm community. He developed a sphere of experience around the pub, where he mainly meets the other villagers. As he engaged a serious relationship with a young woman, he bought a house in the same village, taking for this a loan, as did Jaromir; after breaking up with his partner, however, he assumes alone the expense and the slow renovation of the house. Professionally, Jeronym was trained as car technician and through experience, became an industrial welder, before opening his own workshop in a Říp village where he works for some companies and also to create more artistic pieces. Hence, as many others in the village, he developed his professional sphere of experience over time, progressing through domains of activity that correspond better to his interests and allow creativity. His leisure activities include mountain sports – bike and climbing; some of the biking he does on and around the hill, as training, but for carrying out his climbing sphere of experience, he needs to travel in the country and beyond to Slovakia and Germany – travels which he enjoys very much. Jeronym would love to find climbing or travelling partners; yet his sphere of experience is not shared by anyone in the village, and not really acknowledged. Jeronym has therefore a very ambivalent relationship to the village under Říp: he was attracted by the social life, but the initial welcome did not keep its promises:

> I am actually quite disappointed with the people here lately. But only with this being-too-settled part. It is a bad experience. I used to move a lot and so I pretty much like meeting new people, and since I am here for a long time already, I am missing that. Last year I tried to organize something, and [their reaction] disappointed me a lot. I went to see those guys and told them: Look, your wives sit at home with children, (..) so why don't we go somewhere for a trip together, and they looked at me as if I was not normal. It is an ok life for people who live here with their family, but for people who live alone it is not good. I feel like in prison here.

He develops this point by explaining his loneliness: living alone, working as independent, having his other spheres of experiences alone.... He eventually found through internet some climbing partner in other another Říp village with whom he travels and climbs:

> When we go somewhere, this guy has no limits and I have some; so I need to be pushed, and I feel extraordinary things and am happy with what I experience. When I come back I can live from the experiences I had. And not just be sitting in the pub with those from here. This thing brings me energy. The more I live with people here, the more I want to experience something. So it is a hell at the one hand, to be living here, but it pushes me to do something on the other hand, so maybe it's good for me in some sense as well. It makes me want to live for something and dedicate myself to something. When I want to live something I go climbing or I go with my bike, I try to live something while being here.

Hence, his climbing experiences abroad have, as proximal experiences, an intensity that his life in the village does not have; it is these that become distal experiences strong enough to enrich his local life. It is also by recreating that "living" experience through his biking around Říp.

Asked whether he considered living elsewhere, perhaps in town, Jeronym replied:

> I thought about it a lot. But I have a house here, on which lots of work has been done, a dog, a cat; I could sell the house and buy a flat somewhere, but I don't have enough to buy a house, and with the animals I don't want to live in a flat. One year ago I was seriously thinking about doing that – living in town, getting a flat, letting go of everything, meeting new people again. But there is something with the house that I don't want to give away; lots of work, and I would like to finish that. But I would like to have a small flat where I can go away from all this … So I started to travel, I bought a good sleeping bag [laughs], a waterproof one.

In such a statement, all the ambivalence experienced by Jeronym clearly appears with the successions of "but": he would like to go but cannot leave his house, he would like a flat but cannot leave his animals, he would like to move on but cannot let go. Ambivalence can be the necessary conditions for the emergence of newness (Abbey, 2012); it can also be simply impeding change and force repetition, or liminal hotspots (Greco & Stenner, 2017).

Finally, I asked Jeronym how he saw the future at 5–10 years, and he replied:

> Look, I still see my future in terms of meeting someone, founding a family. I'm a bit afraid that I'm not lucky enough to do so., but... I am definitely continuing traveling. It started to energise me and I think if you live in on the planet Earth, you should know it all, more than just one place. It is our only chance to get to know it, since we are here. And we probably should.

For Jeronym life is organised around a series of spheres of experience which are quite disjoined, and not all fulfilling. His house created the geographical place where he has his home, which lost some of its interest after the break up with his partner, yet got some symbolic value after the work put in there; the village as sphere of experience is attracting, yet he feels rejected by it; he tries as much as he can to get intense experiences in further spheres – climbing, living – yet lacks the company to share it with. Hence, not only can he not really link these spheres of experience, besides bringing back the climbing experience to nourish his proximal spheres; they also have little social recognition.

To sum up, Jeronym's life is anchored in proximal spheres anchored around Říp; yet his distal experiences all pull him away: living elsewhere, climbing or having climbed or exploring the world "as it is our only chance". However, as much as he feels attracted by the world beyond the hill region, he is unable to move away, attached to his house and work. Jeronym's patterns of life around Říp could be represented as centripetal, around the attractor that is the hill (Fig. 6.9): his imagination drives him away, but the hill keeps calling him back to its centre.

Finally, another unstable pattern can be found in Irma's situation. A biologist, she came to live in one of the Říp villages from Prague after having lived abroad in diverse European countries for a few years, attracted by the beauty and the tranquillity of the place. The house reminded her and her partner a Mediterranean house, from where he came from, and so they bought it and had children there. She has learned about the hill as a child, with the school and her parents.

About the hill, she reports the saying that it is meant to have the power to take energy when one has too much and give some when one needs it; she mentions its magnetism and the fact that shamans use it for these powers. She felt these properties herself:

> When I lived here some crises, I had the impression that the hill was stabilizing me, inside me, or in the house…

Finally, like Ester, she discovered having family roots in the region after she moved in; this explained, she believes, her experience of *déjà vu*:

> It was as if I had come back, when I came in here the first time; I felt as if I knew it already, as if I had lived here before. It was strange… as if being at home.

Her professional life brings her to develop collaborations in the nearby towns, to valorise her experience of the ecosystem of the Říp region, and also to present her work in scientific networks in the country and abroad.

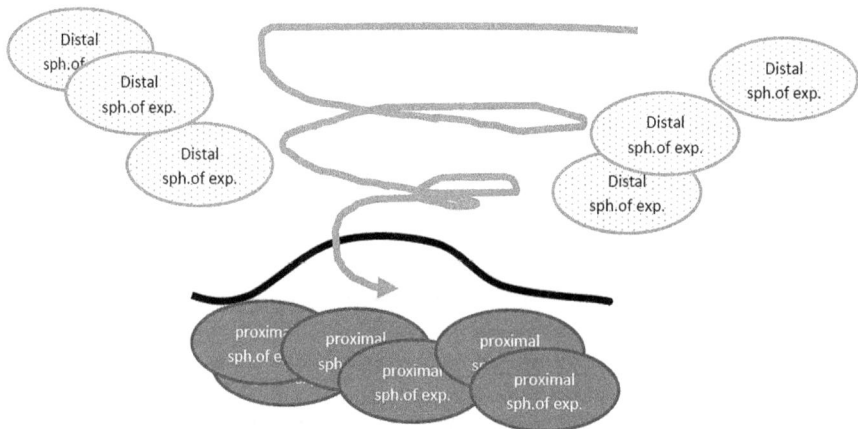

Fig. 6.9 Unstable, centripetal pattern

However, her life under the hill is not so simple. Her children were mocked by other children; some of the neighbouring children broke their home-made toys. She comments:

> I am angry with the people from here, perhaps they think that [we are different], they are a bit primitive at times....

She actually reports that the teachers were telling her that if she was not happy, she could move away; she placed her children in another school, outside of the village.

She however reports making efforts to develop social relationships. With a small group of inhabitants, she created a green association to promote a more organic agriculture, and to object the use of chemicals in the fields around the village; this green initiative was legally countered. This generated a conflict with some inhabitants, which spilled over other activities. She thus refused to go with the children to the villages' burning of the witch and *Masopust*, preferring to take them to the swimming pool in the nearby town.

Hence, Irma moved to the region under hill with a strong attraction, fed with symbolic discourses and personal experience. She could nourish her work with the experience of living under the hill, yet that professional sphere of experience is acknowledged outside of the region. Her past experiences – in town, abroad – render the establishment of social relationships difficult – rather than being resources to meet others, they seem obstacles – and so her social life does also not correspond to the location of her living. The fact that the children attend the local school could have become a facilitator to establish social relationships; however events brought her to send them to schools out of the region. Hence, her family spheres of experience are partly within the house, or out of the region.

To sum up, Irma's spheres of experience are quite diverse; they have little fit with the actual social and material places, and do not find social recognition (Fig. 6.10). Even though she invests the symbolic value of the place, the reality of proximal spheres of experience – the children's school, her work, the antagonism with some neighbours – strongly pull her away. The shape of these patterns could thus be described as centrifugal: although there is a symbolic attractor around the hill and the house, every other spheres of experience seem to push Irma away.

To move a step further, we can now come back to the question of what anchors a stable pattern; just above, I suggested that it may be a coordination of the proximal anchoring of spheres of experience with a personally recreated semiotic field related to the hill. In contrast, Irma and Jeronym both lead many of their proximal spheres of experiences, the ones which are also the more emotionally invested and generating important distal experiences, outside of the Říp region: climbing or a life in town for Jeronym, children's school and international career for Irma. In addition, neither of them integrated the social, mythical or semiotic field associated to Říp in their actual life. Irma was very aware of the mythical, social discourse; but it is not turned into practices taking place on or around the hill. Jeronym was attracted to the hill for the social life and end up biking on the hill alone; his proximal, located experiences have no symbolic correspondence. In other words, Říp is present as a place for them, and perhaps even, as a place with stories; but the social discourses

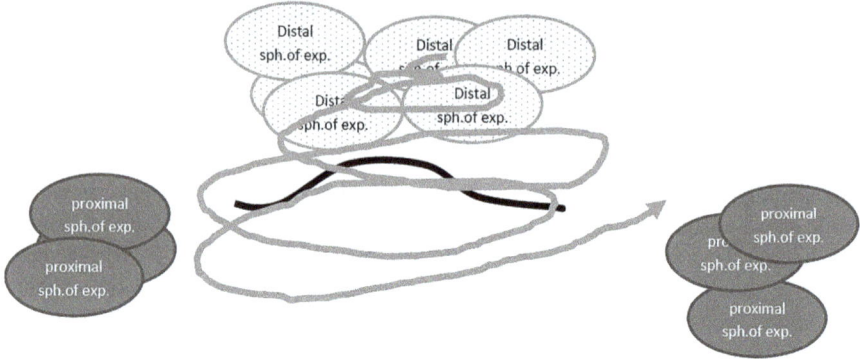

Fig. 6.10 Centrifugal, unstable pattern

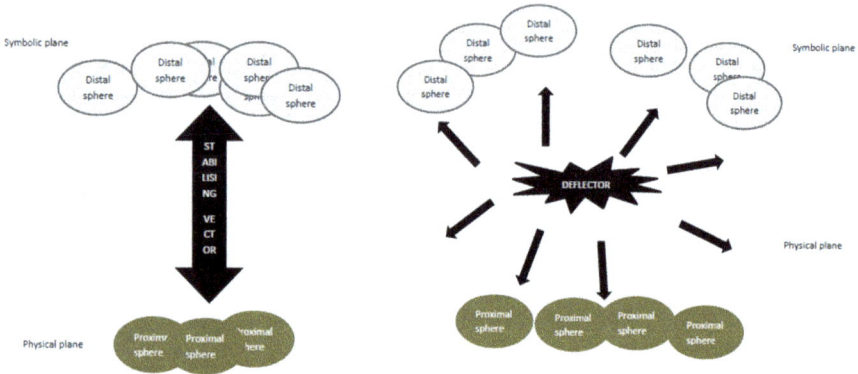

Fig. 6.11 Two types of vectors, in stable vs unstable patterns

associated to it have been little internalised and recreated on a personal plane locally. For Jeronym it is a meaningless place, for Irma it has meaning and sense with no local anchoring. If such reading is correct, then, the hill does not have a full attracting or stabilising power; it is like an axis to which one pole were missing, which would explain its centrifugal or centripetal power.

To summarise, the strength of Říp as an attractor for Jaromir and Ester would be an active personal recreation of the socially shared symbolic nature of the hill, into coordinated distal and proximal spheres of experiences – the attractor is stable because it is an axis, coordinating two planes, and with it, people's spheres of experiences, proximal and distal. Říp does not function as stable attractor when it fails to coordinate these two planes – it is a meaningless place for Jeronym's activities, or a meaning disconnected from its place for Irma – and in that sense, it fails holding together diverse spheres of experiences; it could perhaps even be seen, as such, as a deflector (Fig. 6.11).

6.8   Microgenetic Patterns and the Course of Life

In this chapter, I have tried to describe the life around Říp from different perspectives. First, from a third person's perspective, or a bird's eye, I have tried to describe the villages, the connecting roads and the structure of the population.

Then, still from that outside perspective, I have tried to account for the dynamics organising life around the hill. I have highlighted the temporal, cyclic succession of social and personal events around the hill, which for a large part follow the cyclical nature of the seasons, in an environment where nature is ever present. I have also retraced the circular nature of geographical movements and social networks, by which people build informal exchanges in street, associations in villages, and the circular movement from village to village around the hill, by which people use services and meet professional, friends and families. If these temporal-spatial circulations can be seen as flows – for instance of water – around a hill, these circulations also generate perturbations, streams and divisions. Combining my observation with people's utterances, I thus showed that there seems to be local and temporary boundary divisions within these circulations, around certain specific objects – activities, values, opinions or ways of imagining the village life or its future. Around these divisive points, the gentle flow of everyday life exchange divide, like the flows of the red sea.

Finally, refocusing on people's perspectives, I have tried to retrace the patterns of individual everyday life around the hill. Doing so, I have started to identify four typical dynamic patterns. Two are stable, which means that people have found a way to organise their spheres of experiences, proximal and distal, in such a way that it brings them enough satisfaction, social recognition, positive affective and or aesthetic experiences, and that allow them to imagine their future and engage their daily creativity. The two other patterns could be called unstable. They can be described by a lack of overlap between proximal and distal spheres of experiences, or as lack of social recognition of these spheres within the Říp region; people experiencing these unstable movements seem to feel ambivalence and dissatisfaction. In a centripetal pattern, some forces and dynamics, for instance imagination of self and of possible activities to be actualised elsewhere, push the person away from the hill, while other counterforces pull them strongly back – such as a loan or an attachment to the place. In a centrifugal pattern, some forces attach the person to the place, for instance an imagination and symbolic attachment, while others strongly push them away – such as the actuality of one's professional spheres of experience or a lack of integration in the local and social life. Finally, I have proposed that the resulting force of the combination between configurations of proximal and distal dynamics, and their anchorage in the actual geographical and symbolic space of the region, could thus be seen as creating the valence of the hill – for a person, as attracting, or at the contrary, as deflecting.

Finally, I need to conclude this chapter with two questions. The first question is, if these dynamics appear in a quite clear manner around the hill, how much comparable ones could be observed in other cases? Does a person's internalisation of social discourses and patterns always imply a recreation both at the level of distal and proximal spheres of experience, at both the planes of incarnated and socially located activities, and of semiotic creation? Or put differently, is a person's relation to a place always anchored only if it is charachterised by a double, material and semiotic, recreation? The second question aims at putting back this analysis within the frame of our overall enquiry. In effect, what needs now to be established, is how such a reading combines with the one proposed in Chap. 5, that is, an articulation of sociogenesis with ontogenesis. This is the purpose of Chap. 7; there, I will also explore the generalisation potential of this study.

References

Abbey, E. (2012). Ambivalence and its transformation. In J. Valsiner (Ed.), *Handbook of culture and psychology* (pp. 989–997). Oxford, UK: Oxford University Press.

Bakhtin, M. M. (1982). *The dialogic imagination: Four essays*. Austin, TX: University of Texas Press.

Chester, P., Forrester, S., & Forrester, S. E. S. (1996). *Engendering Slavic literatures*. Bloomington, IN: Indiana University Press.

Dahinden, J., & Zittoun, T. (2013). Religion in meaning making and boundary work: Theoretical explorations. *Integrative Psychological and Behavioral Science, 47*(2), 185–206. https://doi.org/10.1007/s12124-013-9233-3

Freud, S. (1919). The 'Uncanny'. In J. Strachey (Ed.), & A. Strachey (Trans.), *The Standard Edition of the Complete Psychological Works of Sigmund Freud:* Vol. XVII (1917–1919) (pp. 217–256). London: The Hogarth Press and the Institute of Psychoanalysis.

Gibson, J. J. (1986). The theory of affordances. In *The ecological approach to visual perception* (pp. 127–143). Hillsdale, NJ & London: Lawrence Erlbaum.

Gillespie, A. (2006). *Becoming other: From social interaction to self-reflection*. Greenwich, CT: Information Age Publishing.

Gillespie, A., Kadianaki, I., & O'Sullivan-Lago, R. (2012). Encountering alterity: Geographic and semantic movements. In J. Valsiner (Ed.), *Oxford handbook of culture and psychology* (pp. 695–719). Oxford, UK: Oxford University Press.

Greco, M., & Stenner, P. (2017). From paradox to pattern shift: Conceptualising liminal hotspots and their affective dynamics. *Theory & Psychology, 27*(2), 147–166. https://doi.org/10.1177/0959354317693120

Haigron, D. (2017). *The English countryside: Representations, identities, mutations*. Cham, Switzerland: Springer.

Heinen, R. (2017). Family or career: Policies that shaped the roles of Czech women within the family structure (MA thesis, Charles University). Retrieved from https://is.cuni.cz/webapps/zzp/download/120270466

Heintzelman, L. (2016). Gender inequality in the Czech Republic: Institutional and societal barriers to equality. *Perspectives on business and economics*, *34. Post-communist reform in the Czech Republic: Progress and problems*, Paper 7.

Ingold, T. (2012). Introduction. In M. Janowski & T. Ingold (Eds.), *Imagining landscapes: Past, present and future* (1st ed., pp. 1–18). Farnham, Surrey, England; Burlington, VT: Routledge.

James, W. (2009). On a certain blindness in human beings. In *Great Ideas. On a certain blindness in human beings*. (Original 1899, pp. 1–32). London: Penguin.

Lawrence, J. A., & Valsiner, J. (1993). Conceptual roots of internalization: From transmission to transformation. *Human Development, 36*(3), 150–167. https://doi.org/10.1159/000277333

Lawrence, J. A., & Valsiner, J. (2003). Making personal sense: An account of basic internalization and externalization processes. *Theory & Psychology, 13*(6), 723–752. https://doi.org/10.1177/0959354303136001

Perkins, N. D., & Salomon, G. (1994). Transfer of learning. In T. Husen & T. N. Postelwhite (Eds.), *International handbook of educational research* (Vol. 11, 2nd ed., pp. 6452–6457). Oxford, UK: Pergamon Press.

Ruzicka, M. (2012). Continuity or rupture? Roma/Gypsy communities in rural and urban environments under post-socialism. *Journal of Rural Studies, 28*(2), 81–88. https://doi.org/10.1016/j.jrurstud.2012.01.019

Stenner, P. (2017). *Liminality and experience. A transdisciplinary approach to the psychosocial.* London: Palgrave Macmillan.

Valsiner, J. (2019). *Ornamented lives.* Charlotte, NC: Information Age Publishing.

Van Geert, P. (2009). Nonlinear complex dynamical systems in developmental psychology. In S. J. Guastello, M. Koopmans, & D. Pincus (Eds.), *Chaos and complexity in psychology. The theory of nonlinear dynamical systems* (pp. 242–271). New York: Cambridge University Press.

Vesinova-Kalivodova, E. (1998). The vision of Czech women: One eye open (gender roles in Czech society, politics and culture). *Dialectical Anthropology, 23*(4), 361–374.

Wikipedia. (2018). Vietnamese people in the Czech Republic. In *Wikipedia.* Retrieved from https://en.wikipedia.org/w/index.php?title=Vietnamese_people_in_the_Czech_Republic&oldid=849932837

Wimmer, A. (2013). *Ethnic boundary making: Institutions, power, networks.* Oxford, UK: Oxford University Press.

Zavereshneva, E., & van der Veer, R. (2018). *Vygotsky's notebooks. A selection.* Singapore, Singapore: Springer.

Zittoun, T. (2003). The hidden work of symbolic resources in emotions. *Culture & Psychology, 9*(3), 313–329.

Zittoun, T. (2004). Symbolic competencies for developmental transitions: The case of the choice of first names. *Culture & Psychology, 10*(2), 131–161. https://doi.org/10.1177/1354067X04040926

Zittoun, T. (2007). The role of symbolic resources in human lives. In J. Valsiner & A. Rosa (Eds.), *Cambridge handbook of socio-cultural psychology* (pp. 343–361). Cambridge, UK: Cambridge University Press.

Zittoun, T. (2018). Symbolic resources and imagination in the dynamics of life. In A. Rosa & J. Valsiner (Eds.), *Cambridge handbook of sociocultural psychology* (2nd ed., pp. 178–204). Cambridge, UK: Cambridge University Press.

Zittoun, T. (2019). Generalising from a regional case study: A dialogue with a hill. *Culture & Psychology.* https://doi.org/10.1177/1354067X19888187

Zittoun, T., & Gillespie, A. (2015). Integrating experiences: Body and mind moving between contexts. In B. Wagoner, N. Chaudhary, & P. Hviid (Eds.), *Integrating experiences: Body and mind moving between contexts* (pp. 3–49). Charlotte, NC: Information Age Publishing.

Zittoun, T., Levitan, D., & Cangiá, F. (2018). A sociocultural approach to mobile families: A case study. *Peace and Conflict: Journal of Peace Psychology, 24*(4), 424–432.

Chapter 7
Threading: The Making of Lives, the Making of a Region

Generalisation is an ever-new process of signification.

—(Valsiner, 2019a)

Říp is at the centre of the podřipsko region – the region under the hill – which has evolved with time, together with the larger history of the territory that constitutes its environment, and along the lives of individuals and groups that pass through and live within. Approaching the hill as regional case study from a dynamic perspective, I have been sensitive to the rhythms and movements of life, their repetitions, redundancies and disruptions, in both the material and symbolic realms, as can be observed from the outside, and experienced by a few people.

In these pages, I have thus tried to combine three levels of reading. At a sociogenetic level, I have retraced historical movements, both in terms of factual events and material transformations, and that generate an intense symbolic work, from the state and from people, from afar and from within (Chap. 4). At an ontogenetic level, I have read in parallel the life stories of two women, to show how the same historical events around and in the Říp region have affected them in comparable ways, but how, on the more psychological and semiotic plane, each of them has developed unique patterns of sense, translated in contrasting life philosophies (Chap. 5). At a microgenetic level, I have tried to describe the villages under the hill, the time organisation and the movements that characterise the rhythm of life of the communities, as well as the more specific daily lives and circulations of four persons. Here also, I have attempted to distinguish their proximal spheres of experience from the distal ones, and I have observed in what respects these spheres overlapped and corresponded to the sociomaterial and symbolic nature of the hill (Chap. 6).

In other words, I have systematically combined a reading of what happens at the geographical and material level, and what is experienced in semiotic or symbolic terms, both collectively and individually. I will now come back to what we learn from such reading, first by combining the levels of analysis proposed – socio-, micro- and ontogenesis (Sect. 7.1) – and second, by reflecting in more general terms (Sect. 7.2).

© The Author(s), under exclusive license to Springer Nature Switzerland AG 2019

T. Zittoun, *Sociocultural Psychology on the Regional Scale*, SpringerBriefs in Psychology, https://doi.org/10.1007/978-3-030-33066-8_7

149

7.1   Combining Levels of Analysis: A Psychology of Living Under a Hill

For the sake of clarity, the previous chapters foregrounded one scale of dynamics, seeking for consistency and clarity at the level of social dynamics, lifecourses and everyday interactions and activities. However, the whole interest of a sociocultural analysis resides precisely in its capacity to adress the mutual constitution of these dynamics, and at their points of transaction and friction – there, where history becomes ruptures in people's lives (Wagoner, Chaudhary, & Hviid, 2015), where collective activities transform the social world (Wagoner, Moghaddam, & Valsiner, 2018) or where unique sense-making and imagination can reinvent traditions (de Saint-Laurent, 2017; Glăveanu, 2014; Wagner, Duveen, Themel, & Verma, 1999; Zittoun, 2013). These intermeshed dynamics were in the background of all chapters so far; here below, I try to highlight these mutual dynamics, by examining them first two by two – sociogenesis and microgenesis, microgenesis and ontogenesis, sociogenesis and ontogenesis – and then, the three together. For each combination, I highlight the core psychological dynamics identified so far. In doing so, I thus try to develop a series of theoretical insights for sociocultural psychology.

7.1.1   Sociogenetic and Ontogenetic: Ascending and Descending Semiotic Dynamics

The first effort here has been to combine a reading of sociogenetic dynamics with ontogenetic ones. This has brought me, on the one side, to a joint reading of history and life stories in Chap. 5, of how historical events affect the courses of life of specific persons. The interest of such an analysis is that it shows how the same collective and historical events are experienced differently by specific persons, and how such collective events may even not be experienced as ruptures at all. Such reading thus follows a lifecourse approach – considering the role of major historical events at different points of the course of life, likely to have long-term consequences, showing the importance of interrelated lives (Bengston, Elder, & Putney, 2012; Elder, 1994), as well as the specific events which may be experienced differently by two persons and thus act as bifurcation points (Sato & Valsiner, 2010; Sato, Yasuda, Kanzaki, & Valsiner, 2013). Following our past work, the analysis here has shown how people progressively, through recurrent experiences and local sense-making, generalise from their life experience, so as to develop new understandings, and in some cases, unique life-philosophies (de Saint-Laurent, 2017; Zittoun et al., 2013). How these are differentiated depends, however, on the very daily making of lives, and I will come back to this point here later. On the other side, in Chap. 6, listening to people's reasons of coming to live under Říp, as well as to their explanations about their relationships to the hill, we could hear the echoes of social discourses, national narratives and diffuse mythologies: people described impressions of *Déjà vu*, of a home-like feeling and of "magnetic attraction" to the hill. This, I tried to explain in terms of redundant discourses, creating the semiotic background of general and diffuse values, internalised yet not made conscious, by which people then apprehended the hill, creating, thus, this strange feeling of familiarity (Freud, 1919).

In more psychological terms, then, we observed here two opposing movements: on the one hand, life-philosophies result from the slow decantation of life events, felt and experienced, and, across time, progressively generalised. Here, people more or less consciously identify existential-emotional patterns across spheres of experience, and with time and learning from experience, find ways to express these in general terms, per progressive distantiation; proverbs, sayings or locutions give the flesh to the intuitions people abstract from living. Such process can be called *ascending*, as when water is progressively evaporated into more diffused humidity or clouds, to take on Vygotsky's metaphor (Zavereshneva & van der Veer, 2018). On the other hand, in the case of the magic mountain, people are exposed, right from their childhood, to the same stories and the symbolic universe, told and repeated – the semiotic, at nation level, is saturated with the foundational myth of the country. In more psychological terms, this probably also translates into a more psychological way, in general terms, "up-conscious" or diffused values and meanings (Valsiner, 1998), ready to be activated when the person meets concrete occurrences in which these may have a guiding value; these thus become actualised in actual events. Such logic is thus *descending*, as when clouds suddenly precipitate into local rain (Fig. 7.1).

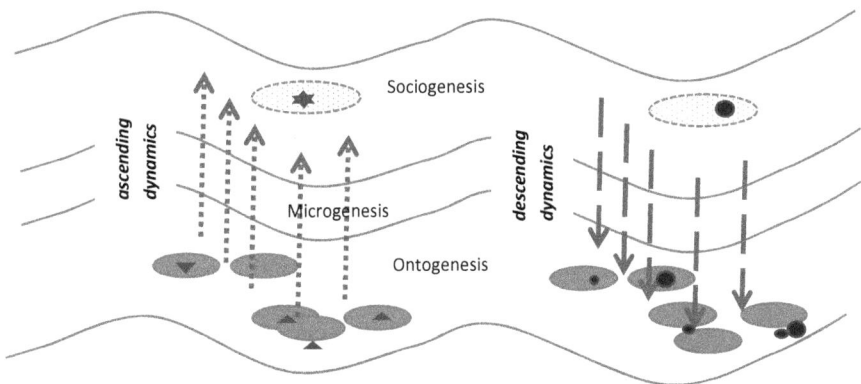

Fig. 7.1 Ascending and descending semiotic dynamics

7.1.2 Sociogenetic and Microgenetic Dynamics: Attractor, Boundary Work and Community

The second combination I proposed was that of an analysis of sociogenetic dynamics, with more microgenetic ones. This was very explicit in Chap. 6, where I tried to highlight how everyday life under Říp could be seen as reflecting wider sociocultural dynamics.

On the one hand, European and nationwide politics, past and present, affect the living conditions in the hill region (Chaps. 4 and 5). This may for instance appear in the position that older people take in relation to the mayor's initiatives – they prefer maintaining small privileges, as was relevant in the war years. It also appears the way in which the middle-aged generation engages in active, entrepreneurial shared actions – such as organising new celebrations or uses of European grants to develop the village, or, in some people's attempts to maintain specific cultural subsystems – the hunters' or the firemen's. One may even say that the anchoring of people's values or systems of orientation in one or the other socio-historical stream may be reflected in intergroup boundary dynamics. We thus observed that "others" appear more different to certain persons if they refer to other layers of historically anchored values. Hence, for the person committed to maintaining the modalities of social life developed as resistance under communist years – informal solidarity and cultivation of cultural subsystem, which are both useful and entertaining, such as hunting or fire sports – people engaged in more EU-oriented entrepreneur developments appear as "bad", while for the latter, such people may rather appear as "old" (Fig. 7.2).

On the other hand, the very historical and geographical organisation of the Říp region brings people to a variety of actual daily circulations and social organisations. In Chaps. 5 and 6, I have thus shown that people not only organise their lives in the villages in small networks of sociality but also across villages under the hill, where people go to meet relatives, work or organise events. Hence, the very socio-material (road system, transports, distribution of services) and symbolic configuration of the region (as vernacular region) brings people to concretely, geographically circulate around the hill. Simultaneously, they develop social networks around various activities, which then participate in the more semiotic development of feelings of belonging, and in the creation of shared and individual memories and life experiences (related to war economy, ballroom dancing or firemen); one thus becomes someone from "under the hill" – as when local people asked me, laughingly, when I would speak "podřipsko", the language from under the hill, not Czech. From such perspective, thus, the hill appears as a centre of gravity that organises the geographical circulation of lives and communities around the hill, but also, as a more semiotic attractor. Both confer a quality of "hill-ness" to all human activities in its range, and diffract, locally, the waves of historical and social movements that affected the region. The geographical hill itself thus becomes a metaphor of its semiotic nature: because of its altitude and geological location, it concentrates and reorganises the clouds brought by winds from the various directions of the planes around; similarly, it attracts, diffracts and

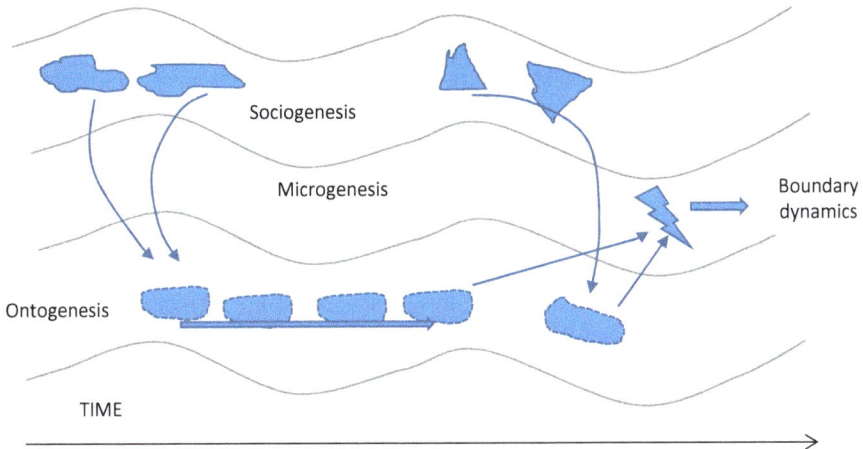

Fig. 7.2 Boundary dynamics in microgenesis resulting from sociogenesis

reorganises multiple layers of socio-historically grounded semiotic streams – hence it functions as an attractor. Of course, such systems of values and communities can be experienced very differently by various people, and this is what needs to now be examined more closely.

7.1.3   Microgenetic and Ontogenetic

I have mainly tried to analyse the junction of microgenetic and ontogenetic dynamics in terms of configurations of spheres of experiences. The notion allows indicating the recurrent experiences and activities in which a person engages on a daily basis and over a lifecourse. Proximal spheres of experiences are taking place in the "real" time and space, and are in principle observable (overt), even if loosely connected to specific settings and social frames. Distal spheres have as main property that they are disjoined from these. As a consequence, a specific person can have her proximal spheres of experience organised more or less closely to the settings in the immediate geographical space, and their distal spheres of experience more or less articulated to these as well, or at the contrary, have them distributed on a wider span. Either way, these spheres can be more or less overlapping with those of people within their close social network.

In Chap. 5, we have thus seen that Zdenka had, as a young woman, most of her proximal experiences distributed between settings of her daily life, that is her father's and her uncle's houses, and then later as an adult, between the village under Říp and her childhood region. As a child, short-lived proximal experience afforded by the school setting, that of sewing, became a distal sphere for most of her life (the dream of becoming a tailor, then a regret), until she could start sewing again as an older woman – in the actual family network of village life, she was the one doing everyone's small textile handwork. Sandra, on the other hand, learnt almost by accident at the end of the war – when the setting demanded her to prove the innocence of her family past - that she had two adult brothers in Germany; from one day to the other, her whole configuration of spheres of experience had to be rearranged, transforming past ones, creating new possible ones – thus enlarging her life space.

The question of spheres of experience becomes even more telling in the analysis proposed in Chap. 6. Here we have seen that the main differences between peoples' relation to the hill region could be described in terms of configurations of spheres of experience: some people, such as Jaromir, have most of their proximal spheres taking place in the social and material settings located on or around the hill (e.g., hunting, working); others have them distributed between the hill and elsewhere – the town, for instance, in Ester's case, or the world, as for Irma. In addition, people can deploy their distal spheres of experience in a symbolic space that is attached to the hill – as with Jaromir, who imagines his future around the hill, or who created new traditions that connect him with an imaginary lineage. Others deploy most of their distal spheres of experience in symbolic spaces disjoined from the social and geographical reality of the hill: Jeronym dreams of hiking; Ester of developing her education.

Such analysis of people's daily lives located in the hill region allowed for the distinction between stable and unstable configurations of spheres of experience. Stable ones group proximal spheres of experience around the hill, or alternate between the hill and a second place; distal experiences are grounded in these, which means that they are partly anchored in the hill. Unstable configurations result from tensions between proximal spheres, and between proximal and distal spheres of experience, some pulling people towards the hill, others pushing them away – what I have called centripetal and centrifugal movements. These overlapping versus disjoined, suiting to the setting or not, more or less balanced configurations of spheres of experience have direct psychological counterparts. People whom I identified as experiencing stable configurations had also a sense of personal continuity and consistency, and of belonging to a community, which seemed to be socially acknowledged. Their imagination of themselves and of their future included personal and shared projects; somehow bound by the limits of the geographical and symbolic context of the hill and their actual lives, they were, however, open and creative, feeling as "adventurers of life". In contrast, unstable configurations were also those of people experimenting high levels of ambivalence about their daily life, their activities and social networks, and who were unsure of their actual belonging. Their distal future or imaginations of themselves were bringing them to other horizons, yet with unclear means; as a consequence, some were also less involved locally.

In other words, to make a theoretical jump, there may be a correspondence between people's actual commitments in their world, the way these are experienced (the spheres) and the way in which these diverse proximal and distal spheres are integrated. Fluid movements in and across spheres which are socially and geographically part of a whole, and even, part of a shared history, may also translate psychologically by a more fluid inner-dialogicality (Zittoun & Levitan, 2019), one that enables one to be daily creative and imaginative, irrigating everyday life. In contrast, when movements across spheres of experience are more problematic – because of inner reasons, or social and material obstacles – distance, lack of social recognition – the whole inner-dialogicality becomes at times more raucous, and imaginations of oneself seem to find a more difficult path to possibly guide one's life.

There is a second aspect to the junction of micro- and ontogenetic dynamics, which I have tried to highlight in Chap. 5. There, the close analysis of life courses has brought me to identify recurrent modes of solving problems, ruptures, or life difficulties. Zdenka was lucky to live, until her teenage years, under the protection and authority of well-respected, talented and powerful men, her father and uncle. They provided her with solutions and guidance, and taught her skills, postures and certain modes of relating to others. I have called this mode of relating vertical, and identified in Zdenka's later posture something similar: once married, she took on that directive and protective role, providing others with guidance and expertise. Sandra, in contrast, learnt soon to rely on a supportive family and then on an extended community and a social-familial network. Resistance to authorities was organised in such cooperative way, as were support for children care, or the burden of daily life; I have called this a horizontal mode of relating. Because I could retrace the two women's modes of making sense of their experience, I could suggest that these preferential forms of preferential social dialogicality were also internalised, and generalised in different modes of apprehending personal and world events.

Put together, these two observations suggest something about the internalisation of social and cultural dynamics. Over the lifecourse, it indicates, people do not only internalise specific values, narrative or semiotic tools; they also internalise modes of relating to others, and modes of moving across experiences; these dialogical and geographical movements become inner-dialogical movements (Marková, 2003, 2016). In addition, this suggests that the very pattern of these social or geographical dynamics translates, in some way, into some modes or patterns of organising experience – vertical or horizontal, stable and oriented towards the future, or more unstable. To clarify, the argument is not that there is a simple translation from the modalities of specific social interactions and dialogues to the mind – as a restricted ideas of dialogicality would suggest, or the naïve idea that because people move in circles around the hill, they simply think in a circular way.

Rather, the idea is twofold. First, because spheres of experiences designate subjectively experienced configurations of manners of doing, feeling, acting, being positioned, etc., these necessarily have a strong psychological existence; from each of them values can be generalised, possible imagination of the future defined, and so on. These may then support, or constrain, vertical and horizontal generalisation and integration. Distal experiences that have a tension of realisation that can never been turned into proximal ones – the dream of climbing with friends, always contradicted by one's co-villagers – can thus become unsatisfied dreams, and as such, turn into frustration or regrets. In some other cases, when these can be, in some ways, joint, the experience is very different; hence, the distant hope of being able to drive racing cars may move closer as a colleague offers us try his car, feeding in both proximal and distal experiences. What has thus been described as centripetal, centrifugal or balanced organisations of spheres of experience, would thus correspond, in some ways, to experiences generating cognitive dissonances or psychological tension – in Spinozian terms, reduction of power (Spinoza, 1677) – while possible integration, mutual enrichment and inner catalysis would correspond to an expansion of spheres of experiencer or the life space – a Spinozian augmentation of power.

The other side of the argument is an extension of Vygotsky's ideas about the internalisation of language and, more generally, cultural tools or art: as speech can be conceived of as water, thought may be considered as clouds; language, once internalised, becomes an ingrown organiser of thinking and sensibility (Vygotsky, 1971; Zavereshneva & van der Veer, 2018). To pursue the Vygotskian metaphor, let us imagine that the stones of a river bed, which, polished by years of river flow, eventually tend to bend the water is certain currents; let us admit that, because of its specific shape, the water that slowly evaporates from that river would also keep something from the specific current and bends from its stream. Hence, the clouds of condensation emanating from a river stream would also, in some ways, be shaped or keep the remnants of the initial water movements – even though these translate in different modes. This principle can be extended from the role of language to any other forms of semiotic, cultural guidance. The idea is thus an extension of the idea presented in Chap. 2: the typical unfolding of social interactions, some modes of resolution of problems, deeply engaging cultural experiences or the more anecdotic exposure to ornaments can all be conceived of as certain forms of external semiotic guidance: these are material, symbolic and humanly guidance of chunks of one's flow of consciousness. What can then be willingly reproduced is the trace of these experiences of having been guided by others from within, and eventually, some form of simplification or abstraction of these movement. In other words, the world provides the person with patterns of organisation of experience and these may become progressively modes of guiding one's stream of experience, from within.

Both ideas together thus suggest that people internalise different active patterns of organising experience, and that these may be, or not be, compatible: if so, they may enrich each other, support each other and catalyse them in more complex or simplified or general modes; if these are not, they may feel as obstructing, blocking or constraining experience.

7.1.4 Socio-, Micro- and Ontogenesis Combined: Patterns of Living

The most difficult and intriguing analytical step consists of combining the three layers of change identified so far (see Chap. 2). The theoretical question is, can we see how sociogenetic co-defines microgenetic dynamics, and how both of these shape ontogenesis, which itself can transform these two first layers of processes? Empirically, these aspects become visible in some of the observations made in Chap. 5, but are mainly visible in Chap. 6, on the background of Chap. 4.

First, in Chap. 4, we identfied historical events which affected the meaning and symbolic constitution of the hill, brought movements of population, transformed the nature of collective life and its daily organisation in terms of activities and networks and finally, were experienced as ruptures, or simply created the setting of people's daily life. Hence, collective events – say, the installation of a harshened communism in the 1950s – directly created ruptures in Sandra and Zdenka's lives, and in addition the muffled effects of the years of this regime may be found in their daily experiences in 2018 – they still were living with very small amounts of money, which they knew how to manage. Such after-effects of history can also be observed in the life trajectories and, therefore, daily experiences of younger people, like Julie – whose studies were still constrained by the remnants of the regime – or even in those of women exposed to an engrained gender inequality, or men keeping active traditions which, without them being aware, were promoted by the communist regime (Chap. 6). Peeple fighting for, or against the boundary dynamics and cultural subsystem, are also still being positioned or trying to correct the historical effects of these communist years, and more generally, the deposits of historical waves in the social fabric.

Second, the history of the hill, its shape and its symbolic uses over centuries have expanded together with the new rise of nationalism, as well as liberalism and tourism. The incredible redundancy of the representations of the hill as well as of the founding forefather all around the hill region reflects the inflation of the symbolic value of the hill. All this has been schematised in the indexical curve designating the hill, the iconic paintings and three-dimensional representations, as well as the endless symbolic guidance. If you are in the hill region, you are constantly reminded of it. The hill becomes a decoration of the hill, and the hill and its representations become reinforced ornaments in the daily life of the hill. This adds to the very geographical organisation of life around the hill, which imposes circular or semicircular movements around the hill. If we follow Valsiner's argument (Valsiner, 2019b), so much "hilliness" and symbolic and physical experiences are likely to be, in some ways, internalised and guide people's experience from within.

We saw many variations of appropriation of the hill in people's lives and discourses. The first occurrence is that of people meeting the hill and having a flash experience – that of a *déjà vu* or an irresistible experience. Here, I suggested, the symbolic nature of the hill was already internalised in a diffuse, non-reflective way by people, and it is the actual meeting in a daily situation of the real hill, usually combined with some opening due to a state of transitionality, that made people attentive to the resonance between the actual hill and their various imaginations and feelings. This meeting or *precipitation* of the symbolic in their daily lives brought people to micro- and ontogenetic changes: they chose to move and live under the hill. Second, for many people, Říp is simply there: it is a component of their lifespace, it is their normal landscape and it defines some specific spheres of experiences – walking to the annual fair, the *Řípska pout'* – but without deep organising effect. In some way, the symbolic aspect of the hill, even if known, has been "neutralised". Third, some people engage in an active appropriation of the symbolic and/or of the material reality of the hill: physically, by biking, climbing or hunting, and symbolically, by trying to turn the shared and symbolic values, as well as those presented in their surroundings, into something personally significant. Here, people engage in actual semiotic work, generating new imaginations of themselves in relation to the hill, and in many cases, connected to real and imagined others, in space and time.

The most interesting finding here is the importance of whether this internalisation occurs at one or two of these layers: did the person internalise only the symbolic value of the hill, or its geographical-material, or both? Indeed, this point joins the previous, on spheres of experiences. If people internalise the symbolic value of hill, it plays a role in their distal experiences; if it is internalised as a more physical experience of the hill, it becomes a proximal, potentially distal experience. Hence a partial internalisation may bring some form of partial reconfiguration of one's spheres of experience. Yet, when someone internalises, or lets the hill grow in at both material and symbolic levels, then it is likely to bring a great consistency between proximal and distal spheres of experiences. Hence, Jaromir recreates a rite of Říp climbing that connects him to a lineage of men in his family. The effect are of course many: such ingrown physical and semiotic values become part of self-definition and of the feeling of belonging (and therefore potentially, exclusion) and also are bound to certain understanding of the local and wider history.

This point thus brought me to the strange hypothesis that this double existence of the hill, physical and symbolic, and people's different experiences and uses, may have either an organising force, or a dissipative force. In the sense, an aligned distal and proximal experience of the hill turns it, for a person, into an attractor, and a stabilising vector. In contrast, for people with no such alignment, or simply no such appropriation and internalisation, the hill may not have such organising force; rather, it may appear as a vector having deflecting properties. In other words, and this is the core idea emerging here, because of its extreme redundancy both perceptually and experientially (its material and geographical reality) and symbolically (its mythical and historical uses), it can become a "semiotic vector" – attractive or dissipative - in people's daily life as well as in the long run of their lifecourse.

To join these observations with those of the previous subsections, what I suggest is that experiences shaped by certain levels of organisation (the spatial and geographical arrangements of the hill, villages and road; or the collective history), experienced physically and psychologically, can then have correspondences in the mind; these can all, in their own ways, be internalised and schematised as specific shapes, incitation of actions or organisers. In other words, patterns of daily living become semiotic patterns organising one's experience.

7.2 Towards Generalisation

Articulating levels of analysis of dynamics taking place at the scale of a region brought me to highlight a series of psychological processes, about the role of one's sociomaterial and symbolic environment in one's mode of experiencing life. One may question the value and, especially, the potential expansions of such propositions. Generalisation can take many directions (Marková, Zadeh, & Zittoun, 2019). The propositions here open up towards three modalities of generalisation: epistemological (about the phenomena to study), theoretical (about psychological processes) and, in terms of research, as process of learning.

7.2.1   Generalising Unit of Analysis

Studying a region, that is, to consider a region as a unit of analysis in psychology was proposed as an extreme case of a theoretically grounded case study – as psychologists, we hardly have the tools to conceptually and methodologically address that size of realities. However, the theoretical interest of a regional case study is great: I hope this case study showed that it offers a unique way to delimitate the sociocultural as a social and geographical reality, and from there, to observe how the layers of socio-, micro and ontogenesis operate. In some way, working at that scale allows a "semio-geology": if we were facing a portion of the ground, we would see lava, stones, and their dynamic transformations; here, we can observe the sedimentation of various layers of semiotic means. We can transform a temporal, fluid reality in to a sociomaterial, observable one. I do believe that this not only allows seeing dynamics, which are otherwise too diffuse, but also realities specific to the scale of a region.

   The first proposed generalisation here thus concerns the type of unit of analysis – regional case studies. These can, but do not need to, be hills; these can be valleys, coasts, islands, localities or a group of localities. They, however, need to be somehow constituted as regions, by its inhabitants and by others, both as geographical entities (even if broadly bound) and symbolic entities. Current attempts to constitute such regions can be observed in many countries in Europe and around the world, often for administrative and touristic purposes. These are also largely studied, in terms of economic changes, social dynamics or cultural transformations, etc, but little in relation to the psychological (experiential, psychosocial, sociocultural) dynamics involved. The proposition is thus to constitute them as a unit of analysis for sociocultural psychological studies, or for other social sciences. For such purpose, it is better for these regions to have a size that makes them accessible to ethnographic study, so as to document the three levels of genesis, as proposed here, and their interrelations: the history or social dynamics active in and through the space; group and boundary dynamics and everyday activities and interactions; and people's courses of lives. However, whether these regions have a very long history, as the hill presented here, or a shorter one; whether their inhabitants are very diverse or considered as homogeneous; and whether there is a high mobility of people or not, may not be relevant. These variations may precisely help to illuminate the various interplays between socio-, micro- and ontogenesis. Whether this type of analysis can be expanded for sociocultural psychology to larger scales and regions, such as the ones currently undergoing claims of independence in Europe and elsewhere, is another question which I cannot solve here; however, smaller case studies, like natural laboratories of social transformation, may be the ground to generate hypothesis about dynamics likely to take place at a wider scale.

Hence, by multiplying this type of case study, and developing further theoretical tools in dialogue with the social sciences, we may move towards a stronger understanding of the mutual making of people and their sociocultural environment, understood not only as cultural systems but also as geographical and sociomaterial evolving realities. At the end, what is at stake here, through the multiplication of such type of case studies and the proposed epistemological stance – multilayer, multiple perspectives, search for interrelations, surprise and patterns – is a general sociocultural psychology, that has as project an understanding the making of mind and societies. Generalising the unit of analysis should be a step towards theoretical generalisation.

7.2.2   Generalising Theoretically

Through this regional case study, I highlighted a portion of the sociocultural and material world in which I could follow some of the dynamics uniting socio-, onto- and microgenetic dynamics. I believe that this allowed, like in a natural laboratory, to highlight and make visible dynamics that take place everywhere, and in more complex manners, as these become more diffused in the multilayered nature of people's experiences. Hence, I have argued that certain modes of practical organisation of life around the hill, as well as the symbolic and mythical discourses accompanying them, become, in some sense, organising psychological life, and especially, that they become patterns for organising semiotic streams. In doing so, my intention is to highlight psychological and semiotic dynamics that may have some theoretical relevance beyond that specific and unique example. I will summarise the four main theoretical propositions made here.

Some of the theoretical distinctions and tools proposed to approach the case study were not new – the three levels approach, the concepts specifically used to capture the phenomenon at each level, and especially lifecourses defined in terms of configurations of spheres of experience. What was less explored is the heuristic interest of distinguishing the sociomaterial and the symbolic nature of a place or a setting, and the analysis of how these two faces of the world participate, independently and jointly, in psychological dynamics.

This leads to a first theoretical proposition. People's proximal sphere of experiences can take place in a limited social and geographical space, or in a wider, or even, open-ended one. Hence, living in a remote village, one is likely to have a closely-knit configuration of proximal spheres of experience; an adult in professional international mobility sees proximal spheres of experience distributed on a much wider geographical space (Levitan, 2018). Also, people's distal spheres of experience can cover a smaller, or wider span – people, in imagination, can explore places and times close to their actual life, or travel to the origins of the earth and imagine a life which is absolutely remote from any reality (Hilppö, Rajala, Zittoun, Kumpulainen, & Lipponen, 2016; Vygotsky, 1931/1994). What becomes interesting is the relation between these, that is, the overall configuration of spheres of experience (Zittoun, in press). So far, indeed, various case studies suggest that there must be different types of configurations, and different ways to create both stability and freedom, or space for creativity. Older people in retirement homes tend to have strongly constrained proximal spheres of experiences, materially enclosed in a controlled space, while they can have their minds that are freer to wander and explore distal spheres of experiences (Zittoun, Grossen, & Salamin Tarrago, in press). Families in repeated mobility have, because of their past trajectories, memories and projects – that is, distal experiences – distributed all around the world; yet to find some form of stability, individually and collectively, families tend to define very stable and transportable proximal spheres of experiences that can be reactivated anywhere (e.g., play cards together in any new house) (Levitan, 2018). Here, we have seen that the consistency of lives around Říp can be explained by certain correspondence between distal and proximal spheres of experience, and the actual sociomaterial and symbolic space of the hill region. Altogether, then, the first general theoretical proposition is that people have to find some balance between the expansion of their proximal spheres and their distal spheres of experience, and the actual span of the social and symbolic spaces to which they have access.

The second proposition follows from the first one: configurations of spheres of experiences can be more or less stable, or rather unstable. Stability may result in integration of spheres of experience and in some generalisation. Instability, even transitory, seems to translate into unquietness, experiences of ambivalence and tension. Some external or internal points can have a stabilising, or destabilising force; these can become attractors. In the case study presented here, the hill can become the only, or one of the attractors stabilising people's lives, practically and symbolically. Instability, or disorganisation, can come either from internal elements – tensions between these spheres, for different reasons, or external forces which disrupt these balances. This opens up the question of what can play the role of a stabilising vector in people's lives; here, I have shown that the hill could play such a role when it was both deeply internalised and experienced, that is, infusing proximal and distal spheres of experience. It also raises the question of how these unstable configurations can transform into more stable ones, and reversely, over time (Zittoun & Gillespie, 2015a).

The third theoretical proposition expands the range of cultural elements that can be internalised and have an organising semiotic force. Besides language, modalities of interactions, symbolic resources, social representations and ornaments, I have proposed that some elements of the sociomaterial and symbolic reality can have the same role – here, "Říp", with all its multiple modes of existence. The redundant nature of these experiences is indeed playing an important role in the fact that these become organisers of experience, in a peripheral or a more central, or more actively creative manner. This opens the road to studying the role, strength and means to psychologically resist the multiple redundancies of our semiosphere – from discourses on fake news to the local recrudescence of rampant nationalisms.

The fourth and last theoretical proposition here is that, when approaching complex and multilayered chunks of the sociocultural world, the very concept of "pattern" may help us to see correspondences, transformations and translations of entities from one layer to the other one – from modes of relating to modes of generalising, from modes of moving circularly to modes of organising one's daily life, etc. This, related to the previous points, thus allowed me to expand our knowledge of internalisation: much more than putting things out there in mind, or reproducing social dialogue in intra-dialogue, it is about adopting a movement, a mode of organisation of a section of one's flow of experience. This is probably the most important theoretical finding here: internalisation does not anymore only designate the psychological guidance offered by specific meanings or signs, but rather, it here designates modes of organising experience, or patterns of guidance – as a symphony can be reduced to music sheets, which can then guide the musician to recreate the melody once heard. This is why films, pieces of art, melodies, interpersonal dynamics, ornaments or landscapes can become psychic organisers, or enable to recreate, in some form of inner modalities, sequences of experiences previously culturally guided (Valsiner, 2019b; Zittoun & Gillespie, 2015b). What is internalised is the propensity of a certain movement; it is a *simplified guidance pattern*. This is why, people rarely "reproduce" a whole artefact or interactions or landscape in their mind or their embodied memory; they rather experience a moment, a movement – a fragment that, precisely, moved them. The implication of this proposition is thus that, across time, people may internalise many of these patterns; these, in some way, may thus become further generalised, or integrated (Zittoun & Gillespie, 2015a) – which calls for further research.

7.2.3   ...and Learning from a Research Experience

Studying a hill, I learnt a few more things about research. "I study a hill" is a slightly awkward answer to the ritual "what do you currently work on?" question mutually addressed in encounters between academic colleagues. I engaged in an object of a scale which defied my earlier practice; I found myself in situations that were relationally and humanly challenging, but also, emotional and thought-provoking; and especially, I attempted to work theoretically, constantly feeling as if being at the fringe of absurdity. Studying a hill was thus an occasion to try to go into the unknown, and to examine if my theoretical toolbox allowed me to do what I consider a core challenge of our field – actually fully embrace the social and cultural nature of people's lived lives. This led me to the series of theoretical propositions summarised above – which, for simple as they seem, put me slightly outside of what I was used to consider as reasonable.

Finally, I also would like to make explicit another of my learning in this project. Many researchers are aware that intuitions – personally or theoretically informed – are a large part of the research process (Valsiner, 2017). But do we know how far to follow them, and when they fail or turn into something else? Here, I approached this study of a hill with two intuitions. The first one was prior to the whole enquiry, and was related to the specific "out of time" nature of the hill (Chap. 1). Hardly a surprise, my analysis actually reveals that there is no such thing: the hill and its habitants are deeply grounded in the history of the country and the region, and whatever forces organise people's life, they are deeply connected to the wider fabric of the environment. Also, although very specific and unique, people's lives and variations under the hill reflect historical and social forces far beyond their cases, and thus, illustrate them – while at the same time, teach us again and again how everyone becomes unique. In some way, the "out of time" nature of the hill reflects more the clarity of these dynamics – out of the noise of urban life, they appear in their simplicity. If my intuition was conducing to anything, it was a naïve light projected ahead of me, which sustained my engagement to the hill.

The second intuition was, as I started to analyse these data, to experience the hill as a sort of volcano from which would pour layers of lava; running downhill, these would stop, slowly freeze, create layers and whirlpools, spread out and crystallise or remain more mobile. This allowed me to be sensitive to the actual dynamics at stake, attractions and dissipation, and interactions between layers of the sociocultural and psychological realm. Again, it had to be abandoned in the face of the diversity of people's daily interactions and lives – but the metaphor carried my exploration for some time. Again, as naïve as the intuition was, it forced me to question what movement was, and how far we can think of one undefined material, social and symbolic, moving reality. If there is such a thing – a general flow – our role will still be to differentiate it in its components if we want, to say anything at all. Whether my analysis made it enough, or adequately, is up to the reader to say.

7.3 To Close and to Open

Closing these pages, the reader may have some idea of what lives may look like under a Czech hill. If my small exploratory case study managed to convey some of my sense of surprise and fascination, I hope it also leaves two open routes for further enquiries in sociocultural psychology. The first one is to pursue case studies the size of a region, so as to hold at once the complexity of human lives, and make visible dynamics otherwise dissolved in the wide fluxes of sociocultural history. The second is a call for a return to the theorisation of the actual psychological and semiotic processes at stake when we study humans in societies. Modestly following the efforts of others before me, I have tried to explore some new aspects of internalisation and cultural guidance; yet, there is still much more to be done, both in terms of accounting for the development of the lifecourse in complex societies, and in terms of theoretical integration. But like any other developmental processes, how facts and theoretical concepts evaporate into diffused clouds of ideas, how they melt through winds and layers of time and space, how they may recompose and condensate into new forms, and eventually, drop back into concepts, words and further dialogues, is unpredictable.

References

Bengston, V. L., Elder, G. H. J., & Putney, N. M. (2012). The life course perspective on ageing: Linked lives, timing, and history. In J. Katz, S. Peace, & S. Spurr (Eds.), *Adult lives. A life course perspective* (pp. 9–17). Bristol, UK: Policy Press.
de Saint-Laurent, C. (2017). Trajectories of resistance and historical reflections. In N. Chaudhary, P. Hviid, G. Marsico, & J. W. Villadsen (Eds.), *Resistance in everyday life: Constructing cultural experiences* (pp. 49–63). https://doi.org/10.1007/978-981-10-3581-4_5
Elder, G. H. J. (1994). Time, human agency, and social change: Perspectives on the life course. *Social Psychology Quarterly, 57*(1), 4–15. https://doi.org/10.2307/2786971
Freud, S. (1919). The 'Uncanny'. In J. Strachey (Ed.), & A. Strachey (Trans.), *The Standard Edition of the Complete Psychological Works of Sigmund Freud*: Vol. XVII (1917-1919) (pp. 217–256). London: The Hogarth Press and the Institute of Psychoanalysis.
Glăveanu, V. P. (2014). *Thinking through creativity and culture. Toward an integrated model*. New Brunswick (NJ) and London: Transaction Publisher.
Hilppö, J. A., Rajala, A., Zittoun, T., Kumpulainen, K., & Lipponen, L. (2016). Interactive dynamics of imagination in a science classroom. *Frontline Learning Research, 4*(4), 20–29. https://doi.org/10.14786/flr.v4i4.213
Levitan, D. (2018). The art of living in transitoriness: Strategies of families in repeated geographical mobility. *Integrative Psychological and Behavioral Science, 53*, 1–25. https://doi.org/10.1007/s12124-018-9448-4
Marková, I. (2003). *Dialogicality and social representations: The dynamics of mind*. Cambridge: Cambridge University Press.
Marková, I. (2016). *The dialogical mind: Common sense and ethics*. Cambridge, UK: Cambridge University Press.
Marková, I., Zadeh, S., & Zittoun, T. (2019). Introduction to the special issue on generalisation from dialogical single case studies. *Culture & Psychology*, 1354067X19888193. https://doi.org/10.1177/1354067X19888193.
Sato, T., & Valsiner, J. (2010). Time in life and life in time: Between experiencing and accounting. *Ritsumeikan Journal of Human Sciences, 20*(1), 79–92.
Sato, T., Yasuda, Y., Kanzaki, M., & Valsiner, J. (2013). From describing to reconstructing life trajectories: How the TEA (Trajectory Equifinality Approach) explicates context-dependent human phenomena. In B. Wagoner, N. Chaudhary, & P. Hviid (Eds.), *Cultural psychology and its future: Complementarity in a new key* (pp. 93–105). Charlotte, NC: Information Age Publishing.
Spinoza, B. de. (1677). *L'éthique*. Paris: Gallimard.
Valsiner, J. (1998). *The guided mind*. Cambridge, MA: Harvard University Press.
Valsiner, J. (2017). *From methodology to methods in human psychology*. Cham (Switzerland): Springer. Retrieved from http://www.springer.com/la/book/9783319610634
Valsiner, J. (2019a). Generalization in science: Abstracting from unique events. In C. Højholt & E. Schraube (Eds.), *Subjectivity and knowledge: Generalization in the psychological study of everyday life*. New York: Springer.
Valsiner, J. (2019b). *Ornamented lives*. Charlotte, NC: Information Age Publishing.
Vygotsky, L. S. (1931/1994). Imagination and creativity of the adolescent. In R. Van der Veer & J. Valsiner (Eds.), *The Vygotsky Reader* (Original publication 1931, pp. 266–288). Oxford: Blackwell Publishing.
Vygotsky, L. S. (1971). *The psychology of art*. Cambridge, MA & London: MIT press.
Wagner, W., Duveen, G., Themel, M., & Verma, J. (1999). The modernization of tradition: Thinking about madness in Patna, India. *Culture & Psychology, 5*(4), 413–445. https://doi.org/10.1177/1354067X9954003
Wagoner, B., Chaudhary, N., & Hviid, P. (Eds.). (2015). *Integrating experiences: Body and mind moving between contexts*. Charlotte, NC: Information Age Publishing.

Wagoner, B., Moghaddam, F. M., & Valsiner, J. (2018). *The psychology of radical social change: From rage to revolution.* Cambridge: Cambridge University Press.

Zavereshneva, E., & van der Veer, R. (2018). *Vygotsky's notebooks. A selection.* Singapore: Springer.

Zittoun, T. (2013). Religious traditions as means of innovation: The use of symbolic resources in the life course. In H. Zock & M. Buitelaar (Eds.), *Religious voices in self-narratives making sense of life in times of transitions* (pp. 129–148). Berlin: Walter de Gruyter.

Zittoun, T. (In press). Imagination in people and societies on the move: A sociocultural psychology perspective. *Culture & Psychology.*

Zittoun, T., & Gillespie, A. (2015a). Integrating experiences: Body and mind moving between contexts. In B. Wagoner, N. Chaudhary, & P. Hviid (Eds.), *Integrating experiences: Body and mind moving between contexts* (pp. 3–49). Charlotte, NC: Information Age Publishing.

Zittoun, T., & Gillespie, A. (2015b). Internalization: How culture becomes mind. *Culture & Psychology, 21*(4), 477–491. https://doi.org/10.1177/1354067X15615809

Zittoun, T., Grossen, M., & Salamin Tarrago, F. (in press). Creativity, imagination and self-continuity in the transition into a nursing home. *Learning, Culture and Social Interaction, Special issue.*

Zittoun, T., & Levitan, D. (2019). A sociocultural psychology of repeated mobility: Dialogical challenges / Una psicología sociocultural de la movilidad repetida: desafíos dialógicos. *Estudios de Psicología, 40*(1), 79–106. https://doi.org/10.1080/02109395.2018.1560025

Zittoun, T., Valsiner, J., Vedeler, D., Salgado, J., Gonçalves, M., & Ferring, D. (2013). *Human development in the lifecourse. Melodies of living.* Cambridge: Cambridge University Press.

Index

© The Author(s), under exclusive license to Springer Nature Switzerland AG 2019
T. Zittoun, *Sociocultural Psychology on the Regional Scale*, SpringerBriefs in
Psychology, https://doi.org/10.1007/978-3-030-33066-8

Printed in the USA
CPSIA information can be obtained
at www.ICGtesting.com
LVHW011256221023
761792LV00001B/37